# Soviet and Post-Soviet Politics and Society (SPPS)

ISSN 1614-3515

Founded in 2004 and refereed since 2007, SPPS makes available affordable English-, German- and Russian-language studies on the history of the countries of the former Soviet bloc from the late Tsarist period to today. It publishes between 5 and 20 volumes per year, and focuses on issues in transitions to and from democracy such as economic crisis, identity formation, civil society development, and constitutional reform in CEE and the NIS. SPPS also aims to highlight so far understudied themes in East European studies such as right-wing radicalism, religious life, higher education, or human rights protection. The authors and titles of all previously published manuscripts are listed at the end of this book. For a full description of the series and reviews of its books, see www.ibidem-verlag.de/red/spps.

**Editorial correspondence & manuscripts** should be sent to: Dr. Andreas Umland, DAAD, German Embassy, vul. Bohdana Khmelnitskoho 25, UA-01901 Kyiv, Ukraine. e-mail: umland@stanfordalumni.org

**Business correspondence & review copy requests** should be sent to: *ibidem*-Verlag, Leuschnerstr. 40, D-30457 Hannover, Germany; tel.: +49(0)511-2622200; fax: +49(0)511-2622201; spps@ibidem-verlag.de.

**Book orders & payments** should be made via the publisher's electronic book shop at: www.ibidem-verlag.de/red/SPPS_EN/

**Authors, reviewers, referees, and editors** for (as well as all other persons sympathetic to) SPPS are invited to join its networks at www.facebook.com/group.php?gid=52638198614 www.linkedin.com/groups?about=&gid=103012 www.xing.com/net/spps-ibidem-verlag/

## Recent Volumes

*Jussi Lassila*

# THE QUEST FOR AN IDEAL YOUTH IN PUTIN'S RUSSIA II

The Search for Distinctive Conformism in the
Political Communication of *Nashi,* 2005-2009

With a foreword by Kirill Postoutenko

*ibidem*-Verlag
Stuttgart

**Bibliographic information published by the Deutsche Nationalbibliothek**

Die Deutsche Nationalbibliothek lists this publication in the Deutsche Nationalbibliografie; detailed bibliographic data are available in the Internet at http://dnb.d-nb.de.

**Bibliografische Information der Deutschen Nationalbibliothek**

Die Deutsche Nationalbibliothek verzeichnet diese Publikation in der Deutschen Nationalbibliografie; detaillierte bibliografische Daten sind im Internet über http://dnb.d-nb.de abrufbar.

Cover Picture:  The "Father Frost and the Snow Maidens" parade within the "Return of the Holiday" (Vozvrashchennyi prazdnik) project by the youth movement Nashi in Moscow on 17 December 2006 © Alena Kaplina.

Second, Revised and Expanded Edition

ISSN: 1614-3515

ISBN-13: 978-3-8382-0585-4

© *ibidem*-Verlag / *ibidem* Press

Stuttgart, Germany 2014

# Contents

"Jussi Lassila's book is a multifaceted and timely contribution about *Nashi*'s political communication strategies, their political rituals, as well as use of image and symbols. This outstanding study demonstrates that, despite its close relation to the Kremlin, *Nashi* wanted to build an ideal youth and tried to have its own voice heard. I strongly recommend this book to scholars interested in communication, as well as in youth culture and politics in contemporary Russia."

*Marlène Laruelle, Research Professor of International Affairs,*
*George Washington University*

# Acknowledgements

The first steps for this book project were made at the Department of Languages of the University of Jyväskylä in the early 2000s. My thanks go especially to Marjatta Vanhala-Aniszewski for her great support and guidance and Erkki Peuranen, who unfortunately is no longer with us, for his inspirational lectures and discussions on Russian culture and literature. I am especially grateful to Markku Kivinen, Markku Kangaspuro, and all the marvelous colleagues of the Aleksanteri Institute of University of Helsinki which has been my academic home since 2006. You provided the best possible input for my output.

I thank Lara Ryazanova-Clarke and Hilary Pilkington; your critique and advice have been helpful in editing this book; thanks to Godfrey Weldhen, Anna Whittington, and Jakob Horstmann who revised my English. I express my sincere gratitude to Regina Smyth, Thomas J. Garza, Pål Kolstø, and Jaakko Turunen who reviewed the first edition of this book (Lassila 2012) and provided invaluable advice.

During these years I have received many valuable comments, criticism, ideas, interest, and support from people of various disciplines. I thank Valerie Sperling, Kirill Postoutenko, Marlene Laruelle, Julie Hemment, Andreas Umland, Ivo Mijnssen, Sanna Turoma, Laura Lyytikäinen, Kaarina Aitamurto, Maija Turunen, Anna-Maria Salmi, Hanna Ruutu, Elina Viljanen, Tapani Kaakuriniemi, Tomi Huttunen, Natalia Baschmakoff, Markku Lonkila, Marianne Liljeström, Sari Autio-Sarasmo, Suvi Salmenniemi, Vladimir Gel'man, Sirke Mäkinen, Alexei Golubev, Saara Ratilainen, Iina Kohonen, Katja Koikkalainen, Sirpa Leppänen, Jan Blommaert, Svetlana Smetanina, Mika Lähteenmäki, Sari Pietikäinen, Natalia Turunen, Vesa Heikkinen, Alexei Yurchak, Miguel Vázquez Liñán, Florian Toepfl, Greg Simons, Nelli Piattoeva, Tatiana Zhurzhenko, Florian Bieber, Rachel Adams, Matti Jutila, Meri Kulmala, Simo Leisti, Maija Jäppinen, Maija Könönen, Ivor Stodolsky, Maya Nadkarni, Riitta Pyykkö, Lea Siilin, Aila Pesonen, Hanna Smith, Svetlana Probirskaja, Maria Petterson and Tintti Klapuri.

I also express my thanks to "Igor," "Oleg," and "Vadim" from Nashi for their approval to share their views and answer my questions, and I thank all my friends and relatives who have suffered my endless stories about Russia.

My greatest gratitude goes to Marika for her ultimate support and patience over these years and to our wonderful sons Into and Oiva. You have been the best possible motivation for dad's work!

# Foreword

When studying Russian youth organizations of the last decade, the reader unused to the peculiarities of post-Soviet politics may find it quite challenging to cast those groups in the mould provided by traditional social sciences and the humanities. These difficulties become less acute if we see the entities in question as institutional bodies and simultaneously resort to a fairly cynical minimalism: "Our social interaction consists very much in telling one another what right thinking is and passing blame on wrong thinking. This is indeed how we build the institutions, squeezing each other's ideas into a common shape so that we can prove rightness by sheer number of independent assent "(*Mary Douglas, How Institutions Think* (1986)). This radical pragmatism finds some support on the discursive and performative level. Indeed, the name Nashi defines the identity of the group not only from, but also *through* its deictic centre—the truth is not "what", but "where" the speaker is: "Self is not only *here* and *now*, but also the origin of the epistemic *true* and the deontic *right*" (*Paul Chilton, Analysing Political Discourse: Theory and Practice* (2004)). Since no other meaningful and stable differentiations between "them" and "us" are provided, membership is not contingent upon specific views or goals but merely consists in echoing the *a priori* "right" sounds coming from the centre (which could be anyone ranging from the local coordinator to the senior officials in the president's administration).

The other brand—*Iduschie vmeste*—seems to be a familiar mixture of synecdoche and allegory: in the place of a goal-oriented behaviour, thinking, or belief there is an overblown self-referentiality—the iconic display of collective performance as such. In fact, both names look like parodies, reducing their absolutist and totalitarian prototypes *ad absurdum*: Even in the least democratic contexts, public self-identifications normally have predicates which *describe* (rather than *point at*) group identities in some way: to be sure, Louis XIV's famous saying *L'État, c'est moi* is a shameless hyperbole, but it explicitly limits the content of the speaker's Self to the sphere of governance (rather

9

than, say, religion or history). In a similar vein, the fascist *Marcia su Roma* in 1922 was not only a simulation of mobility but a journey towards the center of political power with the clear intention of taking it over.

But even if the issue of unfortunate branding is left aside, the questions keep popping up. The ideological vacuity of Nashi, thinly disguised by indiscriminate flashing of "unquestionably positive concepts" (Teun van Dijk) such as "truth" or "tolerance", effectively turns them into secular versions of chiliastic sects. Apparently, moral perfection, hedonist happiness, and other chaotically assembled virtues are only to be achieved as long as Vladimir Putin presides over Russia (and, possibly, the rest of the world as well). Indeed, the meek slogan *Vova, ia s toboi,* unambiguous in its faux ambiguity, attests to the absence of direct communication between the group's members, hopelessly dependent on "external regulation" (Norbert Elias), and their seemingly omnipotent but unreachable super-ego in Kremlin.

This reduction of political loyalty to *Herdentrieb* leads to a peculiar political standing of the youth groups reminiscent of the model outlined by Adolf Hitler in his Reichstag speech on May 21, 1935: as long as 38 million Germans have elected their "single deputy", there is no need to bother about "democracy", parties, and parliaments. Indeed, as long as the state leader, whatever his current title is, grants youth organizations their semi-official status and provides funding, he is indeed their sole constituency and also their major, if not the only, paying member. Unsurprisingly, the only electorate Russian youth groups are really concerned about is that very "single deputy" who makes decisions about their political survival. Needless to say, even in today's Russia this simplified version of "election campaign" may not be to everyone's taste; hence the rules of the game require winners to regularly engage in noisy imitations of grassroots politics, ranging from educating general population to attacking political dissidents.

Unlike many scholars in the field, Jussi Lassila uses "hard facts"—verbal and visual data - to reveal the complexity of his object. His masterful application of various analytical techniques, intertwined with micro-sociological analysis, leaves no stone unturned: Nashi's identit(y)ies and communicative actions are shown to be far more complex than Durkheimian and Habermasian universals would lead us to believe. It would be a shame if general discourse analysts and media scholars would pass over this book due to its Russian specifics: being a must-read for all those who deal with Russian and post-Soviet studies, Lassila's book is also of much use for all those who look for new insights on the crossroads of social and linguistic studies.

*Kirill Postoutenko*
Queen Mary University of London

# I Introduction

In 2007, despite growing international criticism of the Kremlin's aggressive rhetoric,[1] Vladimir Putin enjoyed extraordinarily high domestic support.[2] However, during Putin's third presidential term, that started in May 2012, criticism of his rule has become emphatically domestic as well. The most important moment of change between 2007 and 2012 was the sudden and large-scale blow the regime faced by the protest cycle that started after the parliamentary elections in December 2011 (Gel'man 2013: 167-181). Although the Kremlin managed to suppress the most visible protests over the course of the year, aided by the opposition's organizational incapacity, no large-scale state-patriotic formations, typical for the period before the protests, have since appeared. Although the so called Russian People's Front—originally established as an electoral tool of the United Russia party for the notorious parliamentary elections of 2011—has become more active in responding to the criticism of Putin, its actual organizational and ideological status has remained vague. More importantly, in terms of gaining legitimacy for the regime, the People's Front openly resorts to Putin as a new-old national leader, while "sovereign democracy" and other ideological emphases from the pre-protest era are missing. In short, the regime has become even more dependent on the figure of Putin than before in seeking its political legitimacy.

The reason for the Kremlin's lack of success in finding new substitutes for implementing its formally democratic authoritarian rule can be explained by the crisis of the regime's symbolic politics. In terms of co-optive and coercive strategies of the rule, typical for electoral authoritarian regimes in general

---

[1]  At least three episodes of that year come to mind in particular: Putin's speech at the Munich Security Conference on February 2007 (Putin Says 2007); The Kremlin's hard-line stance towards the EU concerning the so called the Bronze Soldier dispute in Estonia in April-May (see below and Chapter 8), and Russia's pretentious flag planting on the Arctic Seabed in August 2007 in order to prove to the international community that there existed a geological, "natural" connection between the Arctic's seabed and Russian territory (Russians Plant Flag 2007).

[2]  In December 2007 Putin's index of support was 75. That is, 87 percent of Russians approved him while 12 percent did not (87-12 = 75). In November 2013 this index was 24 consisting of 61 percent of those who approved him and 37 percent who did not (Levada 2013, Indeksy).

(Smyth, Sobolev & Soboleva 2013), this is a serious crisis. Various coercive means have been used, for instance when suppressing the protests that occurred with the beginning of Putin's third presidential term. Nevertheless, the major problem of coercive means, including the hidden ones, is that they may become costly if revealed by the public. This was the case in the escalation of protests in December 2011, when large-scale hidden coercion—voter fraud and falsification—was revealed and made public on the Internet. Harder means of coercion—violence against protesters—is even more risky in terms of unpredictable public reactions. Thus, with view of sustaining legitimacy in a semi-authoritarian, formally competitive political system, the usage of open repression must be excluded, and what remains is the usage of seemingly costless symbolic support for the regime. Nonetheless, this kind of support can become costly as well, especially if the regime's overall legitimacy is decreasing. The breakthrough of the Internet as a political venue in Russia since December 2011 has shown that state-driven symbolic politics and spectacles may become not only worthless but also highly harmful for the regime's image, and, consequently, extremely productive for the opposition. Referring to the most skilful opposition figure in this regard, Aleksei Navalny, Regina Smyth, Anton Sobolev and Irina Soboleva point out that "pro-Putin events created the opportunity for more than a million citizens to see (via YouTube etc.) behind the curtain of the constructed support for the president" (2013: 25).

The aim of this book, the youth movement Nashi, is to provide a microcosm of the Putin-era symbolic politics. It was established in 2005 and was to become the largest youth formation since the days of the Soviet Union's Komsomol. The movement's demise over the course of the year 2012 figured as an important symbol of the Kremlin's politics and was a cause for large-scale criticism. However, the actual point of this book is not to scrutinize the movement's last breaths within the regime's general crisis of legitimacy but to show that difficulties of the Kremlin's symbolic politics that came to the fore in the late 2011 can be tracked back to the time when Putin's regime enjoyed levels of support it can now only dream of. For this purpose the book focuses on Nashi during the period of 2005 - 2009, particularly on the movement's activities before its first major re-structuring of early 2008.

In 2014, Nashi can be approached as a textbook case of Putin-era symbolic politics and its flaws. Given Nashi's odd, carnivalistic performances, its symbolic recycling of the Soviet-era volunteer work, and its vulgar and aggressive position against opposition movements, particularly the Kremlin's liberal opposition,[3] it is hardly surprising that the public image of the movement, both in the West and, more importantly, in Russia itself, has been negative. The disappearance of the movement is hardly a coincidence either, considering the regime's arrangements after the protests in December 2011, in particular, the demotion of the movement's administrative founder, Vladislav Surkov, from the Kremlin's top administration to the less prestigious post of Deputy Prime Minister for Economic Modernisation in December 2011. The important point, however, is that Nashi's negative image did not first appear in Russia with Putin's decreased popularity and the beginning of the large-scale protests; rather, this negative image has been manifested throughout the existence of pro-Kremlin youth formations over Putin's political leadership. For instance, the first Putin-era pro-Kremlin youth formation, Idushchie Vmeste, which acted as a sort of predecessor of Nashi, conducted a special book campaign against a few popular Russian writers for the sake of "youth's correct moral values" in 2002. As a result, the action led to the Kremlin's disassociation and official condemnation of Idushchie Vmeste and finally contributed to the accused writers' growing popularity.

Similarly, active and intensive protesting against the removal of the "Bronze Soldier," a Soviet-era statue in Tallinn, in April-May 2007, led to Nashi's reorganization and the closure of the majority of Nashi's regional sections in early 2008. Over the course of the period followed by the re-organization and before its demise in 2012, Nashi's active sub-organization Stal' was responsible for the scandalous installation of "impaled enemies of Russia" in the annual pro-Kremlin youth summer camp in 2010.[4] As a result, Western companies

---

3 The documentary Putin's Kiss offers a devastating insight into Nashi's anti-opposition activities (2011).

4 The issue was about an alley built in the camp and framed by impaled portraits of "anti-Russian" politicians and officials. In relation to this scandal the presidential commission for the development of civil society in Russia demanded Vassili Iakemenko, the former leader of Nashi, and Idushchie Vmeste, since 2008 the head of federal youth affairs in Russia, to explain this incident regarding the theme of the camp in 2010: "Youth issues instead of global ideological missions, such as the fight against Orange Revolution".

sponsoring the 2010-camp, including Daimler AG and Tupperware, announced that they would not sponsor the camp if similar incidents occurred in
the future. Rather than demonstrating well-planned and calculated persistence on patriotism and moral conservatism, these incidents suggest that the
whole pro-Putin youth movement has continuously struggled with its public
image since their idol appeared in Russia's political arena.

If we suppose, as media coverage has often suggested, that Nashi acted
purely as passive servant of the Kremlin policies, an important question remains: Why has its political communication repeatedly failed? To put Nashi
and the Kremlin into a single category is an obvious oversimplification. Naturally, Nashi's scandals could have a potential drawback for the Kremlin's image as well, as the protest cycle in 2011-12 showed. Nevertheless, in order to
examine Nashi's agency within non-intended outcomes of its activities over
the period of Putin's and, to a lesser extent, Medvedev's popularity, it is critical to scrutinize Nashi's political communication as well as the socio-political
conditions under which this communication has emerged. In other words,
what are the socio-political and cultural forces which pose evident obstacles
in Nashi's communication, and how do they appear in the movement's communication? This angle, I argue, sheds light not only on Nashi and pro-
governmental youth activism, but also offers a productive perspective for understanding political practices in post-Soviet Russia more broadly, including
the Kremlin's emerged crisis of legitimacy.

### Conceptual and Theoretical Framework

In addition to considerable interest from Russian and foreign media, Nashi
has also evoked notable academic interest. To mention these earlier studies
on Nashi, Julie Hemment has examined the group's projects as realizations
of post-Soviet Russian civil society practices (2007; 2009; 2012; 2014);
Graeme B. Robertson has evaluated it as an ersatz social movement in relation to Putin's regime, in terms of regulating civil society practices in Russia
(2009). In the same vein, Robert Horvath has approached Nashi as a central

---

Zapadnye kompanii otkrestilis' ot foruma "Seliger" (2010); "29-ia stat'ia Konstitutsii ne
narushena (2010); For more Nashi's connections to the Orange Revolution, see Umland (2009; 2010); Horvath (2011); Lane (2009). See a comprehensive ethnographic
analysis of the Seliger 2010 in Mijnssen's (2012) study.

part of Putin's "preventive counter-orange" strategies (2011); Doug Buchacek has analyzed its early years from the viewpoint of generational mobilization (2006); and Marlene Laruelle has studied youth patriotism and memory politics in relation to official patriotic policies, with a special focus on Nashi as well as the Molodaia Gvardiia (Young Guard), the youth section of Russia's party in power, the United Russia (2009c; 2011). Valerie Sperling has studied Nashi's role in relation to the Kremlin's patriotic policies and Putin's image with a special focus on gendered practices (2009; 2012; 2014); Ivo Mijnssen has treated Nashi's role and ideology through its three nodal points: Orange Revolution, patriotism and memory politics (especially with regard to the "Bronze Soldier"), and the annual youth forum "Seliger" (2012); Maya Atwal has approached the group in terms of activist views in relation to Nashi's official role, and has discussed its conditions of sustainability (2009); Dmitry Andreev has also treated Nashi, as well as its predecessor, Idushchie Vmeste, in terms of the movements' complexity in relation to the Kremlin's official policies (2006) and Ulrich Schmid has paid attention to Nashi's communicative strategies, evaluating them as a continuation of Soviet-era traditions and Soviet-era conceptual art (2006).

Many of these invaluable contributions to the study of Nashi have largely treated this movement as a (sometimes seemingly passive) realization of elite—that is to say, Kremlin—political projects. In comparison with the mentioned contributions the most distinguishable feature of this book, I would argue, is in its detailed focus on the movement's own voice, with the aim to examine the "logic" of this voice within Nashi's socio-political setting; how Nashi communicatively "handles" its position between a reputation as a Kremlin rubber stamp and the cogent mobilization of largely apolitical Russia's youth.

Within the socio-symbolic dimension of Russia's patriotic and nationalistic manifestations over the last fifteen years, this book examines the political communication of Nashi. Brian McNair defines political communication as all of those elements of communication which might be said to constitute a political image or identity (1995: 4-5). Whereas McNair's definition is about political actors' various messages to citizens via the media with feedback effects for the political actors, my principal focus is on the level of a political actor's online publications. In addition to Nashi's representativeness as a Putin-era patriotic youth movement, it represents an insightful case of a political formation whose values meet relatively large support in the Russian society, but at the same time, in terms of the movement's public scandals, Nashi appears as a phenomenon which indicates a clear public reluctance to it. In other words, Russians' relatively widespread support to Putin, his patriotic policies, and conservative values have been evident, but this support is seemingly not present with political actors which align with these values.

My standpoint is that the movement's self-produced official web-texts—as distinct from texts produced in informal forums, e.g. blogs, to say nothing of secondary media writings on Nashi—reveal those communicative strategies by which it aims to manage the tensions and constraints posed by the movement's socio-political position in the largest potential publicity (i.e. the Internet). These online writings can be framed as crystallizations of Nashi's firm voice, choices which supposedly best represent its public image. According to Ralph Negrine, within the Internet social movements can bypass the traditional media by themselves while movements' websites can be seen "as the thing that binds a movement together and gives it coherence" (2012: 34-35). Within this standpoint I approach Nashi's online writings as *the anticipation of an ideal youth*. The verb "anticipate" instead of the verb "construct"—which is relatively common in various discourse analysis approaches—refers to Pierre Bourdieu's observations of language in which communicative agency with various aspects of social uncertainty is the central dimension (1991: 66-89). Hence, Nashi partially produces an ideal youth as well as its own public image, but this is principally an activity which needs to be framed as highly constrained process.

I follow the conceptual framing according to which Nashi's discursive production of an ideal youth includes a tension between *didactics* and *stimulation*, angling to bring these two dimensions into a convincing wholeness. The movement's designation of didactics can thus be defined as official and conformist, especially the educative relatedness of its activities. This concerns, for example, Nashi's discursive production of state patriotism (Sperling 2009; 2012; Mijnssen 2012). Consequently, youth's unresponsiveness towards existing political formations in Russia, which evidently concerns Nashi as well, is at least partially recognized by the movement as the successor of ultimately failed Idushchie Vmeste, and this bad reputation is communicatively related to the didactic dimension. It follows that this recognition activates the need for communicative work that could downplay this reputation. Thus, a demand for stimulating discourse emanates from Nashi's expectations of Russian youth as autonomous and, more precisely, apolitical. The crucial addition to the division between didactic and stimulative dimensions is that the tension between them is not so much a substantive issue; didactics would be exclusively linked, let us say, to patriotic elements and stimulation, to "non-patriotic" ones. On the contrary, the tension particularly lies in Nashi's assumptions of a profitable style to produce "correct" ideal youth, for instance, through patriotism.

Without a theoretical grounding the division between didactics and stimulation is thin, since these definitions are clearly subjective. A didactic instruction can be very stimulative or, vice versa, a "stimulative" signifier may be felt as a didactic political, or cultural, order. To theorize this division accordingly, especially in terms of attaching the concept of anticipation to my approach, I rely on Bourdieu's views on cultural production which are compatible with his notions of language use (1993: 125-141; 1996: 216; 1991). According to Bourdieu, all recognizable artifacts of social reality (e.g. language of political actors) have a particular relation to the aspect of hierarchized cultural production. In terms of artistic contexts, Bourdieu writes (1996: 216-217): "As liberated as the holders of the different kinds of capital may be from external constraints and demands, they are traversed by the necessity of the fields which encompass them: the need for profit, whether economic or political. It follows that they are at any one time at the site of a struggle between two principles of hierarchization: the heteronomous principle which favors those who dominate the field economically or politically (for example "bourgeois art"), and the autonomous principle (for example "art for art's sake")."[5] These two types of hierachizations can also be also called external and internal hierarchizations which clarifies the principles of the field in acting towards other fields (external hierarchization) and towards its own field (internal hierarchization). The internal hierarchization is the same as the field of restricted cultural production, and the external hierarchization is the field of large-scale cultural production.

---

5  To radically condense Bourdieu's theory, it could be called a continuous theoretization of social fields. The most general field division is the division and mutual relation between economic and cultural fields (for more, see Bourdieu 1984).

To transform this framework to Nashi's political communication, the case is about the movement's agency in the given political situation. This situation is between official state policies and the movement's ambition to stimulatively represent this political "didactics" for youth. In this respect, according to Bourdieu's theoretical framing, didactics and stimulation are no longer loose categories that depend on purely subjective judgments. Rather, they orientate to the different fields of Nashi's socio-political reality that stand against each other. It is Nashi's political position that forces it to search for a somewhat cogent balance between these incompatible fields of (political) cultural production. Thus large-scale cultural production (didactics) can be defined as the movements' officially supported cultural production. Youth has only a part in this, albeit an important one, among other elements. This principle is closely linked to the understanding of youth in official policy, including the Soviet legacy within its paternalistic and instructive aspects.[6] Consequently, the restricted cultural production (stimulation) is Nashi's cultural production, which aims to highlight the notion of youth as distinct from adult driven youth practices.

In very general terms the tension between didactics and stimulation can be understood as the tension between adult and youth cultural production in the field of politics. More specifically, this tension comes about as friction between those who have power and authority in terms of symbolic capital to establish particular political projects (like the president, or prime minister in Russia) and those who lack authority and legitimacy to implement these projects. In other words, Nashi definitely operates, on the one hand, as a representative of large-scale cultural production (state policies), but on the other hand this task of representativeness must be carried out in a situation that requires symbolic capital suitable for the rules of restricted cultural production (youth) as well. Consequently, following Bourdieu, it can be assumed that cultural production that relies too heavily either on large-scale, or restricted, production appears to fail, while Nashi's central task is to bring the demands posed by these fields into a convincing wholeness. The task of the state is the

---

6   See, for example, Strategiia gosudarstevennoi molodëzhnoi politiki s kom-mentariiami (2007), Gosudarstvennaia programma Patrioticheskaia vospitanie grazhdan Rossiiskoi Federatsii na 2006-2010 gody (2005).

task of the youth, or vice versa. In sum, the major aim for the movement is to diminish the tension between these two.

When talking about social movements in general and Nashi's failed outcomes in particular, the aspect of mobilization cannot be ignored. There is no movement of any kind without members, but there is hardly a movement without resources (material and immaterial) either. The tension between the didactics and stimulation of Nashi can be understood as the movement's searching for optimal discursive mobilization strategies for the purpose of effective mobilization including resources for this mobilization. These strategies should be profitable, on the one hand, vis-à-vis the didactic demand which crucially resonates with its official side, and the potential effects for sustainability of receiving material resources. On the other hand, the stimulative demand resonates with the movement's capability to produce such communication that could mobilize more members. Although Nashi's online writings figure as an inseparable part of its mobilization strategies, it is worth emphasizing that I am not relying on such resource mobilization theories of social movement studies which reduce all possible material and immaterial aspects—used by a particular movement—into more or less rationally calculated resources for mobilization (Jasper 1997: 29-33). According to this approach, strategies of mobilization (e.g. discursive) are principally regarded as instrumental motives of action in which movements and groups act for strategic advantage and individuals act in pursuit of their own interest. Instead, I rely on James M. Jasper's views on modifying the resource mobilization paradigm, and interpret resource mobilization as "a strategic process of cultural persuasion" (ibid.: 31). In my case this strategic process is Nashi's discursive production of an ideal youth that should resonate with the whole society but principally diminish the tension between, as I argue, incompatible forms of cultural production; between didactics and stimulation.

Mobilization as a strategic process of cultural persuasion understood within Bourdieu's framework is fruitfully compatible with those views of cultural pragmatism that aim to transcend the polarization between structure-oriented and agency-oriented approaches. A special case is the modification of the concept of ritual. Jeffrey C. Alexander points out that social performances, whether individual or collective, can be analogized systematically to theatrical ones (2006: 29): "Rituals are episodes of repeated and simplified cultural communication in which the direct partners to a social interaction, and those observing it, share a mutual belief in the descriptive and prescriptive validity of the communication's symbolic contents and accept the authenticity of one another's intentions. It is because of this shared understanding of intention and content, and in the intrinsic validity of the interaction, that rituals have their effect and affect."

Alexander's description is actually a "ritual-like action" when it is related to modern societies, or ones that can be broadly labeled as nation-states. The difference between rituals and ritual-like actions (the latter is the same as social performances) lies in the fact that in pre-modern societies, the communicative components in various cultures were profoundly ritual (ibid.: 29);[7] they were fused and not institutionally separated in any sense. In other words, the components of a social performance were all blended. Since then, previously combined components of ritualistic communication started to "de-fuse." Along with the emergence of more complex societies and their cultural formations, components of social performances started to institutionalize into separate formations: actors, audiences, representations, and so forth (ibid.: 42-51). In the case of Nashi, this "institutionalization" (separation) in the post-Soviet space can be seen in terms of the de-fusion between an imagined and politically constructed youth, and an autonomous "real" youth. Thus, the most important task for modern, or secular, rituals is to "re-fuse" these more or less institutionalized and separate components of performance into one coherent meaningful whole. In Alexander's words (ibid.: 54-55):

> The goal of secular performances, whether on stage or in society, remains the same as the ambition of sacred ritual. They stand or fall on their ability to produce psychological identification and cultural extension. The aim is to create, via skillful and affecting performance, the emotional connection of audience with actor and text and thereby to create conditions for projecting cultural meaning from performance to audience. To the extent these two conditions have been achieved, one can say that elements of performance have become fused.

---

7   Following Victor Turner's views, Alexander uses the birth of the ancient Greek drama as the initial dividing line between ritual and ritual-like strategy (2006: 29; for more, see Turner 1974). Alexander classifies these components into actors, audiences, representations, means of symbolic production, social powers, and mis en scenes (ibid.: 38-40).

To sum up my intention to approach Nashi's political communication within Bourdieu's "anticipation," and "cultural production," I specify this viewpoint with Nashi's socio-political background as a pro-Kremlin "counter-orange" youth movement when it was established in early 2005. It is not very far-fetched to contextualize Ukraine's Orange Revolution in the late 2004 into the quote above. In addition to youth's central role in Maidan Square in Kiev—the major venue of the Orange Revolution—that event was able to "re-fuse" sep-arate components of this social performance into a one "orange" community. This can be captured in Andrew Wilson's description of the events in Kiev in late 2004 (Wilson via Zherebkin 2009: 199-202): "The mood in the Maidan did not just indicate support for (Viktor) Iushchenko or (Julia) Tymoshenko per-sonally; it was the articulate anger of a people finding their voice…students wanted a change in political culture, the poor wanted a change in political cul-ture, and small and medium-sized businesses wanted a change in political culture." In terms of ritual-like strategy, Iushchenko's camp was able to con-duct "an affecting performance, the emotional connection of audience with ac-tor and text and thereby to create conditions for projecting cultural meaning from performance to audience." This book aims to show that Nashi's political discourse includes a similar ambition, but the crucial difference from Ukraine is that this ambition emanates from a regime-maintaining position. To follow Alexander's formulation, the creation of such emotional connection between didactics and stimulation that could properly oscillate between them is a ma-jor challenge for Nashi. Moreover, despite partially different socio-political cir-cumstances, it was a challenge for its predecessor Idushchie Vmeste, and in more hypothetical vein, it seemingly remains challenge for Nashi's followers.

### Data and the Structure of the Book

For the primary data I chose 38 of Nashi's online publications that appeared between 2005 and 2009, as well as seven texts from predecessor organiza-tion Idushchie Vmeste and a few media publications. In general, these texts show that Nashi has been advocating in favor of and against various social, political, and cultural concerns. On the movement's website, these texts con-cerned various interrelated activities. Patriotism emerges as a particularly strong theme, one that Nashi hopes to incorporate into different spheres of its activities. The sustainability of many of these activities has been limited, culminated by the closure of Nashi's website for several months at the time of writing. When the site was working, new projects and sections often appeared to be terminological innovations that simply restated formerly expressed goals, rather than substantively new projects. Hence, except Nashi's key ideological and recruitment-texts, as well as texts related to the Bronze Soldier theme, I chose the data rather randomly; principally on the basis of how a chosen text partially represents those features that the analysis has partially revealed in the case of previous texts. In this vein, the main logic in collecting a reasonable amount of data is based on the idea of saturation; randomly chosen texts start to produce distinctively enough such results again and again which support the theoretical argument of the study (the tension between didactics and stimulation).

These primary texts were additionally supplemented by discussions with a few insider voices, obtained through three non-structured interviews with activists conducted in May 2008 and March 2009. Each interview lasted approximately 50 minutes. At the time of the interviews two of them worked in top leadership positions in the organization, and the third served as a commissar, the designation that Nashi uses for its activists. I found the first interviewee through a colleague. The next interviewee was found through a Live-Journal blog and was contacted through personal e-mail correspondence. The third interviewee I reached on the advice of the second interviewee. The principal aim of these interviews was to hear their views in terms of joining the movement, the role of the Internet and the main website, as well as the role of image for a social movement. While these interviews work principally as supplementary data, I was satisfied with these three interviews. They add firsthand perspectives that supplement and illustrate trends identified in Nashi's online publications. The interviewees are presented via pseudonyms without mentioning their age.

In terms of the systematic discourse analysis that this book is methodologically about, approximately 40 texts along with interviews lasting almost three hours in total mean that the depth of analyzing the data varies significantly. In addition, data samples differed broadly. The length of Nashi's texts, for example, varies from a couple of sentences to 55 pages. Hence, whereas some of these texts only receive a mention, some are systematically analyzed.

Longer writings have been split into separate samples; altogether, this book is based on 65 numbered data samples.

After this introductory chapter, Chapter 2 contextualizes the concepts of didactics and stimulation by providing an overview to current socio-political position of Russia's youth in light of perestroika and the 1990s. The final section of the chapter, "Values and youth policy in Putin era," sheds light on general value patterns in Russian society over the course of Putin's rule, including youth. Chapter 3 deepens this contextualization by focusing on the role of Nashi in Putin's period. The chapter starts with an overview of Nashi's predecessor Idushchie Vmeste, moves then to Nashi's birth and position vis-à-vis other youth movements and finally locates Nashi into the framework of the political participation of Russia's youth.

Chapter 4 begins the analysis of Nashi's central online writings. Here, I first compare Nashi's ideological outline with its predecessor's key political text and then move to Nashi's recruitment texts. The analysis of Nashi's ideological outline, Manifesto, in light of its commented version, aims to make apparent the constant tension between didactics and stimulation within the movement's recruitment strategies. The chapter ends with in-depth analysis of Nashi's special program for the promotion of the army which provides another case-study of this tension.

In Chapter 5 I take a broader look at Nashi's online writings, first by interviews with Nashi activists concerning their viewpoints of joining the movement, and then by analyzing their views of the Internet. In the final section of the chapter, I contextualize Nashi's dominant practices concerning its online writings with these activist views, and elaborate upon Nashi's communication in light of Soviet-era communication ideals. This chapter provides a preliminary picture of the central discursive strategy of Nashi's political communication within didactics and stimulation, namely Nashi's political ritual, which the following chapter concerns. In this chapter I provide a case-study of Nashi's special cycle-marathon action which blurs certain historical landmarks of national identity and youth activism sensed as modern, and move then to central communicative elements of Nashi's political ritual, its "ritualistic cues." This chapter brings the issue of image preliminarily to the fore, especially in comparison with previous activist views concerning the role of the Internet.

To continue and deepen this discussion, Chapter 7 begins with the examination of the activists' views of image. After that I move toward Nashi's cases in which fashion is harnessed as part of the movement's political communication. Since this chapter aims to show how image and image-fashioning create a sort of pinnacle for the tension between didactics and stimulation, Chapter 8 offers the in-depth analysis of the rupture of Nashi's balancing within this tension: that is, the most well-known and fatal activities of Nashi, the Bronze Soldier, those that followed the removal of the Bronze Soldier statue in Tallinn, Estonia. This chapter adds the aspect of emotion to Nashi's political communication since it plays an important role in the tension between didactics and stimulation. Considering the outcomes of these activities, as well as their connections to Idushcie Vmeste's notorious book campaign, this chapter aims to demonstrate how Nashi's socio-political position results as a failed attempt to reconcile its incompatible communicative demands between the state and apolitical youth. Chapter 9 discusses the findings of the study.

# II Between the State and Apolitical Youth

### From Crisis of Komsomol to Absence of Youth

By their very nature didactics and stimulation applies not only to Nashi, or post-Soviet Russian youth culture, but to youth culture at large. According to Jon Savage, "from the last quarter of the nineteenth century there were many conflicting attempts to envisage and define the status of youth; to regiment adolescents using national policies, or through artistic, prophetic visions that reflected the wish of the young to live by their own rules" (2007: xv). Accordingly the need of control over youth was principally justified by the social concern over juvenile delinquency, and this delinquent behaviour of young people was capable of unleashing moral panics, spread by media in particular, because of the symbolic importance of youth. In brief, the future health of society depended upon the moral health of its youth (Pilkington 1994: 14).

In terms of moral concern, or even panic that youth cultures have always activated in the world of adults, Russia and the Soviet Union are not exceptional from the West (Pilkington 1994: 44). Nonetheless, there are certain crucial differences in the Soviet tradition that provide a special importance for the concepts of didactics and stimulation in the case of post-Soviet Russia. Hilary Pilkington (ibid.) defines three key aspects in this respect which are worth mentioning here: First of these was "the absence of capitalist mode of production in the Soviet Union which principally fostered a market-led youth culture in the West." For instance, this is the case with the invention of suoh marketing term as "teenager" in post-war US (Savage 2007: xv). The second heavily influenced peculiarity in the Soviet Union was "the role of Komsomol (Communist Youth League) as a single, unified and ideologically motivated youth organisation" (Pilkington 1994: 44). The third aspect, elementarily linked to the Komsomol as well, was in the political institution of this official youth league; "not only youth itself but all societal and scientific issues on youth were infiltrated by this massive organisation resulting as a highly monolithic discourse on youth" (ibid.). From this standpoint the control over youth in the Soviet tradition not only lacked the commercial aspect which was a typical opposite-pair in the Western discussions on youth (that is, "youth-as-object-of-social-control" and "youth-as-passive-consumer," or "youth-as-trouble" and "youth-as- fun") but consisted a sort of double concern over youth; "youth-as-constructors-of-communism"    and    "youth-as-victims-of-Western-influence" (ibid.).

During perestroika this double concern was forced into more and more visible negotiations concerning appropriate practices of "rebuilding" of the Komsomol education. In particular it touched public debates on appropriate and inappropriate Western influences along with the crisis of the Soviet system. According to Pilkington between 1987 and 1989 not only emerged a specific perestroika debate on youth—that is, various attempts to modify aforementioned double concern paradigm which was the case during the earlier perestroika—but that debate itself became a central perestroika theme (ibid.: 118). This meant the politicization of social and cultural activity around official (*formaly*) and non-official (*neformaly*) activities, and it was timed with the emerged official discussion on democratization of perestroika (ibid.: 118-119).

The use of public language during this democratization stage of perestroika is an illuminating example in this respect. Michael S. Gorham points out that along with the political demands of "new thinking" (*novoe myshlenie*) and "revitalization" (*obnovlenie*) in order to renew the Soviet system, the language culture of perestroika and its pedagogical principles were reconsidered as well (2000: 617-618). Gorham asserts that "the discourse of perestroika and glasnost shifted the focus on language as an emblem of Soviet patriotism to a model that saw language as a tool for social and political reforms" (ibid.). Pedagogic material written in the years of perestroika generally supported the idea of dialogue of equality (*dialog ravnopraviia*) in which all participants would be active to the same degree instead of the traditional monologic teacher discourse in pre-perestroika school education (ibid.). However, these optimistic expectations of new language and communication practices in the creation of the new, more individual and active Soviet citizen clashed with well grounded concerns about the actual skills of the people: the question was how to express these new visions of democratization with the available communicative and linguistic instruments (ibid). The problem of glasnost was not in glasnost and perestroika itself but rather in the incapability of people to follow the principles of these ideals.

A booklet "Komsomol, Teacher, Pupil," dedicated to the issues education in the Komsomol work and published during in the democratization stage of perestroika in 1989, is a revealing textual artefact of the voices of glasnost, which—from today's point of view—were ultimately incompatible with each other (Vul'fov & Ivanov 1989: 3-4). On the one hand, the booklet reflects the contradiction between the ideals of perestroika and the reality in the schools. On the other hand, it reflects teachers' concerns of such glasnost which seemingly clashes with the ideals of perestroika (ibid.):

> Everybody talks about perestroika, the school reform, XX meeting of the VLKSM[8] but I don't see any changes in the work of my school, or in its Komsomol organization either. Things are not going better but everything is getting worse. How can you explain this?
> We recently had a quarrel in our collective; is it possible that older pupils (starsheklassiki) can be rockers, metallists, etc, and active Komsomol members at the same time? What do you think?

In light of these examples the challenge between perestroika/idealised glasnost and the real glasnost was significantly evident in educational settings where different generations met each other: teachers met their students and pedagogical practices met their actors in the situation where the horizon for unintended results had been irreversibly opened. The authors of the booklet strive to offer reasonable answers using the official discourse stating in many parts, however, that there are no unambiguous answers to such questions as presented above. As a culmination between Soviet authoritative discourse, and the new, and inevitably shocking reality of glasnost, the booklet offers a few summaries of pupils' views for teachers of the Komsomol work on different educational levels. Here is one example (ibid.: 41):

**Teacher!**
Today Komsomol-upper school pupils (*Komsomoltsy-starshe-klassiki*) are concerned about the following questions: I think (and this is not only my opinion) Komsomol has started to lose its idea. Is it not time to change the style of its work? Is it right that in one (Komsomol) organization there are 14-year-old teenagers as well as old boys older than a quarter of a century?

---

8   Abbreviation from Vsesoiuznyi Leninskii Kommunisticheskii Soiuz Molodëzhi (All Soviet Leninist Communist Union of Youth).

Glasnost becomes apparent by explicating challenging discourses (pupils' questions) by which teachers are reminded with the Soviet type of imperatives about their existence and importance in the contemporary (perestroika era) school and Komsomol work. However, the general response to these challenges goes along the lines of the official discourse within its sacred ideological references (Lenin, the constitution of USSR) which hardly diminishes the real conditions of these challenges. In this vein it seems that the authorised side of the society—in this case authorised authors of the official booklet published by official Soviet printing house *Pedagogika* dedicated to educational issues—well admitted the key challenges of the society, here in educational settings. However, admittance appears not in the form of clear answers and solutions but recycling these challenges as new components of official discourse. They were thrown to teachers whose position as official pedagogues could not match the realizations of glasnost that the pupils' views characterise.

### After the Collapse

Along with multiple chaotic aspects of Russian society since the collapse of the Soviet Union in 1991, the issues of youth and youth policy were also characterised by chaos. In certain respects, it seems that in the aftermath of the collapse, perestroika-era tension had diminished in such that the failed ideological regime was not superseded by those discourses which deeply challenged the socialist discursive regime, for example democratic initiatives by youth. Instead, the whole youth issue had become "apparent" by an almost total absence in political practices. In this respect, the youth policy practices of the 1990s can be seen as a continuation of the crisis of the centralized Soviet youth policy that came onto the agenda during perestroika and resulted in a legitimacy crisis for the Komsomol. Pilkington sums up the dramatic change between perestroika and the situation after the collapse of the USSR by pointing out that the previous "constructors-of-communism" element of the Komsomol with its aspect of generational continuity had gone leaving a vision of youth with neither a future nor a present (1994: 193). Quite revealingly, in the constitution of the Russian Federation in 1993, the concept of youth policy is not mentioned at all (Lukov 2006; Omel'chenko 2006).

According to Iuri Korguniuk the ignorance toward youth issues among political parties and movements during the 1990s is not exceptional because in post-Soviet Russia youth was generally regarded as politically indifferent, and hence, useless in the sense of potential supporters of political parties (2000). However, although the absence of youth issues in the 1990s was much more concrete than in the Putin era, it is not correct to argue that the 1990s was an "empty decade" for youth politics in Russia. According to Valery Lukov, during perestroika, in 1987, outlines for the new youth policy of the state began to be formulated (2006: 75). He argues that for the first time in the Soviet history this youth policy was planned to offer possibilities of "self-fulfilment" (*samore-alizatsiia*) for a youngster as distinct from earlier Soviet didactic policies of the communist education. The main problem with this new policy draft which highlighted the solution to everyday challenges of a Soviet youngster instead of former ideological didactics was the time of its establishment; April 1991, that was, less than a year before the end of the empire. Whilst having history as a Soviet document, this new youth policy was inevitably useless for the new leaders of post-Soviet Russia despite its rather individual and liberal pro-gressivity (ibid.). Following Lukov's views, a continuum can be seen from the state youth policy of the perestroika era to 1993 when "the main orientations of the state youth policy"[9] was accepted since the emphasis in these new ori-entations was mainly on youth itself without any explicit references to ac-counts of ideological resource which were the core of the Soviet-era youth programs and policies.

The development from highly didactic underpinnings of the pre-perestroika to the perestroika era liberation, and finally to almost fully individually oriented "youth policy" of the 1990s may offer us rather clear-cut picture of official dis-courses on youth. The collapse of the Soviet Union and the Komsomol did not allow us to argue that the shift towards youth's grass-roots level socio-economic concerns since the late perestroika would have meant the dissolu-

---

[9]   These orientations were 1) guarantee of the rights of youth; 2) guarantee of the rights of youth in labor; 3) collaboration with entrepreneurial activities of youth; 4) state sup-port for young families; 5) guarantee of social benefits; 6) support for talented youth, 7) formulation of conditions which support physical and spiritual development of youth; 8) support for youth and children associations and societies, and 9) collaboration with in-ternational youth exchange programs (Lukov 2006: 76-77).

tion of adult-driven didactics on youth and consequently, march of democratic stimulation of youth. Indeed, Pilkington points out that under the circumstances of disintegrating Soviet system the disengagement of youth led to the rise of a discourse on youth that had always been present, but never dominant: the discourse of social control which stressed the marginal position of youth in contemporary society and the weak authority of all the key socializing institutions (1994: 161-162). In this respect, the weakening of the state actually strengthened the rise of the social control discourse, but this concern paid additional attention to the material position of young people as well as solving de-tabooed problems (drugs, alcoholism, juvenile crime) among youth. Pilkington continues in pessimistic light that despite the old Soviet ideological paradigms of the youth debate were dumped, a new post-Soviet approach had remained the same paternalistic approach than before; youth was seen principally as an object of social policy (ibid.).

In the line with Pilkington's notion, Korguniuk writes that in the 1990s almost all political parties of Russia emphasized the importance of solution of multiple social problems among youth (2000). Especially those parties which more or less relied on nationalistic views of Russia's future saw youth still in light of the Soviet type of didactic control. He identifies the following five theses on youth which were present in the parties' political programs (those political groups are mentioned in brackets which highlight the given thesis): 1) Youth lives in minimal, insufficient, and in horrible conditions (political opposition of Yeltsin from liberals to communists), 2) Youth is one of the categories of the not-yet-capable people, and hence youth must be protected and supported by special social benefits (all political groups), 3) It is necessary to control the youth in all circumstances, protect the youth from alien influences (anti-liberal movements, communists, and national-patriots), 4) Youth is our future, and it is necessary to offer a chance for young people to improve their own possibilities, for example via education (all political groups), and 5) Youth owns messianic position, it is the most energetic population group (youth movements themselves) (ibid.).

Through these five theses Korguniuk defines two main orientations towards youth that the parties had in the 1990s. He calls the first orientation "bureaucratic" while it regards youth only as a category of the population locating at the one of the lowest levels of social hierarchy (ibid.). However, this category occupies a capability to improve social status rather fast, and thus it is extremely important that there is preparedness in society to control the youth because of its potential threat to upper social hierarchies. This orientation is clearly present in the thesis "it is necessary to control the youth in all circumstances, protect the youth from alien influences" which explicitly resembles the Soviet-era paradigm "constructors-of-communism" vs. "victims-of-Western- influences" (Pilkington 1994). Korguniuk calls the second orientation as "intellectual," which means that youth is a part of horizontal evaluation of society, instead of vertical evaluation as in the previous orientation. Intellectual/horizontal orientation underlines equality between the social groups; youth has equal rights and responsibilities as any other social group does have (2000). These political programmatic orientations towards youth, according to Korguniuk, cannot be labelled as "paternalistic" versus "liberal" since those accounts which can be reduced to the bureaucratic orientation—that is, didactic controlling of youth—concerns not only youth but the whole society as well. Liberal instead of horizontal is also problematic since explicitly "Soviet" type of movements of the 1990s with "true" liberals of that time both emphasised equal, i.e. horizontal, evaluation of youth. Korguniuk derives his designations "bureaucratic" and "intellectual/horizontal" from societal and political interests that he labels the interests of two political classes; bureaucrats (who see society and its actors vertically) and intellectuals (who traditionally see society through horizontal connections) (ibid.).

The division between bureaucrats and intellectuals is insightful in terms of didactics and stimulation. The issue is about youth's role in society in circumstances which reveal that the traditional top-down didactics on youth has been recognized, though hardly reflected, as ineffective in stimulating young people into societal and political activities. From this standpoint, didactics and stimulation are forms of political cultural production which stand against each other. My next overview of the Putin-era youth policy illustrates that didactics and stimulation are aimed to be combined, and this reconciliation is principally embraced with a larger national-patriotic shift in the Russian society.

### Values and Youth Policy in Putin Era

According to large-scale sociological polls, the mid 1990s appeared to be a turning point in many Russians' views and associations towards the West.

For example, whereas in late 1991, 60 % of Russians (N=6585) valued the "Western way of life" as positive, in September 1996 (N=2430), 47 % regarded the "traditional Russian way of life" as best, and 22% chose the option "difficult to answer."[10] Boris Dubin writes that due to multiple socioeconomic reasons—one could say social catastrophes in the early 1990s (failed economic reforms, growing poverty and social divisions, and finally the general impression of a bleak image of Russia from an international perspective)—Russians' values moved "backwards" (2001). This meant a shift towards symbols of national wholeness and the prestige of a great power coloured with nostalgic Soviet tones. Of course, such polls should not be interpreted in too straightforward manner although they offer some indication of general tendencies, and more importantly, of controversies between different tendencies. For example, as some polls indicate, there appears to be a respect for the parliamentary practices of politics, for instance, the importance of a true opposition to the president, but at the same time, overwhelming support for the authoritarian rights of the president (Levada 2010: 160).

To put Putin-era patriotic and nationalist youth movements into this picture, including pro-Kremlin youth formations, it is worth adding that Russia's youth was not untouched by the massive social, economic, and cultural changes that took place alongside the collapse of the Soviet system. Young Russians in particular faced the harsh side of new realities of the post-Soviet space which manifested themselves, for instance, in a wave of homeless children, a growing number of juvenile criminals, alarming increases in HIV infection along with rapidly growing traditional youth problems of drug abuse and alcoholism (Pilkington 1998: 380-1). In terms of youth's values, Elena Omel'chenko points out that youth's growing tendency towards "normal," or extreme cases the so-called "yobs" (*gopniki*) in the 1990s as the aggressive manifestation of mainstream "normalcy," was not characteristic of the marginalized, depraved, criminal, or pathogenic portion of Russian youth (2005a: 7). She continues that "this also expresses the interests of the adult majority, who radically reject cultural innovation and are determined to hold on to traditional values under conditions where the direction of social change seems

---

10 These results are based on the sociological polls conducted the research institute "All-Russian Public Opinion Research Centre" VTSIOM (Dubin 2001; see also Dubin 2011).

uncertain. Their auto-definition and practices feed not so much on the popularization of criminal images and values as on the expansion of a narrow-minded economic and cultural psychology which is fostered by the advancement of the market, barbaric capitalism, and the lack of a big idea" (ibid.; see also Omel'chenko 2004; 2005b; Pilkington 1994: 257).

Along with these growing tendencies towards "normalcy" and conservative values among youth, xenophobic attitudes have also become more widespread. Omel'chenko and Natalia Goncharova argue that the economic crisis in 1998 played a key role in activating xenophobic elements among young Russians as alternatives to the feeling of society's lost morality as well as Russia's democratic development (2009: 87). Although the role of the crisis in 1998 should not be underestimated, Lev Gudkov and Boris Dubin, on the basis of sociological polls, point out that in the Russian case the growth of xenophobic attitudes is not so much related to the weakening status of a respondent but to all the changes in a respondent's life (2006: 263). Indeed, during the Putin era these attitudes have been strengthened while the general standard of living grew. These authors see this as "the consolidation against modernization which combines ethnic phobias with imperial mythologies" (ibid.). These tendencies have had impacts on youth's symbolic production as well. For instance, researchers of the Kazan University explored students' pictures of Russia by asking them to draw pictures of the "Motherland" (*Rodina*) in the 1990s, and again in the beginning of the 2000s (Liukshin & Mezhvedilov 2006). During the first half of the 1990s these pictures were overtly negative: Russia was associated with barbed wire, tanks, and other symbols of violence, as well as figures of sad women (ibid.: 39). However, in the second half of the 1990s these associations were replaced by traditional Russian symbols, for example, the plenitude of "birches," "little houses," and "small rivers," referring to local identity instead of certain political or geographical symbols (ibid.: 41).[11]

---

11 These symbolic forms have a connection to the repertoire of the Soviet-era literary movement labeled as "Village Prose." It was active in the beginning of Khrushchev Thaw (the mid 1950s), and one of its most well-known representatives was Vassili Shukshin. In general the movement focused on idealized images of traditional Russian village and countryside. Later, in the 1970s, and '80s, the movement was increasingly associated with Russian nationalism. I am grateful to Kirill Postoutenko for these notions.

During the first years of the 2000s, these traditional, locally oriented, and not explicitly political Russian symbols changed into all-national political symbols signifying national self identity among Russian youth including such symbols as "eagles," "flags," "Kremlins," (either local ones or the Moscow Kremlin) the "residence of the president," as well as some other symbols of "world-power" (*derzhava*) (ibid.: 40). Irina Semenenko has made similar notes concerning the last ten years (2008: 13-14): The unquestionable leader in terms of images of present day Russia among youth has become Vladimir Putin, and in many of these answers Putin was presented along with such state symbols as "the Kremlin," "the Red Square of Moscow," "the capital of Moscow," "coat of arms," "the state flag," and "the double-headed eagle." Moreover, this important shift from the early 2000s to the present can be seen as an increase in the positive associations of Russia and a decrease in the negative ones (ibid.: 14). For instance, when the Russian Academy of Sciences conducted studies in 2002 and 2007 concerning these associations, in 2002 the most common denominator for Russia was "crisis" but in 2007 the clearest winner amongst one-word associations was "patriotism" (ibid.). Dmitry Liukshin and Arif Mezhvedilov argue that "the change from associations of local identity to state level political stereotypes reveals that social change among Russian youth is not happening through some sort of revolutionary and evolutionary change, but instead, it occurs through ways that could be called "tradition," "natural" and "customary"." (2006: 40-41). Since it has become apparent that Putin's political course has been based on patriotic and conformist values, these polls indicate that they are not merely dictated from above but are produced and represented at the grassroots level as well. Nonetheless, Liukshin and Mezhvedilov conclude that young people's growing tendency to use stereotypical state symbols as indicators of national identity makes the apoliticalness of Russian youth apparent, for example, its unwillingness to endorse those who oppose the current political regime (ibid.: 41).

From the viewpoint of pro-Kremlin political commentators, Pavel Danilin points out that young people living in the provinces are more conservative than those who live in cities where, in his words, "politics takes place" (2006: 131-132). He considers that actually urban young people born between 1980 and 1985 can be true locomotives of political change. Quite contrary to the interpretations of Liukshin and Mezhvedilov, Danilin argues that principally young people between the ages of 20 and 25 are more ready for political activism than people in their thirties, that is, those who are regarded as the lost generation (ibid.: 23-24). Similar notes are made by Sergey Markov, a pro-Kremlin political scientist, who sees a fundamental difference between the youth of the 1990s and 2000s (2006: 279). He sees that the main political process of the 1990s was "the shift from communists to liberals" as reflected in the ideals and goals of the 1990s generation; "an individual life with money, career, and night clubs." The generation of the 2000s, on the other hand, is against these ideals, and this resistance expresses itself as political activism (ibid.). Of course, the latter claims are harsh generalizations since a large proportion of Russia's youth of the 2000s no doubt shares the ideals of the 1990s as well. Nevertheless this argued change of values is compatible with the grown patriotic and nationalistic sentiments during the first decade of this millennium. This change arguably frames the main line of the Putin-era youth policy, and the establishment of the pro-Kremlin youth.[12]

One of the brightest manifestations of the state-driven patriotism as part of youth policy is the state program "The Patriotic Upbringing of the Citizens of the Russian Federation" (See Gosudarstvennaia 2005). This program shows a major shift from the 1990s by activating the military practices of the Soviet era's youth upbringing. Even more interestingly, this document shows how an explicitly Soviet-type of didactic and paternalistic discourse on youth with its revival of the Soviet era's compulsory military education in schools are linked to conditions of post-Soviet market practices. For example, by strongly emphasizing the importance of patriotism and patriotic education for the good of society, the program regards the relation between the media and patriotism as follows: "(The need for) the creation of such conditions in the mass media which allow the propaganda for patriotism, the formation of the state demand for the production of patriotically-oriented products by cultural and artistic organizations, and the mass media." In this respect, the discourse of commercial competition and struggle over commercial space is added to a patriotic discourse by the notion of "the formation of the state demand for the production of patriotically-oriented products." This reveals an assumption that the

---

12    A notable feature of the Putin-era policies is the emerged role of various pro-Kremlin think tanks consisting of relatively young ideologists. For more, see Laruelle 2009b.

successful implementation of patriotic values requires a market demand for these values. In the second five-year plan of the program (2006-2010, the first one covered 2001-2005) the connection between patriotism and military activity is highly explicit, reminding the reader in its appendix of various achievements of the Russian army. These are mainly victories (especially the victory in the "Great Patriotic War" 1945) but also including a mention in commemoration of the 20-year anniversary of the Soviet army's withdrawal from Afghanistan in 2009 (ibid.).[13]

The idea of combining state-driven patriotism with market economy seems to be a common discursive practice in the Putin era's youth-related policies. In terms of citizenship education, Nelli Piattoeva (2005: 39) shows that in Russia the notion of good citizenship is complex and contains antithetical ideas. On the one hand, citizenship education is expected to foster democratization and to develop an active civil society. On the other hand, throughout the 1990s and especially since 2000 it has contained a patriotic element, which can be interpreted as an attempt to construct Russia in national rather than political terms (ibid.). In general, for Putin-era policies conservative and patriotic tendencies are not exclusive but intertwined with globally resonating themes. Douglas W. Blum points out that discussion on youth policy in particular during Putin's leadership, has made apparent the tension between seemingly incompatible ideals (2006: 96): "One finds consensual demand for modernity and normalcy, along with the wish to remain culturally distinct and unique in world politics, but one also finds widespread agreement that national development requires creating market institutions and attracting foreign capital, as well as re-socializing the populace to behave like far-sighted, value-maximizing, rational individualists." Through these ideals Blum sums up the major tension in the debate over youth policy: "a demand for civil society and democratic legitimacy, alongside an equally powerful demand for control, stability, and a guaranteed normative order" (ibid.).

Elena Omel'chenko criticizes current official approaches to youth issues by accusing them of practising Soviet type dictates which emphasize societal obligation of youth to the state (2006: 11). However, from a discourse analysis

---

13    For more Putin's patriotic youth initiatives and for a detailed discussion of this program, see Sperling 2009; 2012.

viewpoint with the objective of scrutinizing the symbolic resources of pro-Kremlin youth activities, an interesting point is how these didactic discourses work together with such discourses which aim to focus on youth, or "youth's voice." For instance, it is pointed out in the conclusion of the current official youth policy—"Strategy of State Youth Policy"—that "the state youth policy must become an instrument of the development and reformation of the country" (Strategiia 2007: 45). In other words, youth policy is not explicitly targeted at youth and the problems of youth itself but rather generally defined as "an instrument of national development" in the framework of the need for modernization. In a similar vein the conclusion's mention "targeted at the direct entry of young people for the solution of individual problems" is accompanied by the notion of "all-national tasks." And, in the end of the conclusion, similar "expansions" in youth's role are made in the following remarks: "in the central orientations of the Strategy which are understood and required among youth and in society," and "the conditions for the self-fulfillment of youth and the whole population."

In brief, the current youth policy emphasizes that each time the word "youth" is mentioned, it is immediately accompanied by a concept which expands the category of youth to much broader frames. In relation to Blum's notion of tension between globally oriented rational individualists and desire of a common national idea, these concluding remarks of the Strategy illustrate the presence of seemingly controversial orientations. The policy suggests that youth is not allowed to be presented "alone" with its potentially contingent self-organization, but with various broader, typically national, underpinnings.

The Strategy is also revealing in terms of showing "state intervention" in the definition of youth's role (Strategiia 2007: 17). The basic reason for this intervention is pointed out in the policy with the mention of "unfavourable demographic tendencies" which no doubt exist in the Russian case. More interesting in political terms is the link between youth's vanguard position as the guarantee of Russia's democratic development: "Russia's tempo in moving towards democratic reforms depends on the position of youth, its readiness and activity in tomorrow's society". However, the phrase which follows this discourse that suggests youth's autonomy is clearly didactic, by conditioning youth's invaluable position: "young people must be ready to oppose political manipulation and extremist calls." While the content of political manipulation and extremism is not explicated in the text, it seems that the apoliticalness of youth, which is openly admitted here ("only 2.7 % of youth participates in social organizations"), is the breeding ground for political manipulation and extremism. A noteworthy point is the reference to Western examples in the commentary which seems to be an important ground for the adoption of special measures towards youth by the state.[14] It is pointed out that similar tendencies of youth's political apathy in the US and Europe have become the major justification for state interventions in youth politics in order to activate youth to social and political activities.

In the next chapter I continue to explore the context of Nashi in light of Putin-era youth movements and statistical data concerning youth's political participation. Before that I provide a short overview of Nashi's predecessor Idushchie Vmeste. This movement is an essential background for Nashi in terms of a pro-Kremlin youth movement which began to implement Putin-era political trends.

---

[14] I refer here to the version of the Strategy with commentaries: Various parts of the policy are commented on (written in italics) by its authors in order to explain and justify the points of the policy.

# III Nashi, the Field of Youth Movements and Political Participation of Russia's Youth

## Idushchie Vmeste

The most visible of pro-governmental youth political actions since the days of the Soviet Komsomol took place on May 7, 2001, when thousands of youngsters gathered in the centre of Moscow to celebrate Vladimir Putin's first year in office. Noteworthy in this initiative was not only the high number of people involved but their rather coherent visual image: The vast majority wore t-shirts of Putin's portrait with the intertextual phrase "everything is on track" (*vsio putiom*) referring to order, and to the surname of the president. These people—headed by a former employee of the president's administration Vassili Iakemenko—labeled themselves as members of the youth movement Idushchie Vmeste (Walking, or Marching, Together). The movement was officially registered on July 14, 2000, but through this large scale action in May 2001 it became well known to the broader public as well (Savel'ev 2006: 77; Ivanov 2005; Simons 2003; Iduschie Vmeste 7.5. 2001).

Despite immediate accusations against Idushchie Vmeste that arose concerning its role as a "rubber stamp" for the Kremlin's policies, the movement constantly underscored its spontaneous position as an independent youth organization not belonging to any political party. Consequently, the Kremlin also denied the existence of any formal links between itself and Idushchie Vmeste (Simons 2003: 29). Although the organizational connection between the movement and the Kremlin is obviously more complex than the media's attempt to link the two might suggest, it is clear that Putin was the evident authority for Idushchie Vmeste's support for the national and patriotic aspects of Putin's policy. In this respect, the accusations of a cult of personality that were linked to the activities and public image of Idushchie Vmeste were tackled by arguing that Idushchie Vmeste was supporting Putin in terms of his policy, not vice versa. However, in some other comments Iakemenko said that the organization was set up by Putin (ibid.: 30).

Instead of continuing to speculate on the nature of the connections between Idushchie Vmeste and the Kremlin, I suggest it is more fruitful to scrutinize the nature of the movement's political communication as part of this presumed connection. What is noteworthy in Idushchie Vmeste's ideological support for the Kremlin / Putin are the discourses which draw on Soviet practices. The movement's political agenda offers a rather clear connection to the ideals of the Soviet-era Komsomol as a youth organization which fosters the moral norms of a good youngster. The main text of Idushchie Vmeste—The Moral Codex—is no doubt a conscious reference to "The Moral Code of the Builder of Communism" established in 1961.[15] At least it is rather difficult to avoid such a connotation in post-Soviet Russia, especially in the case of a youth movement which emphasizes strict moral norms. A closer examination of the Codex actually reveals that in many parts it explicitly follows the ideals prescribed for a Soviet youngster: an "active life position" *(aktivnaia zhizennaia pozitsiia)* including a "high level of personal consciousness," "political maturity," "the feeling of patriotism," "high moral," the "priority of immaterial values" instead of material ones, the "rejection of detrimental ways of living," and a "high level of cultural consciousness" (Omel'chenko 2006: 15). These were also central features of *kul'turnost*, which was the cornerstone of Soviet cultural policy. It was introduced soon after the inauguration of socialist realism in 1932, and it largely followed—although with different political attributes—the tsarist era's conservative and normative ideals of culture and education: For example, the importance of acquiring a knowledge of canonical literature, both Russian and foreign, central emblems of the state's culture and history, as well as normative and "correct" Russian language (See, for example, Kenez & Shepherd 1998; Gorham 2003).

Indeed, while the demands for "proletarian internationalism and familiarity with the works of Lenin and the Communist Party" are not mentioned in the Moral Codex, replacing the latter with familiarity with the works of Russian classical literature, we are close to the core of Idushchie Vmeste's political agenda. Moreover, the Komsomol era's coarse definition of youth between

---

15 The Moral Code of the Builder of Communism was a set of twelve codified moral rules in the Soviet Union which every member of the Communist Party of the USSR and every Komsomol member was supposed to follow. It was adopted at the 22nd Congress of the Communist Party of the Soviet Union in 1961, as part of the new Party Program (See Moral Code of the Builder of Communism). In the Moral Codex, the term has been changed to a modified "active civic position" *(aktivanaia grazhdanskaia pozitsiia* (See Moral'nyi kodeks).

the ages 14-30 was also defined by Idushchie Vmeste as their main "target group" (Simons 2003: 33) which clearly shows that the Soviet legacy of youth education plays a major role in the political agenda of the movement. However, regardless of various similarities between Idushchie Vmeste and the Soviet era Komsomol, certain crucial differences exist.

Anne E. Gorsuch asserts that during the 1920s, the period which saw the formation of the Komsomol along with Soviet society, young people joined the organization for many different reasons (2000: 42). The communist youth league offered drama groups, choral societies, sports groups, movies, and concerts providing in this way a variety of communities of peers (ibid.). However, the reason why principally the Komsomol attracted young people to its activities was not so much in its capability to make "unbeatable offers" for youth in comparison with other youth groups. The main reason was the fact that all other youth formations—the Boy Scouts, Menshevik youth groups, and religious youth organizations—were suppressed (ibid.:42-43). In other words, there were no real alternatives to the Komsomol. Indeed during perestroika the Komsomol began to face crucial challenges to its compulsory status with the emergence of alternatives on the youth scene (Pilkington 1994, 89-160). Thus, it is the post-Soviet, or non-Soviet (i.e. non-compulsory), context which is crucial in noting potential similarities between Idushchie Vmeste and the Komsomol. In Putin's Russia Idushchie Vmeste's (and thereafter Nashi's) "alternativelessness" is a socially and politically distinctive option, not a total condition, as was the Komsomol-era's institutional and organizational alternativelessness.[16]

### The aftermath of the "Orange Revolution": Nashi

In late 2004, during the "Orange Revolution" in Ukraine, the first rumors of the new Kremlin supported youth movement began to circulate (Shevchuk & Kamyshev 2005). These rumors proved to be correct as in February 2005 the "Antifascist Democratic Youth Movement Nashi" was officially established (Savel'ev 2006: 86; Savina, Taratuta, & Shevchuk 2008). Its role as the follower of Idushchie Vmeste became immediately clear when Vassili Iakemen-

---

[16] Here I refer to Idushchie Vmeste's Moral'niy Kodeks (Moral Codex) (2007) and Pamiatka Idushchemu, (Instruction for the Walker) (2007).

ko, the leader of Idushchie Vmeste, announced he would be the leader of this new movement. Iakemenko himself stated in late 2006 that "Idushchie Vmeste wonderfully continues its activities, especially in the southern parts of Russia" ("Za "Nashu" pobedu" 2006).

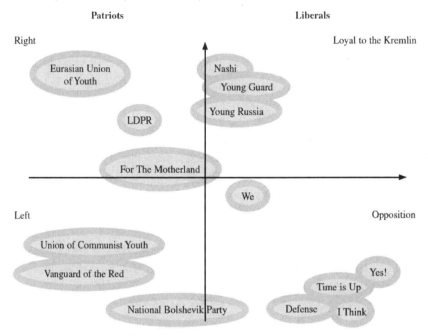

FIGURE 1: Political coordinates of youth movements in Russia in 2005 (Tat'iana Stanovaia 2005).

Indeed, Idushchie Vmeste continued its activities after the establishment of Nashi to some extent until late summer 2008 when the last update to its website was made before the site ceased. However, the moment of the establishment of Nashi rather explicitly indicated that it was meant to replace Idushchie Vmeste. This moment was linked, on the one hand, to changes in the political environment of Russia with potential negative effects for the regime,[17] and, the failure of Idushchie Vmeste due to its notorious campaign in the field of cultural policy, on the other. The most visible change of Nashi from

[17] This change was linked to the Orange Revolution in Ukraine in late 2004 which posed challenging scenarios from the Kremlin's viewpoint (see more in Umland 2010).

its predecessor's emphasis on cultural issues became apparent in Nashi's massive "opening performance" linked to the 60th anniversary of the victory in the Great Patriotic War in May 2005 (Mijnssen 2012). Some scholars and political commentators see that the appearance of Nashi is also linked to the "boom" in youth movements which took place in Russia in 2003-2005 (Kashin 2006: 4-7; Danilin 2006: 38-49; Fedorov 2005). From the viewpoint of political positions, Nashi can be located in the category which Tat'iana Stanovaia (2005) calls "loyal to the Kremlin" (Figure 1).

Besides Nashi,[18] this category includes the youth movements Young Guard, Young Russia, as well as the Moscow-based Locals (the last one is my addition to Stanovaia's category) which work and act according to the Kremlin policies. Those organizations which work to some extent in accordance with the interests of the Kremlin but whose ideology are openly nationalistic or leftist are located in this same category. These include such movements as the *Eurasian Union of Youth* (ESM) headed by the nationalist theorist of geopolitics Alexander Dugin, and the youth organization of the *Liberal Democratic Party of Russia* (LDPR), well known by its populist-nationalist leader Vladimir Zhirinovski. Stanovaia suggests that this category can be divided into "patriots" (ESM and LDPR) and "liberals" (Nashi, Young Guard and Young Russia). The category which is opposite to this one also includes patriots and liberals who can be either leftist or right ones. The leftist opposition includes such movements as *For the Motherland*, which is partly loyal to the Kremlin, the *Union of Communist Youth*, the *Vanguard of the Red Youth*, and the *National Bolshevik Party* (NBP). The last one is partly liberal (or right) in this category and was one of the most well-known Russian youth movements in the mid 2000s (Sokolov 2006). In 2005, such movements of the liberal opposition as *We, the Democratic Altenative Yes!* (DA), *Time is up*, and *I think*, worked mostly virtually without concrete actions. The movement *Defence* (*Oborona*), instead, worked actively as the main youth organization of the political party *Iabloko*, and can be defined as one of the main political opponents of Nashi in its early stages. In sum, Stanovaia argues that the Russian youth movements of the mid 2000s can be defined by two factors: Firstly, by the re-

---

18 Stanovaia does not mention Idushchie Vmeste separately from Nashi, which implies that she treats Nashi as a more or less straightforward follower of Idushchie Vmeste.

lations of a movement to the current political power, that is, to the Kremlin and secondly, by a movement's political color. That is, a movement's position on the left-right axis, as the Figure 1 shows (Stanovaia 2005).

Stanovaia continues that in light of the situation in 2005—and in many ways throughout its existence (my addition)—the most influential and visible youth movement in Russia was Nashi. According to her, the main reason for the creation of Nashi by the Kremlin was to develop a new version of the previous "official" youth movement Idushchie Vmeste after its excessively radical and marginal actions. In addition, the crucial political motivation for the creation of Nashi was the twofold apolitical attitude of contemporary Russian youth from the Kremlin's viewpoint: On the one hand, the ongoing process of the apoliticization of youth and, on the other, the potential consequence of this apoliticization. Stanovaia interprets that the apoliticization of youth actually means the unwanted politicization for the Kremlin, that is, such political activities which are at variance with its interests.[19] In this sense, Nashi is meant to function as a certain type of a motivation system for youth within the official youth policy, and this system must be in symbiosis with such political interests that support the maintenance of the current political power. Hence, all those organizations (e.g. communists, Western-liberals, the extreme-right) which do not fit into this framework are regarded as "apolitical." The biggest challenge for Nashi in its task of mobilization has been students of colleges and universities who have been very sceptical towards such "ready-made systems of motivation" (my formulation and emphasis). Only a few of them can identify with such constructions, and most of them think that movements like Nashi work only as instruments of political manipulation. This skepticism has led to the formation of various local youth movements in Russian institutions of higher education (Stanovaia 2005).

I largely share Stanovaia's views even though her attempt to describe the political positions of youth movements as "patriotic," "liberal," "leftist," etc., cause difficulties in terms of overlapping political positions. Furthermore, although Stanovaia's framing concisely contextualizes the position of Nashi in relation to other youth movements, I think her definition leads too easily to seeing Nashi in terms of a "rubber stamp," or a representative of "virtual de-

---

19 That is, the prevention of the "Orange movements" among youth, see Umland 2010.

mocracy"; a movement which fakes real democratic practices (See Wilson 2005; Robertson 2009). This is not a wrong definition but from the viewpoint of analyzing Nashi's political communication in light of the movement's communicative choices, this is not very productive approach. Stanovaia's account largely follows those two dominant public discourses of Nashi that Maya Atwal has identified among existing portrayals of the movement. On the one hand, the discourse of "creeping authoritarianism" views Nashi as an attempt by the Russian state to undermine the development of independent political youth movements. On the other hand, the discourse of "defending Russia" portrays Nashi as a legitimate response to external threats to the sovereignty of the Russian nation and is favored by the Kremlin (2009: 744). Although Stanovaia's account hardly shows a connection to this second discourse in terms of the Kremlin's right to establish such movements as Nashi, she views Nashi as more or less subordinate to the Kremlin. As Atwal continues, both dominant discourses presume the passivity of Nashi activists and the absolute ability of the state to determine the movements' development (ibid.). Again, although Stanovaia rightly shows those problems which Nashi inevitably faces in its activity—that is, skepticism from the side of Russian youth—she views the movement as a Kremlin project which emphasizes the passivity of the movement in relation to the Kremlin's "orders."

Atwal shows that in reality the development of political engagement among Nashi's activists and their emergence as "politically autonomous beings renders them capable, should they so choose, of sustaining the movement with or without state support" (ibid.: 757). This notion is insightful for my focus on Nashi's (including its predecessor Idushchie Vmeste as well) political communication as it emphasizes the indirect and complex nature between Nashi and the Kremlin. The replacement of Idushchie Vmeste by Nashi instead of it being updated for the changed political environment during late 2004 (especially regarding the "Orange Revolution" in Ukraine) also implies that Idushchie Vmeste was regarded as a failure. In sum, the point is that Nashi and Idushchie Vmeste not only passively prevent such youth initiatives which might contradict the Kremlin's views but their own activities might contradict the Kremlin's guidelines as well.

From the viewpoint of managing the movements' own supposedly invaluable importance in relation to official political guidelines, Dmitry Andreev provides rich insights into the role of Idushchie Vmeste and Nashi in the context of Putin's Russia (2006). According to him, both movements can be described as pure models of "managed passionarity" (*upravliaemaia passionarnost'*) in the context of the managed, or "sovereign democracy,"[20] introduced by Putin's regime (ibid.: 52). By the term "passionarity" Andreev refers to the emotions of such people whose ambition is to serve devotedly the goals given for, or by, them (ibid.: 50). Moreover, for such passionate people the main goal is to organize, or re-organize, everyday life around them with the help of a constructed enemy or with negative examples (ibid.). According to Andreev, post-Soviet Russia creates relatively new context for such an emotionally driven political pursuit. The important addition here is that it is principally the post-Soviet political context that is the new, not the emotional commitment in relation to social and political activity in the Russian socio-cultural context. In the case of the latter, the Soviet-era "construction of socialism/communism" in various settings was definitely loaded with emotional pursuit, propagated by the Communist Party but also felt by countless Soviet citizens. Andreev argues that in post-Soviet Russia features of such passionate movements as the Western student movement, peace movement, or the hippies of the 1960s and 1970s, have appeared rather as elements of "political technology" (*politicheskaia tekhnologiia*) (ibid.: 50-51). Indeed, this term, frequently used in Russia's post-Soviet political life, brilliantly shows the idea of pre-defined politics; politics as technology, which does have certain limits, rules, and instructions to use it, as well as an assumption of managing social and political space with a particular technology.

Andreev asserts that as distinct from previous projects[21] of "managed passionarity," enthusiasm in the case of Nashi and Idushchie Vmeste is some-

---

[20] This concept was said to be the invention of Vladislav Surkov, one of the Kremlin's key ideologists, and the "ideological" founder of Nashi. "Sovereign democracy" aims to be a highly selective constellation of various ideological traits, picking up the best forms from the West, and then connecting them to the most valuable Russian traditions and practices. In this regard, "sovereign" refers to Russia's absolute autonomy to define its own democratic path. For more discussion of sovereign democracy by its ideologists and representatives, see Pro suverennuiu demokratiiu (2007).

[21] According to Andreev there were passionate movements in Russia in the 1990s, for example Lebed (Swan) (2006: 52-53). However, he sees that the passionate elements for these movements emanated from their liberal ideology as distinct from that of

thing deeper than just a creation of particular political stylistics or methods in order to agitate for certain political candidates or parties (ibid.: 56). This enthusiasm is the culture of the "silent majority" and every-day life, striving for the monopolistic power of conformist "common sense". In this respect, the visible campaign against well-known contemporary writers, especially Vladimir Sorokin, by Idushchie Vmeste (see Chapter 8) becomes very understandable, as well as the accusations by Nashi against those who oppose the political course of the Kremlin, or official Russian views, and its condemnation of them as fascists. From the movements' point of view, the enemy is any system of values, ideologies, and actions which do not cover these definitions of passionarity (ibid.). Nevertheless, I disagree with Andreev when he partially downplays "particular political stylistics" in relation to the movements' passionate will to express "the culture of the silent majority". I suggest it is principally a matter of "stylistics" (communication), how this culture is expressed, and more precisely, what are the movements' assumptions about (anticipations of) effective ways for this expression?

As far as it is relevant to treat Nashi as an instrumental movement, Jeff Goodwin, James M. Jasper and Francesca Polletta point out that instrumental movements are also emotional and expressive (2001: 15). Indeed, even the most "professional" and bureaucratic movements necessarily involve emotions and work for emotions and often a great deal of emotion work designed to create the appearance of disinterestedness or objectivity (ibid.). In the case of Nashi this "great deal of emotion work" is principally about looking for supposedly the best possible ways of expressing emotions within its sociopolitical position. It follows that the communicative production of objectiveness and disinterestedness by the movement in its social and political position is easily confronted with such expressions of emotions which might be inappropriate for producing a politically correct feeling of national identity. Adequate tension has been noted by Wodak et al. in their study of the discursive construction of Austrian national identity in which institutional practices were partially in conflict with people's discursive models of identity (1999: 186).

---

Idushchie Vmeste and Nashi, being also more explicitly formed for the promotion of particular political candidates.

Against the backdrop of social movements' emotions, Andreev's notion of passionarity is very illuminating. He argues that although Nashi and Idushchie Vmeste perform as pro-Kremlin movements, and are evidently supported to some extent by it, any type of emotional commitment is "prohibited" in the political guidelines of the Kremlin (ibid.: 58). According to him, this is manifested by the Kremlin's major principle of "economic doubling the Gross Domestic Product," and in ideological terms, this means the possibility of moving from a "superpower quasi-monarchy to liberal oligarchy and from a socially oriented market economy to right neo-conservatism á la Thatcher and Reagan" (ibid.: 59). In short, the Kremlin aims to have total freedom in the field of ideology. It follows that for the current political power passionarity like the political stylistics of Nashi and its predecessor is not only unnecessary but also dangerous if it is to distribute its ideas according to its own administrative vertical (ibid.). Andreev's argumentation leads to such scenarios where these movements start to act on their own, that is, the managed passionarity of the Kremlin becomes the pure passionarity of the movements (ibid.: 59-61). His view is insightful in terms of treating Nashi as a kind of constructor of national identity under uncertainty, or in Bourdieu's terms, Nashi is forced to act between incompatible fields of large-scale and restricted cultural productions. Nonetheless, Andreev does not pay attention to the fact that it was in all probability that passionate activity of Idushchie Vmeste, which obviously failed, that led to the establishment of Nashi with its new communicative strategies, or anticipation of supposedly more profitable strategies. Moreover, Andreev does not pay attention to youth's potential interest or disinterest towards the movements. Next I briefly shed light on the political participation of Russia's youth.

### Overview of the Political Participation of Russia's Youth

Elena Omel'chenko argues that despite the deeply changed social conditions of youth in the post-Soviet space, the current political elite still sees youth, not as a social subject with its own rights, but as a resource (2006: 16). Moreover, she suggests that the argument of youth's apoliticalness in official frames, for example, elections—this view is apparent in the Strategy as well—does not pay any attention to closer features of this "apoliticalness" (ibid.: 18. For example, 15-28 % of those who were for the option of "against all" in elections (regional and federal) are young people. This should show the political elite that the "traditional apoliticalness" might be a new form of politicalness, that is, civil activity, or protest (ibid.).

Perhaps this protest-type of behaviour has been recognized by the political elite but it has certainly not admitted it as a legitimate form of political activity, or an activity with which it should negotiate. Instead, it seems that these kind of activities can be labeled as a result of "political manipulation" and "extremism," as was pointed out in the passage of the Strategy above. In the light of opinion polls conducted by "The Fond of Social Opinion," youth does not fit very smoothly with those views of the Strategy which demand special measures towards youth due to its apoliticalness (FOM 2005; 2008a): According to the 2008 poll, 51 % of Russians (53 % in 2005), and 57 % of the age-group 18-35 (60 % in 2005), considered that "young people (not older than 25) are capable of creating their own political organizations and movements by themselves." Consequently, the clear majority of Russians, 65 %, considered it best that "the state must support youth organizations," while 19 % considered it best that "the state must be familiar only with the point that youth movements work according to the law" (FOM 2008a). These polls do not show how state support for youth movements is actually understood by the respondents. Nevertheless, it becomes clear that a strictly state controlled and selective "ready-made" approach towards youth is not what youth expects from political activity. In relation to the activities of Nashi, and previously of Idushchie Vmeste, I suggest their position between official policy programs and the conditions of youth's actual political participation creates a challenging task in terms of cogent political communication.

The statistical information available related to the population's views on pro-Kremlin youth movements concerns predominantly Nashi, although Idushchie Vmeste is constantly mentioned in this information as well. In March 2005, immediately after the establishment of Nashi, 4 % of the respondents (representing the whole population) announced that they know the movement (VTSIOM 2005). Interestingly, despite this small number, Nashi was the most well known movement. Three percent of the population professed to know Idushchie Vmeste (6 % among the age-group of 18-24 professed to know Nashi, as well as Idushchie Vmeste). The clearest majority, 66 % (56 % in the age-group of 18-24) professed not to know any youth movements. This unresponsiveness towards youth movements dominates public attitudes few years later as well when Nashi had received a large amount of attention in the Russian media. In that poll in which FOM studied Russians' views of youth in relation to politics and political activity, it also asked "what youth movements do you know or have heard about?" (FOM 2008a). The most well known was Nashi but in terms of the percentages, this familiarity with Nashi was not very convincing: only 13 % of Russians announced that "I know or have heard about the movement" (ibid.).[22] The clearest majority of Russians, 75 %, announced that it was "difficult to answer," or said that "I do not know any youth organizations." This is interesting while Nashi's visibility in the Russian media had been overwhelmingly high by the end of the year 2007. According to the Russian print media database Integrum (including also TV- monitoring), the year 2007 was the most active in terms of Nashi's media visibility (Leskinen 2009). This is obviously linked with the Bronze Soldier case, which became the most intensive theme for Nashi before its reorganization (see Chapter 8).

On the basis of the above data, there are very strong grounds to argue that Nashi's relatively low familiarity among the population (including youth) is based on people's unresponsiveness rather than simply a black-out of information. This evidently concerns Idushchie Vmeste as well as it was far less familiar than Nashi during its existence. In other words, people have seen or heard about Nashi but they do not care about what they have seen or heard. Among those who professed to know Nashi, 56 % considered that they did not have any feelings towards the movement (Levada 2008). In FOM's poll the highest percentages, 45 %, were recorded in the categories "I do not have any attitudes towards the mentioned movements" and "difficult to answer." (FOM 2007) The most positive attitudes were recorded for the pro-Kremlin movements, Young Guard and Nashi, but even then only 5-6 % were positive towards these movements. Hence, although this information shows that familiarity of Nashi had grown since its establishment in the beginning of

---

22 According to poll by the Levada centre conducted in November 2007, this figure was clearly higher (26%) among those who professed to know political youth movements. Nashi was the most well known youth movement. Interestingly, Idushchie Vmeste was the fifth famous (8%) in this poll, ahead of many other more active youth movements. However, 66 % announced in this poll that they had not heard of any youth movements (Levada 2008).

2005, the number of negative, as well as unresponsive attitudes has grown at the same time. Especially the number of those who did not know Nashi, or, in all probability, those who did not care, was overwhelmingly high among the Russian population, including young Russians. In this regard, the rapid growth in the familiarity of Nashi in its first year 2005 was still not as high as had been expected.[23]

The unresponsive attitudes towards Nashi as well as youth movements in general find its strongest explanation in statistical information concerning youth's political participation. In the poll of 2005, among all age groups of the population, disinterest in politics was higher than interest in it, but especially among the younger generations (18-35) the disinterest was highest, 65-67 % (FOM 2005). In addition, among the youngest age-group (18-25), 96 % announced that "I have not participated in the activities of any political organizations" (among the whole population the figure was 80 %) (ibid.). In 2008, 75 % of the entire population considered that "there are only a few, if there are any at all, young people who are interested in politics" (FOM 2008a). Among the age-group 18-35 this figure was 76 %, although there were more of those who considered that "there are a lot of politically active young people," 14 %, (while among the whole population the figure was 11 %), and less of those who considered that "there is not a politically active youth at all," 13 %, (while among the whole population the figure was 22 %).

Besides showing youth's apoliticalness, these data support that argument that underlines differences in the understanding of the concept of "political" between the population (predominantly among youth) and the political elite (see Omel'chenko 2006 above). When in 2008 a poll asked "do you think it is necessary or not that young people, not older than 25, participate in politics and the political life of the country," 69 % of Russians considered that it was necessary, and 65 % considered that "participation in politics and political life helps young people to attain a higher position in society" (FOM 2008a). Hence, it seems that attitudes towards politics strongly depend on whether it

---

[23] According to data conducted by VTSIOM in 2005, familiarity of Nashi grew 5 % in three months (in March 2005, 4%, and in June 2005, 9 %). In the light of these dynamics, the author of the report, the director of VTSIOM, Valery Fedorov, assumed that "the day when a youth movement can seriously challenge the older comrades is not far off (2005)."

refers to politics as such, or politics in "practice," that is, existing political structures and organizations. Thus, for example, the highly unresponsive and apolitical attitude becomes apparent in the minimal participation in political organizations (96 % have not participated in any organizations) but, at the same time, there is a relatively positive attitude towards political participation in terms of attaining a high position in society (65 %). The next chapter examines how this socio-political framework and conditions for mobilization are discursively manifested in Nashi's central texts consisting of its Manifesto and some central texts related to the movement's recruitment.

# IV Towards Nashi's Political Style: From Moral Panic to National Megaproject

### Manifesto and Recruitment Texts

In order to frame didactics and stimulation in Nashi's key text, Manifesto, accordingly, Idushchie Vmeste's political program, Moral Codex, figures as an important starting point. This comparison illustrates that the development between these two texts can be condensed as a shift from the exhaustive moral panic to the eclectic patriotic optimism. The following samples illustrate the difference between the topical structuring of these political programmes. Sample 1 shows the headlines of the sections (or paragraphs) of the Moral Codex and Sample 2 shows the headlines of the Manifesto's sections:

1
Respect for parents and the elderly
Abstention (*nedopustimost'*) from killing and torturing animals
Abstention from drunkenness (*pianstvo*)
Abstention from using and distributing drugs
Abstention from cursing
Abstention from nationalistic and chauvinistic ideology
Aim to "be better" ("*byt' luchshe*") everywhere and in everything
Active civic (*grazhdanskaia*) position

2
Historical Perspective
Russia in the Modern World
Russia is the Country of Our Dreams
Changing the Format
At the Start of Modernization
Our Revolution
Our Goals

As the headlines of the Moral Codex's sections suggest in Sample 1, Idushchie Vmeste concentrates on certain special themes of society with a moralistic ethos, including various rejections of, for example, cursing, drinking alcohol, using drugs, or killing animals. In contrast, the headlines of the sections in Nashi's Manifesto (Sample 2) reveal that the goal of the movement is more ambitious, by focusing on proving Russia's leading role in the world. Idushchie Vmeste's Codex implies the sense of hegemonic position which supposedly allows the use of moralistic dictates. Hence, in terms anticipating symbolic capital with such dictates, Idushchie Vmeste believes that this explicitly didactic discourse of particular concerns is a profitable choice for Russian youth, as well as for the political elite. This choice seemingly aims to redeem a supposed need for moral order in the non-order experienced by relying on a Komsomol-type of didactic position, and especially the Soviet legacy of kul'turnost.

The interesting thing is that although the sections in the Codex refer to relatively concrete areas of social activity—for example, opposition to animal abuse—the linguistic (symbolic) production of this activity concentrates on a rather "poetic" description of moral circumstances and conditions. It is also worth adding that animal protection as a theme in the agenda of Idushchie Vmeste explicitly refers to the need and willingness to be "up to date" as a social movement in relation to other Russian and international animal rights movements. The movement's animal protection theme became visible with protests against bullfighting organized in Russia (My protiv korridy 2001) and later, in 2007, when the movement was actually superseded by Nashi, by demonstrating against the Moscovian Boris Surov, who was accused of killing a dog (Miagkii prigovor 2007). In this respect, Idushchie Vmeste's critique against animal abuse can be seen as an attempt to use a felicitous choice between an assumed hegemonic position (i.e. "we are in the position which allows us to issue moral instructions") and the supposed concerns of youth. Let us now take a look at the following passages of Nashi's Manifesto, and then compare them with the Codex (bold paragraph is the formulation in the original Manifesto):[24]

3
**History is a change of generations. Each generation has the chance to carry on unnoticed, or to change the world. Today we, the generation of young Russians, have this choice. We are the ones who believe in the future of Russia and believe that its future is in our hands. We are the youth movement NASHI. We invite you to join the megaproject of our generation, the megaproject of Russia.**
The twentieth century was already the century of Russia. Three times during this century, Russia set the format of world history. The October Revolution was a his-

---

24 The English translation of the Manifesto that I used here is from the SRAS website (The School of Russian and Asian Studies) (SRAS 2012).

torical explosion that, in the end, set the world's political agenda for the twentieth century. Russia's victory in the Great Patriotic War laid the foundations of the world agenda for the second half of the twentieth century. Russia's rejection of the communist system served as a push toward the formation of the twenty-first century world.

By contrast to Idushchie Vmeste, Nashi's choice is to produce a viewpoint which generally implies a shift towards national issues with a stimulative twist; it aims to appeal to Russian youth on the basis of these supposedly important and largely shared issues but without such specified and explicitly instructive sections that are present in the Codex. Russia is typically represented as a central actor in world politics, and especially the way in which Russia has always figured and figures in a glorious manner: For example, by treating the October Revolution as an indicator of Russia's greatness although in the later section of the Manifesto called "At the Start of Modernization" Nashi explicates the importance of Russia's rejection of communism. Nashi's textual simplicity makes constant references to the movement by the use of "we" (which evidently fits the movement's brand name as the possessive pronoun of the Russian "ours") as well as pointing explicitly to a reader (the last sentence of the first paragraph in Sample 3).

Although both political programmes mediate the "clear and unquestionable" state of affairs, they are represented differently: Idushchie Vmeste focuses on the description of negatively valued circumstances without an explicated actor, while Nashi focuses on the description of positively valued circumstances with an explicated actor, either in terms of "we," or Russia. In Nashi's case these two no doubt purposefully overlap with each other (we are Russia, Russia is we). This difference conveys a shift from the didactically driven moral panic of the lost order (the Codex) to the active and stimulatively driven definition of "the new (world) order" (the Manifesto).

Besides differences, both political programmes illustrate an intensive tendency to order the "world" in terms of creating a vision of harmony. This can also be seen as the movements' emotional reaction against the decay of Russian society after the collapse of the Soviet system, the disintegration of previous authorities and orders, the loss of international supremacy, etc. In this respect, Mary Douglas's classical views concerning the connection between symbolic order and socio-cultural purity are very illuminating when she asserts that (1966: 35):

> dirt in culture implies two conditions: a set of ordered relations and a contravention of that order. Dirt then, is never a unique event. Where there is dirt there is system. Dirt is the by-product of a systematic ordering and classification of matter, in so far as ordering involves rejecting inappropriate elements. This idea of dirt takes us straight into the field of symbolism and promises a link-up with more obviously symbolic systems of purity.

This is finely manifested in one of Idushchie Vmeste's first large-scale actions conducted on the anniversary of the Bolshevik Revolution, on November 7 2001. This action titled as "The General Cleaning of Russia" (General'naia uborka Rossii 2001) was primarily targeted against the communists, but, in larger terms, this voluntary cleaning of the streets of Moscow evidently symbolized Idushchie Vmeste's ambition to clean away all that "dirt in which we are living," including the communists.

Although the aspect of purity and danger is more evident in Idushchie Vmeste's Moral Codex, I regard Nashi's tendency to construct "the world" with simple sentences in its Manifesto as a structurally similar attempt to "avoid" the disorder of things, that is, "socio-cultural dirt and danger." The disorder/dirt of things, followed by a sense of danger, is never manifested as such but within particular relations of things. Following Douglas, "shoes are not dirty themselves but they are dirty on the dining-room table; food is not dirty in itself, but it is dirty to leave cooking utensils in the bedroom; similarly, bathroom equipment is not appropriate in the drawing room, out-door things in-doors, and so forth" (1966: 35-36).

From the viewpoint of mobilization the difference between the move-ments' harmonious worlds offers an interesting insight: Although the topics of the Codex may be closer to the everyday life of a contemporary Russian youngster (e.g. drinking habits, or animal protection), they focus on moral specifications with a pejorative and highly paternalistic tone without explicit references to a potential reader. In the Manifesto the case is almost the opposite in this sense: the explicit reference to "you" in the beginning of the text, and the whole Manifesto strongly relies on the reader's capability to create some coherence out of the short sentences. However, the topics which are described by these relatively simple and short sentences are in many ways related to "high politics"; Russia's history and future in globalization, Russia's international relations, etc. Next, to continue the Nashi's emphasis on stimulation as distinct from Idushchie Vmeste's Codex, Nashi's recruitment announcements are revealing documents in terms of poising between didactics and stimulation (formulation is from the original):

4
# YOU

do you want to realize your own project?
do you want to change the world around you?
do you want to influence the future of your country?
do you want that the world would remember you?
do you search your place in your life?
You have a chance to change your life, influence the world politics, to come new intellectual elite
Our people are already in the Public Chamber, political state organs and in the biggest Russian companies.
Are you worth the higher education in our university with the best teachers of the country?
Are you worth a traineeship in the company you want, in Russia, or abroad?
Are you worth realizing your own project?
Prove it! Fill the form!
Come to our team.

This recruitment announcement which Nashi used until November 2009 when its website was updated, exhibits that an important part of Nashi's stimulative discourse is based on the presupposition of the reader's natural attraction to becoming part of the national elite. In terms of shifting presuppositions that are targeted at this supposed attraction Nashi's discursive strategy can be elaborated by Louis Althusser's (1971) concept of interpellation. For Althusser all an individual's activities are consequences of social practices and this is manifested in the individual's role as a subject. Besides the economic and politico-legal structures with their social practices, ideological practices determine the subjects' values, desires, and preferences. According to Althusserian reasoning ideologies constitute subjects and this occurs in terms of interpellation; "subjects are interpellated by those who believe that they can do so, and those who are interpellated are thus transformed into subjects."[25] This

---

[25] A case of interpellation is, for instance, the situation when an individual walks on a

transformation requires that "images" of subjects exist before subjects can transform into them. The instances that conduct this ideological reproduction—in Althusser's terminology, "ideological state apparatuses"—are all those central institutions of a society; for example, family, religious organizations, the media, and especially the educational system (ibid.).

Although Althusser's totalizing theory of ideology is hardly suitable for analyzing the language of a political movement as a channel of ideological state apparatuses (it describes everything and thus explains nothing), I suggest that the concept of interpellation elaborates the idea of how Nashi anticipates profitable symbolic practices. While for Althusser (ibid.) ideology has no history, and the individual is always an already ideological subject (see the footnote above), the point is not so much how Nashi "interpellates" its reader-subjects from their point of view (i.e. how Nashi works as a kind of ideological state apparatus). Rather this interpellation as a concept is useful to illustrate Nashi's belief that it is part of an all embracing ideology; how Nashi believes that ideology legitimizes the movement to act particular way, and more precisely, how this interpellation with "language as ideology" should be done in the best possible way. Thus, shifts between Nashi's presuppositions targeted at readers reveal how "subjects" should be constituted. I suggest that in this sense the concept of interpellation specifies the shifts between the aforementioned presuppositions, but more importantly, it specifies how didactic and stimulative discourses are linked to a particular discursive production of reader-"subjects."

For example, the shift from individual possibilities to seemingly dictated possibilities given the supposed compatibility between these two—that is, a sort of combination between stimulative and didactic discourses—is profoundly expressed in the announcement. First by narrating the prestige instances where "our" people work, and finally by changing the repetitive question "do you want to" to the question "are you worth?" Both rhetorical ques-

_____

street and hears that a policeman shouts "Hey you there!" The individual responds by turning around, and in this simple movement of his body he is transformed into a subject. This is possible because the person being hailed recognizes himself as the subject of the hail, and knows to respond. Even though there was nothing suspicious about his walking in the street, he recognizes it is indeed he himself that is being hailed. This shows, according to Althusser, that individuals are "already-ideological subjects" before they are, and thus can be, "interpellated" into subjects (Althusser: 1971).

tions can be seen as forms of interpellation which constitute subjects according to an individualistic discourse, or "individualistic ideology." In the case of "do you want to"- questions, Nashi constitutes subjects on the basis of the individual's capacity to contribute to this ideology in terms of individual possibilities. In the latter case, these possibilities are explicated as ex officio "images" of subjects, which allows one to ask whether the constituted subjects are actually worthy of these "images". While it probably sounds that my logic of interpretation is stuck in Althusserian ideological determinism, it actually explains how Nashi believes in constituting its potential reader-members from its sociopolitical ("ideological") position. Individual possibility which is constituted by stimulative discourse, is not contrasted, nor downplayed against didactic discourse, but it is constituted in a way which allows the didactic position as well. In sum, the platform which Nashi here offers for individual possibilities is so appealing that a reader must think, is s/he actually worthy of these. The final separate imperatives "Prove!" and "Fill the form!," followed by the call "Come to our team" written in larger fonts, underscores this point by suggesting particular "compulsory" free will: Nashi speaks as if an addressee reacts in the way "this is so good offer that I cannot refuse."

In the website version, updated in November 2009, Nashi offers even greater promise for potential members. The portraits of Dmitry Medvedev and Vladimir Putin are presented at the top of the main website as explicated authorities—implying their ex officio didactic position—accompanied with the question, "Are you gonna be the third?" (*Tret'im budesh'?*). On the right side of this ambitious question, which resonates with colloquial youth language, is the flashing word "join", and below that the link to the Manifesto. The actual recruitment text which is behind the "join"- link is more informative than the previous one by contextualizing the importance of the movement with the points from the Manifesto.[26] Nevertheless, it also anticipates a reader's supposed moves by interpellating the options that a reader can make, that is to refuse, or to become member through the four paragraphs of the announce-

---

[26] Indeed, after the protests related to the Duma elections in December 2011, followed by the removal Vladislav Surkov in to the post of a deputy prime minister, Nashi updated its Manifesto. This version was clearly shorter than the original one, and repeatedly emphasized the notion of modernization.

ment.[27] However, in this latest version the option to refuse is given as the first choice, and joining as the second. The announcement ends as follows (formulation is from the original):

5
**Did you think about it?**
Now you have two routes:

FIRST                          SECOND

| you close the site and nothing is going to change, everything goes on in the same way, all the way to your old age. |
|---|

| you fill the form and your life starts to change |
|---|

Well, now think about it...go to the form...or don't.
**GOOD LUCK AND KEEP IN TOUCH.**

Althusser's concept of interpellation has been applied in analyses of advertisements in terms of scrutinizing how ideology functions through "the interpellation of the viewers" in advertising discourse (see, for example, Pajnik & Lesjak-Tušek 2002). From this viewpoint, there is a discourse of the inner voice used in advertisements that addresses the reader as "you," continuously telling you what you want and need; advertising, as an ideological practice, interpellates individuals as subjects (ibid.: 279). Following Althusser, it is capitalist ideology which presumably allows for advertisements to conduct this subject-constitution, for example, in terms of a "society of spectacle," allowing all kinds of communicative practices (ibid.: 280). A more insightful interpretation, which is partially compatible with Althusser's ideology-driven view, is given by Veijo Hietala, who argues that associations in contemporary advertisements emanate from the value patterns linked to cultural myths which potentially guarantee that there is no need to justify the symbols used in the advertisements (1996: 134-137). In this sense, the highly emphasized "you", written at the top of the announcement (sample 4), figures as a common national myth within particular visual allusion to "The Great Patriotic War" (see e.g. Tumarkin 1994; Dubin 2004) in terms of interpellating the readers. It is an

---

[27] The first paragraph of the announcement is titled "Dear friend!," the second "For whom and why this is needed?," the third "How it will be?," and the fourth (Sample 5) "Did you think about it?"

explicit referent to the well known Soviet propaganda poster of the Civil War and Second World War eras in which a Red Army soldier points to the viewer with the text *TY, zapisalsia dobrovol'tsem?*("Have you volunteered?").[28] In terms of cultural myths used in advertisements, this historical reference is justifiable as such, and does not need to be further elaborated. In this light, it has a loose logical connection to the war era recruitments (logical in the case of a patriotic movement) but more importantly, it figures as a choice of cultural myths which justify their use in the different contexts defined. The change of this Soviet-era reference to portraits of Medvedev and Putin within a growing sense of simulating a dialogue with a reader in Nashi's latest website version can be interpreted as a more stimulative discursive practice of "interpellation." Nevertheless, the mythic component seemingly remains: there is no need to justify these symbols, that is, the leaders (Medvedev and Putin) of the country.

Nashi's recruiting announcements are not unique in terms of utilizing the repertoires of contemporary advertising for the purposes of mobilization. There are plenty of social and political movements in the world which use these kinds of communicative strategies in order to mobilize supporters and sponsors. However, these strategies reveal the tension in relation to the official youth policy: the tension between the concomitant demand of individual possibilities and strict national order (Blum 2006). The intertwinedness of stimulative and didactic discourses has two dimensions here. On the one hand, Nashi's sociopolitical position in a manner of speaking allows it to reconcile the didactic and stimulative "constitution of subjects." On the other hand, Nashi's recruitment announcements reveal the communicative demands of the movement's sociopolitical position; the didactic discourses of the pro-power movement are influenced by the demand of potentially challenging (individual) youth discourses. An advertising method[29] of constituting

---

[28] This was one of the most well known Soviet propaganda posters and was created by the Soviet poster artist and caricaturist Dmitry Stakhievich Moor (1883-1946), during the Russian Civil War (1917-1923) in 1920 and was reprinted during the Second World War, or in Russian patriotic terms, "The Great Patriotic War" in 1941-1945.

[29] Alexei Yurchak points out that in post-Soviet Russia a new Western type of advertising, strongly referring to individual "almighty," creates a division in relation to previous Soviet authoritative discourses (2003: 77-78). This new type of advertising uses personalised and active linguistic forms, such as active verbs, imperatives, pseudo-intransitives,

individual's subject-images is aimed at being combined with natural obligatory instances, for example respective state institutions and high quality education. Nashi's version of Manifesto which includes commentaries is an illuminating case in showing Nashi's position between these two realms.

## Manifesto with Commentaries

Along with Nashi's primary (first) Manifesto there is also the "Manifesto with commentaries" (*Manifest s kommentariiami*) in which various concepts mentioned in the original one are clarified and completed. While the primary Manifesto has approximately 9 pages, the Manifesto with commentaries is approximately 55 pages long. I argue that the coexistence of these two documents, which both serve the same function—self-produced manifestation of the movement and its goals in relation to mobilization—reveals Nashi's particular uncertainty in its struggle between legitimate forms of political communication. Moreover, the choices in the Manifesto with commentaries itself make apparent Nashi's anticipation of symbolic capital between various "objective facts," and politically subjective accounts—the latter already pointed out in the primary Manifesto—which calls into question the whole function of the version with commentaries. In the introduction to the version with commentaries Nashi clarifies the role of the document as follows (Manifest s kommentariiami):

6
The manifesto is a special genre. It is not an article, not an analysis. It is a civic (*grazhdanskaia*) position, a call to action. It is a conviction of those who view the fate of the country and the world approximately in the same way; it is a handbook of action for those who are ready not only to talk but to act as well. A manifesto isn't like money, it is not supposed to please everyone; it is not supposed to have indifferent, well-meaning readers but supporters or opponents. Either there are those

---

the pronoun *ty* and reflexives (ibid.). For similar features in the Russian media discourse in terms of conversationalization, see Vanhala-Aniszewski 2007; 2005b; see also Smetanina 2002. In the context of nation building, Ryazanova-Clarke applies Bourdieu's views of legitimate forms of expression in relation to post-Soviet representations of the Victory Day celebrations of the Great Patriotic War in the Russian press (2008). She argues that the shift from relatively free and creative representations of the Victory in the 1990s to highly controlled and patriotic representations during the Putin era can be conceptualized as a struggle between discourses of heterodoxia and orthodoxy after the heretical break which occurred in the Russian linguistic market immediately after the collapse of the Soviet Union (ibid.: 224-226; see also Bourdieu 1991: 128-129).

who agree with it and share its political position at some point, or there are opponents; those who are at some point against it. Well, some may not have decided yet but there are less and less of those.

The most famous manifesto in history was the 'Communist Manifesto' of Marx and Engels, which turned the world on its head. With it, people went to the barricades, to prison and even to their death. They went, risking everything because they believed in the ideas set forth in that Manifesto. We wrote this Manifesto because we believe in its ideas, and because we are ready to act and fight for the realization of these ideas in life.

However, not everything can be included in the manifesto, it is a very condensed document, it requires clarifications.

clarifications which explain one or another political concepts that are used in the Manifesto.

information which deploys and illustrates the theses of the (main) Manifesto in greater detail.

This is why the reader finds commentaries in this brochure together with the main Manifesto. These commentaries are not neutral politically, they have been written from the viewpoint of NASHI. Its (Nashi's) goal is not to explain but to put <u>an ideological weapon in the hands of its political fighters.</u> And, the political fighters—members of the movement NASHI—can use it in a debate with their political opponents in the battle that has not been won or lost.

The youth goes into politics. There is soon no place for the neutral, indecisive and politically indifferent among the active, clever and strong. There will be a fight for the first mentioned. The Manifesto and its commentaries must convince the hesitant about the validity of the movement NASHI in terms of that WE (NASHI) express the most essential interests of the whole generation, and fight for Russia and its rebirth. The Manifesto and commentaries must show political opponents that they are wrong, and in the name of Russia's rebirth, they have to think over, and become OUR (NASHIkh) political allies of US

I argue that the principal reason for commentaries (55 pages) on their own ideological outline is the fact that Nashi does not trust its subjective and political discourse produced in the primary Manifesto (and the recruitment announcements). This uncertainty can be seen in the sentence after the second paragraph in which it is pointed out that "however, not everything can be included in the manifesto, it is a very condensed document, it requires clarifications." However, a bit later, in the third full paragraph, it is pointed out that "Its goal is not to explain but to put <u>an ideological weapon in the hands of its political fighters.</u>" This partially underlined sentence emphasizes the politically subjective importance of the commentaries. This, however, clearly contradicts the earlier statement which justifies the function of the commentaries on the basis of the first Manifesto's brevity. Although Nashi uses here different verbs/nominalizations which can be translated as "clarification" (*poias-nenie*) and "to explain" *(ob'iasnit)*, they ultimately mean the same; when we clarify something, we typically explain this something in other terms, or when we explain something, we supposedly clarify this something as well. Next I examine Nashi's balancing act between the "subjective political weapon" and "objective explanations/clarifications" which goes on throughout this document of 55 pages.

The metaphor "ideological weapon" that Nashi uses above presumably refers to Nashi's intention to conduct own, invaluably experienced, political and ideological work. To adopt Quentin Skinner's (1974) term, an "innovative ideologist" aims to legitimize his/her "dubious" political activities with this ideological weapon. In terms of didactics and stimulation, this metaphor no doubt aims to work for the purpose of stimulation. Nevertheless, the discursive practice of this "weapon" strongly draws on the encyclopedic type of authoritative discourse. This is the case, for example, in the elaboration of the following concepts mentioned in the first Manifesto (Manifest s kommentariiami):

> 7
> World development, globalization, globalism, colonies, modernization, postindustrial society, the right of all nations to self-determination, isolationism, clash of civilizations, separatism, Sikhism, sovereignty, politics of assimilation, sovereign democracy, geopolitics

In addition to these concepts, various forms of democracy, oligarchy, liberalism as well as an explanation of a couple of extreme right-wing organizations in Russia (The Russian National Unity, The National-Bolshevik Party, and skinheads) are elaborated by using the encyclopedic type of discourse. To illustrate this discourse, the second paragraph of the primary Manifesto ("The world development is the competition of the nations") is cited in this commented upon version as such, and then the four following concepts of "competition" are commented upon (italics, underlining, and bold letters are in the original):

> 8
> **Competition** (from the Latin verb *concurre*—to clash)—in everyday use: A rivalry between economic subjects for better conditions of production, purchase and sale of products.

*Competition*—in classical economic theory: An element of market mechanism that allows the balancing of supply and demand.

*Competition*—in biology: Antagonistic relations, defined by the effort of the best and fastest to achieve some objective compared to other members of the community. Competition arises for space, food, light, shelter, mates, etc. Competition is a manifestation of the struggle for existence.

*Global Competition*—competition at a world scale: Global competition is the realization and the result of globalization.

This sort of representation clearly resorts to "objective" dimensions of the word, and locates Nashi in a didactic position. After these four "objective" classifications, the concept of "globalization" is presented according to a similar encyclopedic discourse but it is also completed by some further elaborations, for example, by referring to the well known sociologist Ulrich Beck (Manifest s kommentariiami). A reference to a famous scientific authority along with resorting to the "objective" discourse of encyclopedias reflects Nashi's willingness to explicate its own cultural capital. References to various socio-cultural authorities make apparent tensions which these authorities imply when they are related to Nashi's general political agenda as a pro-power youth movement. This is, for example, the case with Nashi's comments on the concept of globalism (Manifest s kommentariiami):

9

**Globalism:** theory, ideology and politics concerning the progress of globalization, mainly of violent progress.

This is a doctrine that is foremost developed by an American political class, and targeted at the progress of a global world as an American project. Globalism is the project of the strengthening of the US hegemony in today's world. At the same time, the concept of *mondialisation* (*italics* added by J.L.) arose in the European thought: globalization as an objective process in which all nations must be involved. A global movement of anti-globalists arose who stand against globalization since it destroys cultural specificities of nations. A global movement of alter-globalists arose who think that globalization must be social; it must be dislodged from the subjection of transnational corporations and put into a control of a global civil society in order to serve people. Globalization is the objective historical process. There is no chance to hide from it, it must be approached as fast as possible and (it must) reserve the most fortunate positions in it. There is a global battle over what globalization should be. Our task is to make Russia a leader in globalization.

This quote shows the basic tension in Nashi's ideological orientation: The co-existent orientation towards on the one hand plural and democratic models of globalization and world politics, but at the same time, towards essentialist views according to which there can be only one ruler, or even hegemony, in each period of world history.[30] Both orientations are targeted at the hegemonic position of the US in the global world. While the first emphasizes the more or less democratic and multipolar development of globalization,[31] the second regards globalization as an onerous struggle in which acting in one's own interest is the only rule. As was the case with the examples above, so here the meaning of "globalism" is given as an objective account in the form of an encyclopedic discourse. However, the paragraph which follows this encyclopedic description is evidently "Nashi's view" although it partially follows the relational structure of an encyclopedic discourse.[32] This is about a doctrine connected with an American political class, and then expressed as the project of American hegemony.

Nashi's critical responses to "globalism" are tied together by the generic expressions "arose" (*vozniklo*) by which Nashi aims to emphasize the magnitude of processes which are against globalism, that is, American hegemony. However, in the last three sentences Nashi makes apparent its own position on this "positive" globalization. This appears, not in the sense of democratic globalization, but as a space of objective struggle in which we (Russia) should receive as good a position as possible. Although Nashi clearly orientates towards "European thoughts" of globalization (i.e. mondialization) by repetitive appearances of such thoughts, the movement does not explicate its own and Russia's engagement with them. Instead, it states that "Our task is to make Russia a leader of globalization."

---

[30] Mijnssen discusses this tension in terms of agonism and antagonism (2012).

[31] The issue of multipolarity as a manifestation against the US became apparent in a personal e-mail response (23 February 2007) that I received from Nashi. In the beginning of 2007 I sent an e-mail to Nashi in order to find out problems that had occurred in the main web-site of Nashi at that time. The answer was immediately shifted from "my personal micro-level problems" to macro-level of world politics with a reference to a speech by Vladimir Putin in Germany a couple of days earlier. In that speech Putin mentioned the "dangers of a unipolar world" referring to the hegemonic position of the U.S in world politics.

[32] Relational structure refers to simplified verbal connections between things, creating an essentialistic worldview, in the sense "x is y, and that's it." A similar authenticity is produced in the case of the globalization- commentary by referring to the already mentioned Ulrich Beck, as well as figures of the Brazilian car industry, and domestic airplane industry (Manifest s kommentariiami).

Nashi clearly anticipates those sentiments of post-Soviet Russian nationalism which rely on civilizational, eurasianistic, and explicitly anti-American accounts, partially theorized with the help of Samuel Huntington's *Clash of Civilizations* (see sample 7; Shnirel'man 2006; 2009; Scherrer 2009; Laruelle 2009a). However, Nashi's partially positive account of globalization is different from these profoundly negative views. Serguei Oushakine argues that Andrei Parshev's book "Why Russia is not America" *(Pochemu Rossiia ne Amerika)* published in 2001 became a major contribution to a national-indigenous understanding of Russia's role in globalization in post-Soviet Russia (2009: 59-61). The focus of the book is on Russia's geographical, climatologic, and economic "facts" supported by the idea of Russia's doomed destiny in the sense of the inconvertibility of Russia's national values (ibid.: 62). In short, Parshev's book illustrates the division between Russia's "natural destiny" with its "good national values" and "bad globalization/ Americanization."

In relation to these negative and nationalistic accounts towards globalization, Nashi's ideological position can be somehow described as a supportive of globalization in the sense of Russia's globalism: The only way to attend globalization is to lead it, otherwise you lose it. The Manifesto with commentaries for the most part aims to legitimize these zero-sum game-driven ideological slogans by referring to "neutral" and "objective" elements. This is accomplished by referring to historical events and scientific authorities, including encyclopedic discourse and authoritative persons. In terms of authoritative scientists Nashi principally resorts to Western scientists (for example, Arnold J. Toynbee, Ulrich Beck, Fernand Braudel) whose views are converted to Nashi's own views. This is also an interesting difference from those Russian nationalists (e.g. representatives of the Eurasian movement) who exclusively rely on Russian theorists (Oushakine 2009; Shnirel'man 2009; an important exception in this regard seems to be Samuel Huntington, see, for example, Schnirel'man 2006). This implies that Nashi aims to show the global resonance of its own political views by referring to non-Russian authorities. After all, it seems that Nashi's "ideological weapon" is, if anything, explicated by resorting to didactic symbolic practices, such as encyclopedias or dictionaries, which are often used in didactic approaches. This is the case, for example, in the following explanation (Manifest s kommentariiami):

10
**Colonies:** countries and territories that are under the power of a foreign state (metropolis), have no political and economical independence, and are governed by a special regime.
In 1914, 42.9 % of the world's territories were colonies of the West, where 32.3% of the world's population lived. However, in addition to official colonies, there were countries that had been forced into the dependence from the West, for example, China. In 1914, colonies and dependent countries covered almost 66.8 % of territories and 60 % of peoples on the globe. For instance, from 1876 to 1914, Great Britain seized 9.7 million square kilometers consisting of 49 million people; Germany: 2.9 million square kilometers, 12.3 million people, USA: 0.3 million square kilometers, 9.7 million people, Japan: 0.3 million square kilometers, 19.2 million people. Almost the whole African continent became the victim of colonial slavery. Only one independent state remained, Ethiopia.

The placement of the Colonies paragraph in the Manifesto with commentaries implies that its probable function is motivated by the need to emphasize that in history the majority of countries under Western rule became colonies. However, the section in which this statement is given also emphasizes the close relations between Russia and the West. Hence, it appears that the ideological and identity-related tension between Russia's own way, that is, "our way" (see e.g. Dubin 2001; 2011) and Western oriented accounts (Western authorities and modernization) is managed by offering an implicit warning of the potential consequences of Western influences: Russia might become the West's colony. Discursively this is achieved by offering a highly exact, and "authentic sounding" numeral listing[33] of the consequences of colonialism. Moreover, the mention of Ethiopia is anything but a coincidence here despite the fact it remained outside straight colonial oppression: Ethiopia has been the closest partner and ally of Russia/Soviet Union in the African Continent. This kind of fact-driven description reveals, on the one hand, Nashi's knowledge (cultural) capital, and on the other, allows it to hide its own voice in relation to this ideological/identity tension; we, in a manner of speaking, are

---

[33] The use of numbers and quantitative statistical data as indicators of "truth" is widely used in different politically motivated discourses, see, for example, the article by Elaine Campbell concerning criminal issues in Britain (2000). In the context of Russia, the power of numbers and quantitative indicators has been pointed out by Evgeny Golovko and Nikolai Vakhtin in the case of official discourse in the Soviet Union (2004: 209-212). Serguei Oushakine has interestingly pointed out that among post-Soviet youth issues of style are often represented by using discourse of quantitative indicators (2000).

not saying that Russia would become a colony ruled by others (e.g. by the West) but we show this option in the light of historical and "objective" numbers.

As some of the discussed concepts have shown, the use of the encyclopedic discourse is not only limited to seemingly complex concepts but is used in the case of the following relatively familiar concepts as well (Manifesto s kommentariiami):

11
Generation, competition, leader, West, way of life, agenda, global view, national view, values, Cold War, North America, European Union, South Asia, Western and Eastern Christianity, Islam, Buddhism, civilization, justice (spavedlivost'), solidarity, fascism, dictatorship

I dare argue that most of these concepts are more or less familiar for those who are generally interested in participating in social or political organizations, at least for those whom Nashi regards ideal members. The desired features of these members are finely presented at the end of the primary Manifesto where it is pointed out that the movement must formulate a new generation of leaders who have a sense of patriotism, historical optimism, strategic thinking, social responsibility, openness to the new, the capability to be constructive, leadership qualities, and a high degree of professionalism (see Manifesto). The founder of Nashi (and Idushchie Vmeste), Vassili Iakemenko articulated this view in *Komsomol'skaia Pravda* in 2005 as follows (Komsomol'skaia Pravda 2005):

12
The future is for those who are at now 16-20 years old. They don't know what is the geopolitical defeat. We teach them to win. We produce them according to the system "patriot, leader, specialist." We collect the best guys from streets and teach them in our institutes. The best specialists are dealing with them. After few years we'll have couple of tens of thousands of guys who will think in another way that those who are in power at now.[34]

---

[34] Iakemenko's claim of the obliviousness among the age group 16-20 concerning the recent past is partially true at least in the light of some sociological results. Arseni Svynarenko points out that particularly the generation of perestroika is "gone" in the sense of patriotic-optimistic expectations of Russia (2005: 87 - 94). The generation between 18-22 years old, on the contrary, is close to older generations in terms of respecting national and patriotic values (ibid.).

Although the notion of Bourdieu's class is not the focus of my analysis, Iake-menko's views highlight the point that his ideal youth is clearly classed: there is capable youth, that is, "our youth of the forthcoming elite," and there is in-capable youth, that is, "the generation of losers." It is also fascinating how these overly simplified classifications seem to occupy Nashi activists' views regarding their views to participate in the movement. For instance, Ivo Mijnssen's respondent Andrei repeats the above mentioned views of Iake-menko ("patriot," "leader," "specialist") literally as well as Julie Hemment's re-spondent Kirill (Mijnssen 2012: 69; Hemment 2014: chapter on Nashi). The movement's Manifesto seems to occupy at least as authoritative role as the leader's words, as the interviews in the next chapter illustrate. In terms of Al-thusser's interpellation, Nashi's, and Iakemenko's in particular, sociopolitical position allows the movement to constitute subjects according to ready-made subject-images in which "the most talented youngsters" can transform them-selves. This is tangibly apparent, for example, in the following passage of the Manifesto with commentaries in which *lider*, a widely used loan word in the Russian language, is commented upon (Manifesto s kommentariiami):

13
Lider (In English *leader*: to head, to direct, from *to lead*, to take [*vesti*]): Literally a person who takes others with himself.

This elaboration hardly yields any new information about this word. Instead, such encyclopedic-dictionary- discourse reveals Nashi's sense of interpellat-ing a leader as a "ready-made subject"; a supposedly stimulative figure which is compatible with Nashi's didactic position. This position emphasizes Nashi's careerist side, and may cause negative impacts among "youth resources," from which Nashi (in Iakemenko's words) wants to pick the best individuals. Iakemenko's idealistic and forceful view—expressed by short active sentenc-es—shows an overly resource-oriented and didactic attitude towards "the most talented guys" who "Nashi chooses from the streets," and then "edu-cates in our institutes with the best specialists."[35] Interestingly, and somehow

---

35 Here Iakemenko obviously refers to the "National Institute of Administration" (Natsion-al'nyi institut Vysshaia Shkola Upravleniia) which was established in 2004, and is close-ly linked to the Kremlin, and official educational policies. During its first years with the birth of Nashi, the connection between educational programs and the movement was explicit. Since then the hyperlinks to each other's sites disappeared from both the Insti-

opaquely Iakemenko contrasts the future's new elite against those who are in power now. On the one hand, this hardly means Nashi's "benefactors," that is, the Kremlin-related political elite, particularly around the president, but probably those who, from Nashi's viewpoint, (still) have too much power of opposing Kremlin policies. Yet, regarding Russia's overly president-driven political system, Iakemenko's vision of changing those who are in power now, sounds strange. On the other hand, such contrasting is compatible with the points made by Andreev (2006) as well as Atwal (2009) that I discussed in the previous chapter: It implies Nashi's "passionate" willingness to conduct officially related policies in its own way, and this seemingly results in autonomous and potentially incompatible strategies in relation to "adult-driven policies."

The commented version shows various nationalistic but similarly relatively conciliatory concepts (e.g. accounts of "good" global-ization in terms of "Russia's globalism"). A vivid realization of the attempt to combine these two aspects is present in the part of the version with commentaries in which the aforementioned, didactically framed stimulation of the leader in the previous sample is given:

14
Russia, it is our Motherland and we see our mission, our thought of social life, to enable Russia to become the great, modern (*sovremennyi*), free and righteous empire, which would head the most progressive processes of the modern world, and would become a global leader itself.

Especially noteworthy is the part in which "freedom" and "righteousness" as generally accepted qualities of Russia are attached to an overly nationalistic concept of "world-power" (*derzhava*). In sum, the Manifesto with commentaries makes apparent the seemingly unsolved political communication between the didactic and stimulative approaches. On the one hand, an orientation towards official conventions of cultural (symbolic and discursive) production results in a didactic sense of educating, or "interpellating" youth. On the other hand, from the viewpoint of the primary Manifesto and the recruitment announcements, Nashi has a clear desire and willingness to orientate itself towards supposedly youth-driven expectations; that is, to conduct its "patriotic

tute's, and Nashi's sites. However, the ideological connection between these two is still evident in terms of creating new administrative and business elites for Russia.

political project" in a way which would allow space for "your talented activities." Next we turn to Nashi's special project "OUR Army" which illustrates this issue.

## The Didactics and Stimulation of "Our Army"

Nashi's special project "OUR Army" was launched at the turn of 2006-2007, and its main goal was to offer an attractive image of the Russian army. The role of the army in Russia has been controversial because of the tension between its socio-cultural dimensions and actual practices. In terms of socio-cultural values, the army in Russia is one of the three institutions which are generally trusted along with Putin and the church. Trust towards the army is essentially linked with the patriotic underpinnings of the greatest national celebration, "Victory in the Great Patriotic War." However, in terms of actual practices linked with the army—that is, compulsory military service for male citizens—people generally prefer to avoid the army. In 2007, 47 % of citizens shared this view. The main reason has been *dedovshchina*, a particularly cruel form of hazing and bullying conducted by older conscripts and military staff (Lonkila 2008, 1127-1129; See also Sperling 2009).

Whereas the army and military service is always connected with various compulsory admonitions—"your country needs you," "you are needed for the freedom of your country"—Nashi's role is significantly twofold: On the one hand, Nashi explicitly reveals its own position as a conductor of a state level program, which partially calls into question the independent position that the movement wants to emphasize.[36] On the other hand, Nashi seemingly seeks to prove that, from its socio-political position, it is the correct conductor of this project.

As a major part of marketing this project, Nashi made public an approximately eight minute long and openly propagandistic video on the Internet in February 2007 (Nasha armiia video 2007;"Nashe" interv'iu 2007). In order to facilitate my analysis, I divided the video into the following twelve parts:

---

36 On different occasions Nashi has underscored its spontaneous position as a pro-power youth movement, or in Iakemenko's words in the interview in the Moskovskii Komsomolets (2006), "Nashi is an independent all-Russian youth movement." See also Savel'ev 2006: 94.

(1) introduction, (2) general contextual framing, (3) specified contextual framing, (4) more specified contextual framing, (5) example voice, (6) request and guarantee, (7) example voice, (8) example story, (9) example voice, (10) the most specified contextual framing and request, (11) example voice, and (12) information announcement.

The introduction of the video gains from rather traditional visual images widely used in different settings of Western driven global fiction: thunder and rocky landscape. Through these images the logo of Nashi is constructed, followed by a quotation in Russian from the *Los Angeles Times*, written in white letters on a black background. This quotation, which discusses the miserable situation of the Russian army, figures in at least two senses: On the one hand, the construction of the threat of Americans and the US (which is followed by the introduction) is launched by a source of "the other", which Nashi aims to show as wrong. On the other hand, the degradation of the Russian army, including evading military service, is obviously the central starting point for the "Our army" project. Hence, in order to diminish this degradation the movement wants to play the vanguard role, and the quotation of the *Los Angeles Times* works as a supposedly cogent forum of the presented fact.

The second part of the video, general contextual framing, constructs the world from the viewpoint of organic life cycles, according to which the actions of states is the same as searching for food. Accordingly, the death or blossoming of states depends on their capability to find food. In this light, the US appears as an ever-spreading monster to which other states are subordinate. Russia up to now has remained out of this situation but in all probability is the next target of the US because of the vast amount of America's food located in Russia (i.e. oil which is not yet explicated here). This essentialist and stereotyping discourse of the US and Americans is interesting in two ways by describing Americans and their government, on the one hand, as a like-minded mass ("every American wants a powerful car, fashionable clothes, and big shiny new house")[37] who consider Russians as simple drunkards ("Americans believe we inhabited a godforsaken wild village full of moonshine drinking, little bears"), and they are already on our borders with threatening intentions:

---

[37] These quotes are English subtitles of the video which was available on YouTube (In May 2012 video was only available at RuTube without subtitles). The subtitles appeared to be correct and acute when I compared them with the original.

15
They're already right next door; in the Baltic states, in Ukraine, in Georgia. They already have military bases located there along with their rockets. And guess who's in the crosshairs?

On the other hand, a couple of sentences before this quote, the intentions of the Americans are considered natural, not as an adversary action, although their natural need (i.e. search for oil) seems to be the same thing as a military attack, that is, "if we offer them a chance":

16
They're coming for the food. They can't afford not to. Not because they don't like us or they are our enemies, no. They just want to eat. Their government wants to eat <...> We won't have to go to war with America on one condition; only if they are sure that our army is, at least, not weaker than theirs. Otherwise, given even the slightest opportunity, they will do everything they can to overcome us.

In the following part, specified contextual framing, the male voice narrat-or partially shifts the story onto the viewer by mentioning people who still understand the meaning of the army, namely, the defense of the motherland. This argument is legitimized by stating that people who do not do their military service bring closer a situation similar to what is happening in Iraq (in 2007). This is because only a fool thinks that the Americans are in Iraq in order to spread democracy. The analogy which then follows is that the Americans, who actually are in Iraq because of the oil, will be in Russia next because of its much larger reserves of oil. In general, this part follows a rather emphasized didactic discourse by showing clear and simple reasons for the importance of the army, emanating from an essentialist understanding of world politics. In other words, the narrator as the authority-seer tells how things actually are.

The next part—more specified contextual framing—projects the argumentation, as well as didactic discourse, on the viewer more intensively than the earlier part by constructing a paradox. According to it "everybody knows the importance of the army but when the issue comes to you, you evade the army." The paradox is emphasized by various troubles which follow this evasion. Consequently, these troubles aim to show the absurdity of the paradox:

17
They make you afraid to apply for an international passport. They make you hide in an unnecessary university and then an even more unnecessary graduate school.

Then they make you start to think you are sick, think up diseases, and stay at home in bed. And all this is for the sake of what? Think about it, it's all in an effort to avoid defending your motherland.

In addition, an implicit allegation—which is rather contradictory from the viewpoint of widespread evasion of the army—is made by mentioning that:

18
Thousands like you are already standing guard. What makes them any different from you? Maybe they were simply more honest.

The allegation is not followed by more accusations but a discursive break "Well, okay" (Nu, ladno), which shifts the focus on the reasons why people evade military service. The most common reasons are hazing, and the waste of time which are emphasized on the screen by rotating these words. The following part, the example voice, starts with a conscript talking about his colleague who had left the army without any explanation. This account is completed by the narrator's voice who tells about "the new revolutionary program of Nasha armiia established by Nashi in association with the ministry of defense," and this statement is completed by the talk of the conscript who confirms that it is easier in the army when you are together with others.

The clearest shift towards stimulation is made in the next part—request and guarantee—which constructs viewers of the video as particularly "capable clients." Various routines of military service are presented as alternatives from which "you" can choose the most interesting ones, for example, assembling a team of friends, the possibility of checking out the battalion for your service, as well as the possibility of picking a nice place for your service with your own books and computer. Moving from these advantages, protection against hazing is constructed by "the support of the largest youth movement Nashi which is ready to protect you on all levels."[38] The presumable stimulativeness of this army program—especially in this part of the video—is explicitly secured by the parent organization, that is, the movement Nashi. In light of network marketing discourses the aspect of security is intrinsically linked with the notion of justice. In addition, what is essential in the aspect of "justice" in the new management discourse is the notion of a justificatory regime built from con-

---

[38] The similar strategy of securing was used by Idushchie Vmeste in its special recruitment text "Instruction for a Walker" (See Lassila 2011a).

trasting, or adversarial linguistic elements targeted at an individual (Chiapello & Fairclough 2002: 198-199). Eve Chiapello and Norman Fairclough write that the "grammar" of justificatory regimes—a defining feature in popular management discourses—incorporates a contrast and a relation between "the great ones" and "the small ones" (ibid.: 199). As the earlier samples of Nashi have shown, this division is typically manifested as "we the capable" elite as distinct from "the not capable", "the generation of losers."

The eighth part—the example story—reveals the identity of the example voice, "the great one," continuing the supposed stimulation in relation to security as well as justice. The example voice of the conscript is Lokha Chernykhin who attends the project "Our army". The narrator repeats the elements of security through the case of Chernykhin, and hence aims to stimulate interest towards military service and national duty:

> 19
> He doesn't have to worry about trying to think up some way of weaseling out of military service, or saving money for temporary documents. And his international passport is all in order. He serves his country because he knows: If someone like him doesn't go and serve today…Tomorrow who knows who's going to protect his family and his motherland?

This statement is emphasized by a short part of the example voice in which Lokha states that "if a country doesn't have an army of its own then it will have a foreign army." The tenth part—the most specified contextual framing and request—makes apparent the contrasting and adversarial elements of the video: the "justificatory regime of the army" by dividing "the great us" from "their wrong assumptions":

> 20
> They say our generation hasn't done anything. They say the army isn't worth it. They say there's no end to military hazing. Let's give it a shot. It's within our power to change.

However, this adversarial logic seems to be very ephemeral. Immediately after this seemingly "wrong" assumption of "theirs," this assumption is projected as the most common way of doing things. It seems that this common way of doing things creates a situation from which "you" can distinguish yourself, to do things differently in relation to the past. As Chiapello and Fairclough point out, the "great ones" are systematically associated with the future while the "small ones", with the past, on the basis of a banal ideology of progress (ibid.: 199):

> 21
> It's easiest of all to sit around the stove and do nothing. But this doesn't solve any-thing. This is what the majority of people you know already do. They sit and drink beer in the courtyard while someone else is defending their ass. It's much more dif-ficult to go and change something with your own hands. This is the road of a person who doesn't take the easy way out. The road of a warrior. Be one of the people that will be talked about someday, be one of the first. The people that will help make our army stronger. The people that will make Russia different. It was harder for them than anybody else but they did it anyway. Come to be a part of the program Nasha armiia.

Now at least the unquestionable legitimacy of the army along with its didactic discourse is transformed into a stimulation of the viewer with youth-resonating expressions (e.g. "someone else is defending their ass"): The army needs you, not only because of the general need of the mass but "because of the special and capable people who can change the situation." In this respect, the role of Nashi, again, appears interestingly twofold: On the one hand, the ob-vious idea of the video, as well as the "Our army" project, is to stimulate as many young Russian males to do military service as possible but, on the oth-er, the common service does not seem to be enough. It must be conducted better than that. This view is present in Lokha's last comment followed by the information text attending the project:

> 22
> We want the program to keep developing. If we get 1,000 people this spring then we'll get 5,000 in the fall. I see people on the street who say half-heartedly: "yeah, I served. It was so and so" but I can honestly say I served, and served proudly. What they did was noble, but it wasn't smart.

The video itself is not outside the attention space where Nashi acts but it is an initial part of it. Nashi seemingly assumes that the "rules of a contemporary video" targeted at young males supposedly include particular visual and sonic devices. As part of a supposedly stimulative discursive practice, these devic-es play an essential role, although they may call into question the serious-ness of the topic of the video. This comes about by overtly caricaturing the visual side of the video. For example, at the beginning of the video the con-struction of the threat of the US is not represented just by various documentary snapshots of military actions and equipment, which can be regarded as the products of traditional visual military discourse. Instead, various humorous animations are used as well; nations of the world as stereotypic (and racist) figures, the US in the figure of a fat giant with huge tentacles, and Americans' views of Russians as wandering drunk bears. Elements from rock music videos are intensively used; for example, repetitive heavy metal type guitar riffs along with sudden appearances of Nashi's logo. The appearances of the logo divide the narrative into separate sections and arrange a traditional military catalogue of officers and facilities into a rhythmic and dramatic form. A culmination of this stimulation appears in the part in which an orthodox priest, visualized with the alteration of fastened and delayed motions, blesses conscripts standing on guard, having a sharp and distorted synthesizer sound as the incidental music.

Visual and sonic devices are crucial definers of a cultural product such as a music-video. However, applying Bourdieu, when the message of the video goes beyond "restricted youth culture forms," the role of these devices become different, and definitely more vulnerable in terms of a "rigorous evaluation of the anticipations of symbolic profit" (Bourdieu 1991: 81). In other words, I suggest that in the given combination of cultural products and practices, the outcome easily becomes infelicitous while those who generally rely on official instances of military education are not familiar enough with the products of youth culture. Consequently, the target group of the video, namely, those young males who are to be stimulated into joining the military may evaluate this use of "youth culture tools" (e.g. music-video elements) as inappropriate and / or ridiculous.

The aspect of propaganda—which is not difficult to avoid in the case of this video—illustrates the above mentioned incompatibility. Labeling the video propagandistic was not only due to the general response of the public[39] but was also by the author of the video, the former press-secretary of the movement, and later a Duma-member Robert Schlegel. While for the majority of viewers propaganda was seen in pejorative terms, Schlegel explains the function of propaganda as follows (Nashe interv'iu 2007):

---

39   According to the Internet publication Aktsija online, by the end of March 2007 sixteen thousand people had seen the video (Nashe interv'iu 2007).

23
And why not? I think that a person, or to be more precise, the state and then the individual, must create, right from the beginning, an example of an idealistic picture of the army, what it is and what it must be. Then, on the basis of this model, society is constructed. Roughly speaking, a group of people who talk, well, here's the picture, you must go here and there, and then it becomes clear where you go and what you have to do...If the army will become as we see it within the project and as I showed it in the footage, then it will be a great success.

Schlegel's point here is that instead of giving any sort of objective account of the army and its role, the video aims to offer an idealistic picture as a starting point according to which people and society may then begin to construct themselves. He shows a rather straightforward belief in the power of the examples over people in the sense that these examples are perceived as they are intended to be perceived. In this respect, I interpret that the generally negative perception of the video shows that Bourdieu's argument concerning probable breakdowns of original experimentations within practices of restricted and large-scale cultural productions is certainly true (Nashe interv'iu 2007; Bourdieu 1993: 129). In addition, I would add that the combination of these two fields is simply infelicitous in general, and in this case operates in both directions; propaganda on behalf of the army targeted at "passive youth" (of the restricted cultural production) from the viewpoint of the large-scale cultural production (in this case, the army) are inaccessible to those who are familiar with its valuable practices (i.e. particular practices of music-videos).

Andreev's view of Nashi (and of Idushchie Vmeste) as passionate movements which enthusiastically search for enemies is illuminating with regard to "Our army" (2006). Following Andreev's definition, the enemy is any value or feature (e.g. passivity) that is incompatible with the movement's ambitions. However, a specific problem for Nashi in this respect seems to be the need for culturally and nationally stimulative enemies, but at the same time, the need to avoid enemies which would be associated too much with Russia's nationalistic anti-Western images. "Our army" shows that Nashi, as a pro-governmental youth formation between state-policies and apolitical youth, is in a difficult position in terms of balancing between conformist didactics and unrestrained nationalistic stimulation. Let us now examine how Nashi's activists see their role in the movement, and consider the movement in terms of distributing its ideas on the Internet.

# V  Projecting the Movement Onwards

### Reasons for Joining

In March 2009, a Nashi leader referred to here by the pseudonym Oleg explained me his reasons to join the group:

> 24
>
> (Oleg): Why did I join? Well, this is difficult and simple question at the same time (laughing)…difficult because…because I don't know why I joined eventually …it's difficult…in that time I already had experience in youth political activities and they had affected me extremely negatively…because…I had enough, it wasn't interesting.
>
> (Jussi): Why?
>
> (Oleg): Why…well, you know, each youth organization has a particular adult organization…the Komsomol had, and still has RSM KPRF (the youth movement of Russia's Communist Party), although less than the Komsomol of the KPSS (the Communist Party of the Soviet Union)…the Young Guard has the United Russia, and that is always a very….complex enough relationship. And, from the viewpoint of progressivity, youth is repeatedly linked to this progress in the country, but adults, on the one hand, somehow systematize and….intervene, on the other hand …there is the federal youth leadership, there are adults with their own tasks, but in this region. And there is a kind of dilemma in the administration…well, the matrix's structure (*matrichnaia struktura*) is not in balance, it's not very…effective, or correctly speaking, it is non-balanced…the central operatives are not nice. Well, in sum, I had enough. I joined Nashi…because I was one of its founders, first in one region, and then in another…we sat down together…and decided to do something despite that negative experience. Difficult to say [I joined] perhaps because there were no adults at any time.

Oleg's partially wavering explanation of his reasons for joining the movement reveals a combination of didactic "adult" discourse and autonomous "youth" discourse. The didactic discourse comes about implicitly as his major negative experience and as the most probable reason why he actually joined Nashi. Here Oleg identifies himself as "non-adult," that is, a representative of youth, representing different practices from those that had caused his highly negative experience. However, the specification that elaborates his negative experience, and hence ground for joining Nashi, interestingly assumes a rather bureaucratic vocabulary, that is, markers of a discourse that could be termed "adult" as distinct from "youth": "there is the federal youth leadership", "dilemma in the administration", or "the matrix's structure is not balanced, it is not effective, correctly speaking, non-balanced." Such wording reveals that Oleg sees youth political activity principally in organizational terms with effective or non-effective results, but leaves open to what this effectiveness or ineffectiveness is attached. Since he is a leader of a pro-Kremlin youth movement, it can be assumed that this bureaucratic vocabulary actually reveals Oleg's understanding of Nashi's role vis-à-vis official policies. As distinct from these "negative and ineffective/non-balanced" adult practices, Oleg mentions those youth movements that appear more or less as political opponents, or at least competitors, of Nashi (LDPR, KPRF, *Rodina*). In addition, he also puts the youth section Young Guard of "Putin's party," Edinaya Rossiia, in this same group as well. Hence, Oleg regards Nashi as something different from all of these, allowing more space for youth without adult "systematization" and "interference". This implies that Nashi represents, or allows its members, that progressivity which is often linked to youth. Indeed, this comes about in Oleg's reply to my additional question as to whether Nashi is purely a youth movement:

> 25
> Yes, yes, clearly youth [movement] that LDPR, KPRF, Rodina do not have at all at the moment ...well, on the other hand, if we view this question simply. Why simply? Because I saw the possibility to do something real in the movement. And that pleased me. This possibility was not only related to my own region, but it was a possibility to do something on the scale of the country...to be part of some kind of megaproject...and most important, I clearly understood that this project allows me personal improvement as well. I saw the educational program...and I really liked it, it was...and is interesting.

In short, Oleg sees Nashi as the movement in which he can do something real. This "real" is something that allows activities not only at the regional level, but on the scale of the whole country by using the term "megaproject," a term that is mentioned in the first lines of the movement's manifesto (see Sample 3). For him, Nashi represents a youth movement in which he can be part of "big issues" and undergo personal development, and this option is contrasted against adult practices.

This single sample from a leader of the movement does not allow one to draw overly wide conclusions of Nashi's viewpoint in relation to official policies. However, Oleg's views illustrate the movement's aptitude to be something unique along with the official political conformism. Similar views that draw on the movement's uniqueness and individual capabilities, as well as views that are compatible with official policies can be tracked in Vadim's reasons to join the movement. One of the early leaders of the movement, he was interviewed in May 2008, also using a pseudonym. While Vadim regards my question about reasons of joining the movement very nicely, he specifies:

> 26
> First, I did not join Nashi. There were few people…people who found the Nashi movement…and I joined this process…when I found out that there is a group of people in Moscow with whom my personal ideas are completely compatible (*sovpadayut na sto protsentov*)…That's why I joined the process.

By seeing the establishment of the movement as a process that was compatible with his own ideas and interests—a process that he found—he constructs himself as a leader distinct from those who joined the movement later and continue to join it now. Or as he puts it in another part of the interview: "I joined the movement because I had a possibility to be a part of its establishment." In addition, Vadim's individual interests are seemingly compatible with official discourse, since he mentions that among Nashi's goals he saw the idea of "maintaining the country's sovereignty" (*sokhranenie suvereniteta strany*) around the "orange events" (*oranzhevye sobytiia*) as principally important. Although Vadim does not contrast his and Nashi's interests with "adult practices" as explicitly as Oleg does, his views on Nashi's uniqueness are clearly contrasted with other pro-Kremlin activities as well:

> 27
> There was the youth movement Idushchie Vmeste, a pro-Putin one…I experienced it, to say honestly, very negatively. I knew it well, but it did not appeal to me. I did not join the party United Russia either…it was not interesting.

Although Vadim does not specify why Idushchie Vmeste appeared to him in a very negative way, it can be assumed that the issues that Idushchie Vmeste propagated were incompatible with his own (*sobstvennye*) ideas. Moreover, by mentioning an "adults' party" (United Russia) in this respect, Vadim's view implies that Nashi differs from it. This difference refers in all probability to organizational and practical aspects, rather than ideological ones, as the United Russia is the key actor in propagating ideas of maintaining Russia's sovereignty, which Vadim regards as most important for Nashi, as well.

Oleg's and Vadim's views illustrate Nashi's ambition to act as a sovereign conductor of official political views. In terms of communicating these views throughout the movement, the question is about Nashi's own commitment in relation to official political guidelines. Nashi appears to be a movement that allows space for personal views in relation to official policies, and this possibility is contrasted with "adult practices." Following Andreev's (2006) views of Nashi as passionate movement, this evident grass-roots commitment may also appear contradictory in relation to official political guidelines.

A somewhat different justification for joining the movement is given by Igor from St. Petersburg (pseudonym, interviewed in May 2008). He frames his background in youth politics by mentioning his central role in the Western-oriented oppositional youth movement DA (*Demokraticheskaia Alternativa*) (see Stanovaia's classification above). However, he distanced himself from it after the movement began to work with "natsbols".[40] This was a turning point for Igor in his joining Nashi:

28

After one and a half weeks I was phone-called by "Nashi" of Moscow and they asked me to come to work with them. I agreed. In that time we had either orange movements, or NASHI. Young Guard appeared much later in St. Petersburg than in Russia...Young Russia, if you have heard about this movement, was not represented in St. Petersburg at all.

So, for Igor, Nashi appeared as the only choice in a situation where there were only "orange" movements and Nashi. By mentioning that he was phone-called by Nashi, he seemingly emphasizes his importance as a member in the movement, although he is not in a leader-position as are Oleg and Vadim. As distinct from Oleg and Vadim—who both emphasize Nashi's uniqueness in relation to other pro-Kremlin movements—Igor justifies joining Nashi on the basis of the situation in St. Petersburg: Nashi was the only "non-orange" (i.e. pro-Kremlin) movement in the city at that time.

These passages from the interviews with three Nashi activists show how a personal position is intertwined with aspects of official policies. They provide

---

40 These "natsbols" refer to members and supporters of the National Bolshevik Party (NBP) which appeared as one of the most well-known youth movements in Russia in the mid 2000s. In addition, with its diverse, anarchist, and deeply non-conformist ideology it has been a major enemy for Nashi. For more about NBP, see Sokolov 2006.

a grassroots insight into the tension which became apparent in the official youth policy: A combination of national-patriotic discourses and youth's autonomous position, which results in a conceptual broadening of the term "youth." This appears, for example, in the following view by Oleg in which he elaborates on Nashi's activities as follows:

29
Well, we talk that you must gain personal success but it must be linked to the state's success. If you're a successful constructor of airplanes...the country will be glad about that, it will have good airplanes, right? You can be a talented artist, doctor, or poet, it doesn't matter...but the whole society wins. Here I don't see any point in separating the country, the state and society. I think they all can unite. That's what we think about that.

This quote is clearly compatible with the notions of the official youth policy in which the concept of youth is almost always accompanied with a certain conceptual broadening, typically with the state, the country, and the society. It follows that such an account activates the background of youth's apoliticalness which is well recognized by all the interviewed activists. It appears implicitly through that discourse by which Oleg, Vadim, and Igor highlight their own active and seemingly model position as distinct from other, passive youth. Youth's apoliticalness is also explicitly mentioned by all of them, although they show some reservations when explicating this. Igor sees Russia's youth as apolitical at least in St. Petersburg, which is his primary location. Oleg calls into question the youth's apoliticalness by stating that "youth is interested in that part of social-political life in which it participates. In this sense it is active." However, a bit later Oleg admits that "I can say that many [young people, who graduate from universities and institutes of higher education] are not ready for true relationships in terms of employment." Consequently, Vadim explains that especially urban youth is not so apolitical as is generally claimed although he thinks only approximately 10% are really active youth (presumably including himself). From this standpoint he defines his role in Nashi in terms of "leading the maximum number of (active) young people to the social-political life."

### Internet

Nashi activists follow the didactic discourse from their individual and partially elite position. However, from this position—especially contrasted with adult practices by Oleg—Nashi appeared as a stimulating choice for the activists, but more importantly, as Vadim's last account suggests, this stimulation must be projected on potentially capable youth. Nashi's previous examples from Manifesto and of recruitment strategies have illustrated that this projection seems to be a difficult task. The activists' views of the major forum of their self-produced information—the Internet and the movement's website—are quite revealing in this regard. As Oleg's following quote shows, his positive attitude toward the Internet is principally linked to its effectiveness:

30

> From the viewpoint of a youth movement, the Internet is a very convenient (*udobnyi*) instrument in the two senses: for the outer and the inner work. I like the Internet because through the Internet, I can receive information that I need for effective work. It is obvious that a modern youth movement cannot work effectively without the Internet...There is a big number of information flows in which you must participate if you want to change the environment...well, in order to know and change (things) through them. And, it must be acknowledged that in recent times it is a means of geopolitical struggle.
> (Jussi): In this respect, your main website is for the outer communication in particular, am I right?
> Yes, exclusively for the outer communication because it is...a virtual face of the movement. We had a form of it that we closed, and for the inner messages we have a separate form...the closed one, that's a normal thing...Once, I found that all messages I had sent were available to unknown addresses (laugh). So, to open your own inner information channels is not a clever move. That's why we use the Internet as a working instrument but it is not connected with the site at all. The site is only a tool to tell about yourself.

Therefore, the Internet is principally associated with the kind of technical pragmatism which is used amongst the movement's members. Consequently, this (internal) working instrument has nothing to do with the (external) main website. The division between open (for example, various web-blogs), and closed forms, is presumably justified by the problem of hacking of websites, as Oleg's account with a laugh reveals. However, Oleg does not explain further the choices that are made in the interest of the main site, which he calls "the virtual face of the movement." A similar technical and pragmatic understanding of the web becomes apparent in the next view by Igor in which he describes the role of the Internet in the work of the social movement. The following quote brings home the notion of hacking as well, but as distinct from Oleg's positive attitude towards the Internet, Igor reveals his personal disappointment with it:

> 31
> Well, you know, first, the Internet is a mechanism. It cannot be the goal as paper is not the goal of a newspaper. It is only a place where you can write something...it is a tool...To carry propaganda on the Internet in these days is not very healthy thing to do. If you work through, let us say, *ZhZh*, you will be immediately bored by 20 natsbols who start to talk rubbish. That's a minimum. That's why it is absolute senseless to debate.

For Igor, while considering the Internet purely as mechanism, this mechanism is currently useless for distributing propaganda (see the next section in which this term will be discussed) because of "bullshitting natsbols" (see the previous footnote) with whom it is now impossible to argue. An important addition here is that Igor, as Oleg above, principally perceives the Internet not through the movement's main site but through the chat. As Igor has his own web-blog, his answer suggests that his interests in the web are more likely to be linked to the blog context than the movement's main site. This view has wider dimensions in the Russian Internet as well. In the Russian case, a web-blog is generally understood as *Zhivoi Zhurnal*, in everyday use *ZhZh*, which is a straight translation of the "Live Journal" blogging site (Gorny 2006: 75). While in the West, the use of the Live Journal is less popular than, for example Facebook, in Russia, Live Journal has almost become a synonym for the Internet (ibid.).[41] It is also the key forum for various social and political actions organized and discussed in the Russian web-space (ibid.: 76; Lonkila 2008: 1140-1142). In this regard, Igor's understanding of the web is primarily linked to personal blogging, and its disappointments due to "cyber-hooliganism," while the main website is seen as somehow beyond the Internet. This view is strengthened in Igor's answer concerning my question of the "image" and style of Nashi's main website:

---

[41] In 2012 Vkontakte appeared to be the most popular social networking website and Live Journal was the second (Top Sites Blog 2012).

32

I don't know how a foreigner views the style of our site. From my point of view, it is a natural thing that we have a certain template of messages…It is a basic issue of any professional journalism, it is natural…Well, yes, there are prohibited words. For instance, it is prohibited…prohibited to use guys' words… That's why there is a standard formula for commissars, activists of the Nashi movement.

Hence, for Igor the construction of the public image in the main website—which is arguably the broadest public forum for Nashi in this respect—is not articulated through any elaboration of the communicative devices that are used in the main site. Instead, the site is articulated as a technical and natural "journalistic practice" for Russian users, while Igor reveals his unresponsiveness towards how a foreigner might perceive the site. In addition, his comment reflects a particular didactic position by emphasizing the unsuitability of "using guys' words" in their official communication.

The role of the main site in relation to the Internet seems to be relatively insignificant for Vadim, too. Although he cordially explains Nashi's professionalism in the sphere of the Internet, Vadim, like Igor above, thinks that there was a "good" Internet as compared to today's Internet:

33

I won't hide the fact that Nashi has, indeed, great specialists in the field of the Internet. At some point a special attention was paid into this direction. A special program was established for people who purposefully worked in the Internet. The so-called blogs were created, our own sites were written.[42] However, I think that a good outlook on the Internet—it is important, of course—[but] it is not…a primary thing. If you have a good look only on the Internet, a movement won't go far.
(Jussi): So, besides a virtual position, you have to have a concrete position as well?
Yes, there must be…a real position, "offline," everything else comes only after that. Although, beyond Russia's borders, supposedly, the perception of Nashi is formulated foremost by the media, and then by the site of the movement…though there is no version in English available. After all, I have a skeptical attitude toward the Internet. There was a period in 2006 when the Internet, or our Live Journal, Zhivoi Zhurnal, was a platform, a platform for debates, negotiations, disagreements…it was a very interesting phenomenon. However, already by 2007 this was gone, and now

---

[42] Here Vadim references the competition organized in the annual educational summer camp of Nashi and other pro-Kremlin youth movements in Seliger (in this case in 2007) in which the Internet specialists of Nashi were the fastest in the creation of various Internet facilities. For example, the competitors from Young Russia-movement were slower (see Stanovaia's categorization of youth movements above).

there are only all kinds of fanatics and marginals left. Today, I think, the Internet...it is a sphere for a private communication...not for a social action.

Although Vadim regards the "offline", that is, "real" position of the movement as more important than the virtual, "online" position, he points out that in all probability abroad, besides the media, the picture of Nashi is formulated via their main website. However, after this remark he makes an immediate addition that there is no version in English available.[43] This addition implies, on the one hand, that foreigners cannot obtain trustworthy information from Nashi's website because there is no English version available, implying that foreigners do not know Russian. On the other hand, in relation to Vadim's skeptical attitudes towards the web, the lack of an English version may imply the movement's resources are insufficient in this respect.

However, this latter implication is relatively lame in relation to Vadim's earlier account in which he cordially mentions the movement's professionalism in the sphere of the web. Instead, the first implication of his seeing the information provided for foreigners via the non-English main site as being "naturally" insufficient is revealing in terms of the movement's public image. Just as Igor made clear that the template of messages used in the main website is a natural journalistic practice—showing Igor's unresponsiveness towards that how foreigners may read Nashi's main site—Vadim's views also illustrate the inarticulate nature of the main site in relation to its actual communicative practices. Moreover, Vadim makes no mention of the foreigners, including me, and in all probability almost all who visit the main site of Nashi, who know Russian, to say nothing about how Russian youth might perceive the image of the movement through the main site.

It is, of course, impossible on the basis of three activists' views to make a larger generalization about Nashi's activists' attitudes towards the movement's web-communication and especially the main website. However, I suggest that these accounts offer an indication of how the Internet figures in the

---

43 In this part of the interview another activist of Nashi who participated in the interview, and was largely silent during the whole interview, tried to add something to this point but Vadim interrupted by saying "that's not necessary" (eto ne nado). If this interruption was about English version of the main site, it is worth noting that there was actually a section in the site that included a few announcements in English in 2007-2008, obviously targeted at the foreign media, but since then this section has disappeared.

movement. It is principally a technical and pragmatic tool for spreading the movement's agenda; for Oleg in a positive light while for Igor and Vadim more tentatively. However, all the interviewed activists see a division between the internal and individual "Internet" (i.e. blogging), and the main website; it seems the latter is not associated with the Internet. Thus, the technically developed and relatively professional appearance of Nashi's website is not articulated as symbolic capital (followed by potential conversion to some other capital, e.g. political), which is seen as worth emphasizing when a foreign scholar urges about the movement's web-communication. Nor was it emphasized in other parts of my interviews when the discussion touched youth's political participation/passivity, or Nashi's activities in general. Quite the contrary, for Igor and especially for Vadim, the Internet is partially contrasted with the "true activity" of the movement. This view implies that if there is too much investment in the Internet in terms of the movement's public image, it may appear as false by hiding its true (for Vadim "offline") activity. Next I briefly contextualize these views with an overview to Nashi's web-texts in light of Soviet information practices.

### Nashi's Online-Reporting and the Legacy of the Soviet Information Practices

During his interview Igor pointed out that the local branches of Nashi forward their texts to the Moscow main office which masters the main website. Igor described this hierarchical practice as purely technical. Or, as he put above, Nashi's special template of messages is "a natural practice in any professional journalism." The next sample elaborates what this template is about:

34
Headlines picked from the archive section of Nashi's website concerning actions conducted on March 16 2008 (time, headline, Nashi's section behind the report)[44]
19:53        Iaroslavl: "NASHI" collect "pampers" for invalid children (Social direction)

---

[44] Original reports from above: Iaroslavl: "NASHI" cobiraiut (2008); Iaroslavl': Neobkhodimoe delo (2008); Moskva: Rytsarskoe posviashchenie patriotov (2008); Vorotynsk: "Bronzovye soldaty" (2008); Professiia zhurnalist (2008); Kodopoga: A ty znaesh Kondopogu? (2008); Naryshkino: Chto ty khochesh (2008); Priazha: davayte znakomiatsia (2008); Tula: Bronzovaia kniga (2008); Livny: Urok patriotizmy (2008); Voronezh: Snova v nashem zale (2008); Rybinsk: Vmeste—protiv fashizma (2008).

| | |
|---|---|
| 19:49 | Iaroslavl': A necessary thing (Social direction) |
| 19:24 | Moscow: A chivalrous initiation of patriots (http://nashi.su/) |
| 19:11 | Vorotynsk: "Bronze soldiers" on streets of the town (Small towns) |
| 19:06 | Journalism as a profession. History of success (http://Nashi.su/) |
| 19:02 | Kondopoga: Do you know Kondopoga? (Small towns) |
| 18:59 | Naryshkino: What do you want, youth? (Small towns) |
| 18:57 | Pryazha: Let's introduce yourself |
| 18:56 | Tula: The bronze book as a memory of heroes' feats of valor (http://Nashi.su/) |
| 18:51 | Livny: A lesson of patriotism for high school students (Small towns) |
| 18:40 | Voronezh: Again there were no empty seats in our auditorium (http://Nashi.su/) |
| 17:55 | Rybinsk: Together against fascism (Small towns) |

Within the vast number of Nashi's web-page reports,[45] these twelve head-lines—referring to patriotism, professional success and socio-political volun-teering—from a single day reveal the dynamics of report-ing: approximately one report at intervals of five, ten minutes. In stylistic terms these headlines illustrate the movement's repetitive style of creating reports. This becomes apparent by using of place-names and colons in web-texts' headlines as these headlines illustrate. Reports behind these headlines are relatively short, mainly written in the past tense for indirect narration[46] with a relatively norma-tive lexicon, simple and grammatically full sentences. In addition, repetitive variation with the grammatical possibilities of the name Nashi[47] with the use of capital letters is a frequent feature of Nashi's texts which distinguish them from purely official discourse.

This repetitiveness, or intertextuality, is supported by the arrangement of texts within various hyperlinks which give a systematic and well organ-ized image to the website. It supposedly creates a picture of systematic, effective,

---

[45] In February-March 2012 Nashi's website included approximately 33,000 reports. Over the course of the year 2013—that is, after the movement's demise—the site was work-ing though last occasional updates were made in 2012.

[46] An example of direct narration (representation, or discourse) would be as follows, on the basis of a report from Nashi: "Commissars point out: "The support for Nashi's ac-tions in France was guaranteed by the leaders of the party." In other words, in direct representation a "direct" citing of one's words are used, while in indirect representation one's views are given by an author with his words (see, for example, in Fairclough 1992: 107-108).

[47] In particular this means the conflation of the movement's brand name with the posses-sive pronoun "our" in Russian.

and well organized actions by the movement. The feature which is also almost a rule than an exception in Nashi's reports is the addition of the signature IA REGNUM at the end of the reports. This is the case, for instance, in all
the reports mentioned in the sample above. This relatively well-known Russian news agency is said to be a non-official news agency which sometimes
mediates anti-Western views (Open Source Center of the US Director of National Intelligence 2007). Nashi's use of this signature might suggest that
there are close organizational connections between the Regnum and Nashi.
Nonetheless, Nashi's website appeared to be the only forum where these reports have been published. This became apparent when I entered the titles of
Nashi's reports mentioned in the sample in the search box of Google. The
complete results of these searches referred exclusively to Nashi's website
without indicating any other sites where these reports could be found (e.g.
Regnum's own portal, or the media that use Regnum's news). In any case,
inserting the name IA REGNUM shows that Nashi wants to exhibit the symbolic capital of its reports by adding the signature of a widely known news
agency which is ideologically compatible with Nashi's views. ⚹

Nashi's rather professional contribution to its website in technical terms,
which clearly distinct the movement from its predecessor, Idushchie Vmeste,
can be framed by the broader context of the Russian Internet. Schmidt and
Teubener write about a particular "monumentalism" of the Russian Internet in
this respect (2006). They point out that official discourse on the Internet, as
expressed in various official documents (e.g. in the youth policy), appears to
be both polyphonic and contradictory (ibid.: 51; see Strategiia 2007: 20-25).
An attempt has been made to integrate the Internet into official cultural values
and achievements, for example, in the sphere of "high culture" (Schmidt and
Teubener 2006). However, at the same time, the Internet is seen as the place
of "cultural dirt," or, as the long-time Moscow mayor Iuri Luzhkov has put it, "a
weapon of mass destruction" (ibid.: 52). The "monumentalism" of the Internet
can thus be described as a form of tension between ideal,[48] and actual reali-

---

[48] In relation to a study of Internet users in St. Peterburg in 2000 and 2001, Nafus describes how a local city minister describes the need for an Information Society in Russia by arguing that it is "a scientific fact that the Information Society is the next step in
economic development" which, according to Nafus, shows "an interesting combination
of the techno-enthusiasm of a la 90s style management consultant and Marxian-
Hegelian determinism" (2003: 200).

zations of the Internet. In other words, the Internet as a phenomenon and a symbol of technological modernization is considered to be highly positive but from the viewpoint of its actual communicative practices, it is seen as a true challenge to, and potentially threatening for, the ideals of cultural harmony. In terms of cultural and symbolic production, this means that officially related political and cultural goals face true challenges in producing cogent communication in a space which is remarkably contingent and fragmentary (Kratasjuk 2006: 47-48). This view is certainly the case with Vadim's and Igor's disappointments with the web, as well as all the interviewed activists' way to separate the main website from the Internet.

In the current official youth policy, which was published in 2007, the ideal aspect of the Internet is linked to the goals of developing of youth related information (Strategiia 2007: 24-25). However, an obvious controversy here is that these youth related information practices, for example, blogging, could potentially be regarded as harmful and dangerous for the official cultural and political practices. Indeed, the emergence of mass protests via mobilizational capacities of the Internet's social networks in late 2011 showed that this fear became true (Bode& Makarychev 2013; Lonkila 2012). In the light of illustrating "youth forms" of web-communication, a special section of activists' blogs appeared in the November 2009 version of the website. It is not far-fetched to see here Nashi's anticipation within its web-blog section in relation to president Medvedev's highly positive views on the Internet that he has stated in public. In addition, Medvedev has his own web-blog.

As a whole Nashi's evident cultural (here in terms of technical skills) and economic capital is not articulated by the interviewed activists. They see the Internet largely as an individual activity (especially through the Live Journal), and thus the main website is seen somehow as being beyond this sphere. The Internet appears as a technical and pragmatic tool for spreading the movement's agenda although there are variations between the activists' positive, or tentative, or even negative associations towards this tool. To some extent the aspect of image, however, is associated with the discussion on the movement's main website. For Oleg it is "the virtual face of the movement" while for Igor and Vadim this dimension seemingly activates the need to emphasize the true activity beyond the Internet, implying that the Internet is insignificant in nature. These accounts are compatible with the notion of the Internet's momumentalism in Russia: In official contexts the Russian Internet figures principally as a symbol of technological modernization (e.g. Vadim's points about Nashi's skills in the sphere of the Internet) but its actual content and practices are not elaborated, causing negative responses. Nashi's explicitly repetitive web-page reports along with the activists' technically oriented but substantially inarticulate views of the main website are a connection the Soviet-era information practices.

Frank Ellis writes that in comparison with the ideas of what constituted newsworthiness in the capitalistic West where news was and is profoundly based on entertaining novelties, in the Soviet Union "anything which can be used to illustrate current Party policy or economic progress was considered worthy of publication, and almost anything else is considered unimportant and unworthy" (Hollander via Ellis 1998: 212). It is, of course, important to point out that the division between the West's "scandal and sensation" and the Soviet era "Party advertisements" is not as clear as Ellis's formulation might imply. Actually we can easily find several examples in Western journalism in which repetitively constructed sensational novelties are connected with different political motivations (see e.g. Fairclough 1995 and Chouliaraki & Fairclough 1999 concerning the effects of consumerism on late modern media discourses). However, the function of news as well as the idea of mass communication as a central part of a particular political and ideological project gave distinctive role to the Soviet information culture in comparison with practices in capitalist societies. According to Ellis the foundation of Soviet media theory can be found in Lenin's works "What to do?" (*Chto delat'?*), "Where to begin?" (*S chego nachat'*), and "The Party Organization and the Party Literature" (*Partiininaia organizatsiia i partiinaia literatura*) (1998: 192). Common to these was Lenin's conviction that the task of the media in Soviet society was to create the new Soviet man by educating, mobilizing, and indoctrinating its readers into a new socialist consciousness (ibid.: 193). This dimension became highly apparent, for example, in the activities of the Komsomol (e.g. Gorsuch 2000), as well as in the formulation of *kul'turnost* (Kenez & Shepherd, 1998; Kelly 2001).

This total coverage of ideological education had a clear impact on the understanding of the function of public information in society. It is possible to suggest at this point that many representatives of Western "infotainment" prefer

to receive the language and topics of the media through a more or less neutral discourse.[49] In the Soviet Union, largely through Lenin's ideas, the situation was quite the opposite. The key elements for spreading political consciousness were "agitation" and "propaganda", and these had far reaching
socio-cultural consequences (Ellis 1998: 197): "News, in the sense in which
that is understood in the West, or in which *novosti* had been understood before the Revolution, i.e. the attempt objectively to record events as soon as
possible after their occurrence, disappeared from Russian print culture for the
best part of seven decades." This particular and seemingly long standing impact of Soviet era information practices is worth elaborating on here. The issue is about two predominant Soviet media models. The first of these was
"the hypodermic effect model" whose material and technocratic assumption of
social reality is shocking: According to this model, information is received in
the form it is given (ibid.: 216-218). Although the second model, "the two-step
flow theory," is a bit more sophisticated than the hypodermic one in that it assumes that people with a higher education were more exposed to the media
and would pass on their understanding, this model too had hardly any real
equivalents. As Ellis says, this messenger-model actually had the opposite
effect: "It was precisely the better-educated who tended to be the most critical
of the Soviet government and most active in organizing opposition to it" (ibid.:
218).

These models imply the influence of natural scientific and technologically-
driven views which were hard currency in the Soviet modernization project. A
special role was played by cybernetics and its impacts on communication
theory (Gerovitch 2002). According Slava Gerovitch, the role of cybernetics
within the Soviet ideological dogmas created a peculiar combination between
ideologically motivated newspeak and mathematically-oriented cybernetics,
and resulted as a kind of "cyberspeak." Furthermore, while this cyberspeak
was embedded with changing ideological emphases within the Soviet political
system, "it eventually began to control its masters. After they (cyberneticians)
had fashioned cyberspeak as a universal, objective, precise language, it became very difficult for them to step outside the cybernetic discourse and criti-

---

[49] Indeed, this "disguise of neutrality" actually figures an important task of revealing a hidden agenda in the media's supposed neutrality in critical discourse studies (See, for instance, Fairclough 1992; 1995; Chouliaraki & Fairclough 1999).

cally examine its limitations" (ibid.: 295). This kind of technical, "mathematical," as well as partially antagonistic, communication ideal can be grasped in the following quote by Vassili Iakemenko in Seliger youth forum 2011:

35
In order to solve Russian (*rossiiski*) problems within the Seliger section "Politics," the so-called "civil campaigns" will be established. Each member of the section must itemize one minor problem in his/her town, describe it in five words (maximum), find the "enemy," guarantee "media visibility" (*mediinost'*) of the problem, define the necessary sum of money for the problem's solution, and describe an adequate action plan to solve the problem (Putin i burundiki 2010).

Although this view was provided by a secondary source (in this case online publication Lenta.ru), it reveals Iakemenko's teleological view according to which regional, and ultimately, state-level problems could be solved as a kind of "obvious societal equation." Moreover, as Iakemenko's description partially implies in terms of the legacy of Soviet era communication patterns, the disappearance of news and the establishment of a highly simplistic and technocratic understanding of information flows in society were accompanied by an even more important and broader cultural factor—the Russian language under the new regime, influenced by Lenin's language use. Continuing his discussion on Lenin's impact on the information culture in Soviet society, Frank Ellis writes that "Lenin effortlessly churned out pejorative neologisms against his enemies; clarity, precision, and brevity were frequently sacrificed to endless tautologies and periphrasis in an attempt to browbeat the ideological opponent" (1998: 199). Of course, the browbeating of ideological opponents is not a peculiarity of Soviet era political communication as such but widely used in social movements' communication in general. For example, Marsa L. Vanderford points out that vilification has a key function among social movements in the US which have labeled their opponents as either anti-abortion, or "pro-abortion" (i.e. pro-choice) movements in their struggle with each other (1989). Rather than regarding opponents as good people who have different opinions, vilification delegitimizes them through characterizations of their intentions, actions, purposes, and identities (ibid.: 166). Such "eliminating with words" can be found in propaganda in general. For example, Paul Chilton shows how Hitler constructed the conceptual connection, or blending, between parasites and Jews in the sense that both must "naturally" be eliminated, as "we all know" that parasites must be eliminated (2005).

Political browbeating or even symbolic eliminating of enemies can be seen in non-totalitarian contexts as well,[50] as Vanderford's example illustrates. Indeed, this account orientates to a critical evaluation of "totalitarian communication" in general (Postoutenko 2010). To shift this background to Nashi on the basis of Bourdieu's framework, my standpoint is that the browbeating of political opponents and the casting of them in terms of black-and-whiteness largely draws from the Russian linguistic market in seeing it as a supposedly legitimate practice in the field of politics. In Bourdieu's words, "specialized discourses (e.g. agitation, vilification, or propaganda) can derive their efficacy from the hidden correspondence between the structure of the social space within which they are produced (e.g. political field) and the structure of the field of social classes within which the recipients are situated and in relation to which they interpret the message" (1991: 41. I treat Nashi's socio-political position in the same role as Bourdieu's "field of social classes" here). The change and development from Idushchie Vmeste to Nashi, and finally Idushchie Vmeste's replacement by Nashi, suggest that the emotionally colored discourse which particularly prevailed in Idushchie Vmeste's Moral Codex has affected Nashi's recognition of the appropriateness of such discourse in the discursive production of an ideal youth. In short, Idushchie Vmeste's communication appeared to be ultimately ineffective and unsuitable.

Nonetheless, if there is any recognition, it has certainly not abandoned the major problem of Nashi. On the one hand, a partial reason for Nashi's miserable image in comparison with Putin is that Nashi's social and political position as "a youth movement" cannot redeem its symbolic production to the extent that "the leader" Putin can.[51] On the other hand, it is relevant to assume that Nashi's position as a youth movement may allow it to conduct such symbolic production which is principally suitable for youth, and not for "adult politi-

---

[50] Chilton's study of Hitler's propaganda is thus exceptional as this linguistic-cognitive elimination of the Jews is concretely related to the Jews' true elimination.

[51] An important dimension of Putin's success has based on his masculine and youth-driven habitus in comparison to weak and old Yeltsin, for example, in terms of his "macho-outputs" in talk and appearance in particular (See, for example, Gorham 2005; Sperling 2012; Sperling 2014).

cians." For instance, Oleg highlighted the distinction between adults and youth. However, the movement's role as "semi-official" seemingly deepens that uncertainty which prevails between "non-youth" and "youth," that is, between the didactic and stimulative approaches. For example, Nashi's choice to produce explicit propaganda for recruitment into army, strengthened by Robert Schlegel's justification to choose a propagandistic approach as the natural choice for the video (see Sample 23) shows that Nashi's anticipation of symbolic profit hardly worked as planned: The majority of responses from the public to this choice was negative (Nashe interv'iu, 2007). Even though propaganda can be seen as a more "natural" and appropriate choice for a social and political movement (see Igor's comment in Sample 31) it appeared to have failed. The Soviet legacy of information practices, however, includes more nuanced aspects than just explicit propaganda and vilification. Let us take a look at the following sample which is Nashi's report on Russian education.

36
**Ryazan: Russian education: the best in the world!**
OUR economists organized a round table discussion on a selected theme. Today it was education in Russia.
Activists discussed about all pluses and minuses of today's education. According to them, (two) pluses are the annual enlargement of learning levels and choices of study places. A minus is that today it is too expensive to receive education.
The economists also pondered why the education with tuition fees is more popular today than free education.
In the beginning the discussion went peacefully on but then the opposition came to the fore. Commissars and supporters (of Nashi) expressed their own opinion absolutely without hesitation.
Some thought that the education with tuition fees is chosen because young people (*abiturienty*) do not trust themselves and their ability to pass entrance exams. Other talked that this happens because it is impossible to gain entrance without money, and in any case, all study places free of payment have been bought.
However, despite all minuses of Russian education, commissars concluded that it is still the best in the world (Ryazan: Rossiiskoe obrazovanie 2007).

One feature in Nashi's report, which also owes something to Soviet-era discursive practices,[52] becomes apparent in the point that Alexei Yurchak dis-

---

52 In addition to the element of intertextuality that becomes apparent in the headlines of Nashi's reports, the headline in this sample offers a relatively clear intertextual link to Soviet era slogans. According to Yurchak, Soviet slogans during late socialism fell into

cusses in terms of "rhetorical circularity" (2006: 72). This means that various official texts during late socialism (e.g. newspaper articles roughly during the period between 1960s-1980s) often suggested that a particular task has been achieved (e.g. we have built communism), but, at the same time, these texts paradoxically suggested that this same task still remained to be fully achieved (e.g. we need to build communism) (ibid.). It is not in order to construct an analogy between Nashi and late socialism but rather to evaluate Nashi's discursive practice in relation to the rhetorical circularity. This angle opens up a perspective which helps to deepen our understanding of the complex relationship between Nashi's didactic and stimulative approaches. In this respect, Nashi's rhetorical circularity comes about in the contradiction between the frames and the actual content of the report. The frames of the report are constructed by the explicit definition of the excellence of Russian education which is a given starting point, and then, the conclusion of the text refers to this successfulness more or less explicitly (the repetition of the headline's claim). Hence, a reflection of rhetorical circularity becomes clear when the headline and the end are related to the content between them: It is explicated that there are some things in the Russian educational system that are not so good (e.g. "today it is too expensive to receive education" or "all study places free of payment have been bought,") and these presumably suggest that something must be done. In this case, the content between the ultimate success, proposed in the beginning and the end of the report, can be seen as a space in which Nashi struggles with appropriate discursive forms to reveal these unfortunate qualities of Russian education.

Nashi's reports' repetitive, formal, and relatively controlled nature finds partial explanation in relation to the Soviet era's communication ideals concerning

---

three categories as part of a larger unified interdiscursive (intertextually constitutive) system that Yurchak calls a "hegemony of representation" (2006: 57). The first category of slogans included the most general and context-independent slogans such as "People and Party are United!" The second category included more time and context-specified slogans, such as "Long Live May First!" while the third category included the more localized and contextualized slogans that hung in factories, stadiums, schools, etc., such as "Sportsmen of Leningrad, hold higher the banner of Soviet sport!" Nashi's headlines are closest to the second and third categories with various localized topics and contexts, although it is not helpful to consider them as similar to the Soviet-era slogans due to the different discursive regimes between late-socialism and Putin's Russia. Nevertheless, this element is a partial legacy of Soviet-era discursive practices.

information's ideological correctness supported by highly formal textual practices.[53] The headline and the closure which can be seen as didactic mediate the official harmony and purposefulness of educational policies, now in relation to national dignity. From this viewpoint the harmonic framing of the report can also be seen as stimulative, while in the post-Soviet space it evidently aims to reproduce the issue of national dignity and even a particular Soviet nostalgia (Nadkarni & Shevchenko 2004; Levada 2004; Dubin 2004; Gudkov 2002). Consequently, the content of the report, which focuses on a discussion on Russian education by Nashi's "commissars" and supporters (in the beginning of the report these are defined as "economists" with the hyperlink to the economy-related section of Nashi's activities), evidently anticipates a model civic activity in which own opinions are not hidden: "Commissars and supporters expressed their own opinion absolutely without hesitation."

Nashi's explicit attempt to exhibit its own importance and supposedly model activity inevitably creates a contrast with those who are not acting in this way. In this particular case, these implicit "enemies" (i.e. passive ones in relation to this education discussion) were probably present in the round table session which Nashi activists and supporters attended. However, the formal and harmonious intent to produce discursively such a report easily vitiates the commissars' true will to express their own opinions about educational issues in Russia. A Soviet type of harmonious report may work stimulatively when it encompasses national dignity, but in this explicitly youth related topic, this is a very hesitant option. Rather, such didactic and formal discourse easily vitiates the stimulative potential (a theme which truly speaks to young people) that the content between the headline and the closure touches upon.

---

53 Andrei Romanenko describes this nature of the Soviet official language by using the term "Soviet document" (2003). The key principle of this document as a rule of communication was the use of highly standardized words signifying the absolute denial of metaphors, and all such figures of speech which might lead to multiple interpretations of a text were forbidden. In a comprehensive study of the formation of early Soviet language culture, Michael S. Gorham shows how this growing need for formality in the new proletarian language caused an ideological struggle with the "people's" communication, that is, the original proletarian language (2003). This was linked to the dilemma of Soviet modernization vis-à-vis proletarian ideology. For example, Maxim Gorky, the central authority for this formalization, or "purification," of the official language deeply admired "writers from the people" but was deeply critical of their colloquial speech and hackneyed phrases which, for him, showed their rural backwardness (ibid.: 108).

Nashi's struggle with appropriate discursive forms on its official website in this particular case can be contextualized by an "unofficial" account by a Nashi's activist Makar Vikhliantsev on the website www.nashi33.ru (Reforma vysshego obrazovaniia 2006). This was Nashi's other important website in 2006, and briefly acted as the main site during the large-scale updating of the www.Nashi.su site at the turn of 2006-2007. After that the Nashi33.ru site disappeared. In his account Vikhliantsev writes, "We're used to talking about Russian education as if it were the best in the world. By talking in this way, we distort the facts...Each year Russian institutes of higher education spit out millions of non-professionals, masters of skills that nobody needs" (ibid.). In this explicit accusation Vikhliantsev strongly demands radical measures from the state in order openly to ideologize the Russian higher education in terms of educating only the necessary people for the state: "The state, I think, can and must proclaim higher education as the most important stage for the ideological struggle, and activate work with the aim of high level ideologization (*sverkhideologizatsii*) of the best representatives of our youth" (ibid.).

Vikhliantsev's account is illuminating in two senses. First, it shows that the spectrum of opinions among Nashi's activists is definitely rather broad, which is a common challenge to any movement's ideological coherence. Second, and more importantly in this case, Nashi's web-texts as items of Nashi's official communication obviously try to find a balance between various ideological views and emotional emphases that could be harnessed for the purpose of stimulation. Since Vikhliantsev's account was present in the temporary main site but then disappeared when the nashi.su site was reopened in an updated form, it seems that Nashi's sense of political correctness is uncertain:[54] Nashi's socio-political position is ultimately seen in the way in which it does not allow the downplaying of conformist didactics to the extent that

---

[54] Deborah Cameron points out that the term political correctness is highly controversial. Instead of speculating as to what it might contain, the term itself is vivid proof of the power of words (1995: 122): "If anything makes the case that words are powerful and definitions are political—exactly as the so-called politically correct have claimed, and as their critics have ridiculed them for claiming—it is the history of the term —political correctness itself" (ibid.). Suffice it to say that political correctness is a tangible case of a struggle over cultural definitions as well as appropriate words, or forms of action and being. Moreover, perhaps the most interesting aspect of the term is that its limits are never completely defined for, and by anyone.

Vikhliantsev's potentially stimulative call for ideological education suggests. As a result, the texts in the main site are relatively controlled, manifested as "Soviet type" harmonious reports of "successfully conducted actions." This can be seen in the following two samples which ideologically reflect rather different views of journalism:

37

### Tver: journalists of BBC held an open master-class in Our school of young journalists

In June 30 journalists from the leading analytical program of the television channel BBC "Night News" held an open master-class for listeners of the school of young journalists, commissars and supporters of the movement "Nashi."

The lesson was organized within the form "question-answer." The main themes that arose during the discussion concerned problems related to freedom of expression in journalism, objectivity of information, tendencies of development in contemporary journalism, and many more. As a result, the discussion made clear that Great Britain and Russia share similar problems and tasks since we are locating in the unite information field of the European civilization.

A BBC camera crew arrived at Tver to explore our country from the viewpoint of the young Russian generation, and to make a documentary film about Russia in today on the basis of the selected material. For that purpose they spent one week together with the movement "Nashi" (Tver: Zhurnalisty BBC, 30 June 2006, 13:34).

38

### Saransk: Journalists must be capable to manipulate

Activists of the information section passed the course of VShU[55] "Technologies of social manipulation and methods to act against them." Within the course, the guys (*rebiata*) learned many new things:

Where are mass sentiments drawn from?

Why does personality lose its individual features in the mass, and become vulnerable for influences?

How do mechanisms of suggestion, imitation and defilement work?

How to analyze sentiments and aims of people redirected into a certain course?

The exam session was about discussion on the issues of the course. Everyone was given the possibility to speak out. After the discussion "journalists" filled their notebooks. At the end the teacher acknowledged guys for attending in the lessons and actively participating in them (Saransk: Zhurnalisty dolzhen, November 29, 2007, 17:06).

---

55   See the footnote related to Sample 13.

In the analysis of Nashi's manifesto with commentaries I pointed out that one of its repetitive features is the constant use of authoritative symbolic forms, especially encyclopedic discourses and the constant resort to foreign scientific authors. In sample 37 Nashi produces a similar anti-cipation by showing its "social capital" vis-à-vis well-known actors in the field of journalism: Some supposed symbolic capital derives from the visit of journalists from the *British Broadcasting Company*, and its program *BBC Night News*. Here Nashi defines its role as "the voice of Russia" and sharing the same interests as the UK because "we are locating in the unite information field of the European civilization." Nashi strongly orientates itself towards Western ideals of journalism by emphasizing a "common Europeanness," with its presumable concerns: namely, "freedom of expression," "the objectivity of information," as well as "tendencies of development in contemporary journalism." Interestingly, on the one hand, the conclusion of this "concern-list"—made by the addition "and many more"—suggests that there were lot of issues under discussion. On the other hand, this expression allows the downplaying of topics which may be not suitable for state-driven didactic discourse: For example, not to specify any critique of the shutting of those elements of the Russian media which criticize the Kremlin.

The report exhibits an explicitly formal and naïve formulation of a supposedly stimulative structure in that the visit of the BBC was held in the school of "our young journalists": "The event was organized in the form "question-answer"." In short, it aimed to prove that the master-class by the BBC journalists allowed open discussion in terms of questions and answers. In addition to Nashi's attempt to figure as a voice speaking on the behalf of Russia, the last paragraph strives to prove that the movement has a key role in representing Russian youth in particular. While it is reported that the BBC arrived in Russia in order to make a documentary film about Russian youth, the report closes with the sense that Nashi had successfully conducted an action: "For that purpose they spent one week together with the movement "Nashi"."

In sample 37 Nashi anticipates those views of journalism that aims to prove Russia's role as a modern actor in the world, and with "the modern world," constantly referred to in the movement's Manifesto. In sample 38, however, this anticipation towards "the West" appears with rather different ideals. Here the ideal journalist is urged not to worry about "freedom of expression," or the "objectivity of information," but to perceive the role of a journalist as that of a conscious educator of a given ideology (presumably the official state policy). The field of journalism and information is seen as a psychological and ideological battlefield of various, in all probability Western, influences. In other words, this view is not very far from the media practices of the Soviet era mentioned by Frank Ellis above, in which the key ideals were agitation and propaganda. The content of the text is overly didactic in which the narrator (Nashi) empowers itself as the educator, for example by putting the word "journalists" in quotation marks, and telling how these "trainees" dutifully filled their notebooks in the lesson. Consequently, in the same report a tiny explication in relation to "voices of youth" (i.e. supposed stimulation) is made by stating that "Everyone was allowed a possibility to speak out."

Nashi's willingness to emphasize its own model activity—represented by this Soviet type of discourse—presumably downplays any potential pitfalls that might arise out of ideological flexibility; whether the issue is about "Western values" of journalism, or education for the sake of manipulative journalism. In both cases Nashi works together with the harmonic and flawless world of ideal youth. This is finely manifested by the closures of the reports which highlight their successful purposefulness: In sample 37 by pointing to the BBC's interest in spending time with Nashi, and especially in sample 38 by the phrase: "At the end the teacher acknowledged guys for attending in the lessons and actively participating in them." Nonetheless, this strategy hardly diminishes the evident tension between the cultural (symbolic) production linked to official power, and the cultural (symbolic) production linked to autonomous (e.g. socio-economic) needs of youth. In the light of the activists' interviews along with the information concerning youth's political participation/passivity, there are hints of this challenge in the official web-reporting as well, as a sample of Russian education illustrated. In the next sample this challenge is clearly explicated:

39
**Kaliningrad: We know it by ourselves, we tell it others**
What is the state of affairs in our educational institutes in terms of teaching youth to plan projects? This question was discussed today in a round table session by students of the "Project management" courses. After a lively discussion guys made a conclusion that there are only a few students in institutes of higher education who

know basic knowledge of planning projects. Of course, there are attempts to develop project planning, but attempts to develop this orientation are not sufficient. Young people have an idea to create a project which would help to solve a certain problem. However, at the same time, they cannot agree with the fact they have to study this issue much more by themselves (19 November 2007, 19:18).

As the headline shows, Nashi makes a clear separation from other, or "common" youth by suggesting that Nashi knows how the things should be and this knowledge is then distributed forwards. Again, the participation of "guys in lively discussion"[56] shows Nashi's intention to highlight a sort of civic activity in terms of debating. In contrast to previous reports, here the content is not framed by the flawless harmony in which all the participants were active and model youngsters. Instead, it is pointed out that "there are only a few students in institutes of higher education who know basic knowledge of planning projects", and "attempts to develop this orientation are not sufficient." In relation to Soviet media models, the headline explicitly follows, on the one hand, the ideal of the two-step model,[57] but, on the other, the result of this model is facing serious challenges which are here (rather exceptionally) explicated by the movement.

To follow Dmitry Andreev's definition, that for Nashi (and Idushchie Vmeste) the enemy is any value or feature (e.g. passivity) that is incompatible with the movement's ambitions—see also Mijnssen's discussion on Nashi's in terms of agonistic and antagonistic positions (2012) –, it is the explication of enemies in terms of distinguishing itself from "others" that figures as an important aspect in the creation of the stimulation (Andreev 2006). In this regard, Nashi's reports with their harmonious, conformist, and positive purposefulness as forms of didactic discourse that resonate with cultural forms of power may vitiate the potential of this "enemy-distinction", as the sample concerning education in Russia illustrated. In this vein, while Nashi's web-reports aims to harmonize various ideological controversies (e.g. a controversy be-

---

[56] The expression "guys", rebiata, no doubt aims to provide a stimulative twist to the report's general normative vocabulary.

[57] See above. Ellis points out that the two-step model of Soviet communication theory and practice was predicated on the assumption that educated people, that is, those with a higher education or specialized training were more exposed to the media because they were better qualified to understand the information and hence likely to be more interested in it (1998: 218).

tween journalism reports), they also narrow Nashi's ability to produce "neces-sary" enemy-images. A strategy which seemingly compensates this narrowed ability to produce enemies is to highlight the movement's model role by pro-ducing an elite-position inside the common conformist goal (Sample 39). However, this strategy is also risky in that it may result in tilting too much in the direction of distant elitism and away from the viewpoint of youth, or in moving too far from the official guidelines of power. In the next chapter I ex-amine Nashi's major communicative strategy by which it aims to manage the tension in its discursive production of ideal youth.

# VI Nashi's Political Rituals

## Modern Cycling through the Time of Troubles

Jeffrey C. Alexander and Jason L. Mast point out that in order to be practical and effective in action, that is, to have a successful performance, actors must be able to make the meanings of the culture structures stick (2006: 4). In this vein, ritual (or ritual-like strategy) as social performance completes Bourdieu's "field struggles" by habituses by adding a communicative dimension to these struggles in which a diverse, or "de-fused," starting point prevails. It is in order here to follow theatre metaphors insomuch as ritual is discussed in Victor Turner's tradition (Turner 1974; Alexander 2006; Alexander & Mast 2006). Against this backdrop, Nashi's communication can be described as the actor's evident will to re-fuse a de-fused stage according to his/her own script. In terms of Bourdieu's "anticipation of symbolic capital," the elements which Nashi aims to re-fuse into a stimulative wholeness without downplaying too much the demand of didactics can be justifiably termed as "anticipations." This is because, I suggest, Nashi's recognition between the ideal script and the real-life constraints is emphatically uncertain.

Intertextuality—the concept I touched in the previous chapter with regard to Nashi's repetitive style in creating its online writings—treats texts historically as transforming the past with its conventions and prior texts into the present (Fairclough 1992: 85). Moreover, the degree of "ritualness," or the success/felicity of ritual, can be defined by the coherence of its components. Thus, the issue is about how "smoothly" an intertextual constellation can be put together to form a coherent wholeness. From the critical (linguistic) analysis viewpoint, coherence is ultimately an interpretive category, and hence various textual devices that are made in a text for the sake of coherence are not grammatical-textual necessities but ideologically related "cues" which orientate readers-interpreters to a "correct" perception of texts (Heikkinen 1999: 168; Fairclough 1997: 159-161). In this light, it is precisely these cues which are produced in designed and more or less well-planned official web-texts that offer a good insight into Nashi's sense of creating re-fusion, and hence, the anticipation of ideal youth.

It is crucial to add that Nashi's texts are principally narrated, or re-produced, "rituals." In other words, they are descriptions of activities that have already happened, but which could be analyzed as "here-and-now" performances as well. However, it is impossible to know exactly to what extent the real-time, or "first hand", social performances have actually taken place (some of them were probably cancelled). In this regard, these online writings as "second hand" performances offer an insight into how textual re-fusion can, and supposedly should, be done in the official website. In the following table I condense the ritual-like social performance as follows, followed by a sample of Nashi's narrated ritual-like strategy (Alexander 2006):

TABLE 1. Components of Nashi's ritual-like strategy

| De-fused actor | Nashi which aims to be re-fused with |
|---|---|
| De-fused audience | youth and the citizens of Russia, with |
| De-fused representations | chosen agendas and topics within |
| De-fused means of symbolic production | particular language and semiotic choices, which supposedly can re-fuse |
| De-fused social powers | didactics and stimulation in |
| De-fused mis en scène | Nashi's main website on the Internet |

40
**The Road of Freedom: The Cycle Marathon Accomplished in Moscow**
The finish of the open historical patriotic cycle marathon "The Road of Freedom—2007," organized by the movement "NASHI", took place on the Vassiliev square in 25 August, on the anniversary of the first victory of the Home Guard in 1612 against Polish-Lithuanian invaders. The cycle run was dedicated to the 395-year feat of valor by the Home Guard of Minin and Pozharskiy.
Over two weeks, five hundred cyclists from 35 regions of Russia traveled more than 1150 kilometers. They slept in tents, ate in open-air circumstances on the road of the Home Guard of the year 1612, from Nizhny Novgorod through Kostroma and Yaroslavl' to Moscow.
In the village of Purekh—the hereditary estate of the prince Pozharskiy—the consecrated replica of the flag of the Home Guard was presented at the Savior-Transfiguration Cathedral (*Spaso-Preobrazhenskiy sobor*). The memorial cross was erected in the churchyard (*na rodovom pogoste*) of the Family Susaniny in the village of Isupovo of the Kostroma region.

The final competition according to the Home Guard multiathlon (mnogobor'be) was organized on 22 August, on Russian Flag Day, at the lake of Pleshcheevo. It included archery, air rifle, rafting (*gonki na raftakh*), and orienteering with the satellite navigation. In August 24th the multiathlon was accomplished within the exam of patriotic history (*eksamen po otechestvennoy istorii*). The map of the patriotic route was established with the help of the Russian navigation system GLONASS.

On 25 August, Nashi ideologist Evgeniy Ivanov saluted participants of the cycle marathon on Vassiliev square. After that he solemnly announced the winners of the Home Guard multiathlon. Evgeniy Pozharskiy, a descended of Dmitry Pozharskiy, carried the flag of the Home Guard to the monument of the citizen Minina and the prince Pozharskiy. After him the participants of cycle marathon brought carnations to the monument ("Doroga svobody": Velomarafon zavershilsia 2007).

Let us now go into this text using the classifications mentioned in the table, and examine how this strategy is manifested.

*The actor*: The text makes it clear that the organizer, not the actual actor, of the event is "The movement "NASHI." Hence, this official choice—instead of Nashi's common language game between the proper name and the possessive pronoun—orientates the reader to a particular benefactor-like position of the movement: Nashi officially organized and made this event possible. In this respect, Nashi is only part of the actor who also include the participants in the cycle marathon. The text blurs, that is, aims to re-fuse, the background sender/actor (Nashi's text and action in its own website) with the actual actors of the text, that is, the cyclists, who thus can also be seen as representatives of the audience.

*The audience*:[58] According to the text, the cyclists are not exclusively young Russians but "cyclists from 35 regions of Russia." Another text about

---

58 The issue of the audience is problematic in the case of ritual-like actions, including "reported rituals" which I am discussing here. In his study of Willy Brandt's famous act of kneeling in front of the Warsaw Ghetto Memorial in 1970 from the viewpoint of ritual-like action, Valentin Rauer elaborates on the concept of audience in terms of "first," "second," and "third-order audiences" (2006: 260-261): "The first-order audience" includes those who experience the actual performance, or event. "The second-order audience" is the media which encode the event, and "the third-order audience" includes those who view these media (ibid.).However, in real life, especially within the new media (reality-TV, Internet, etc) these classifications are complexly intertwined. In my case, interpreting Rauer's elaboration, the first-order audience is the participants and organizers of the event, and the second-order audience is Nashi which reports this performance. The third-order audience, instead, belongs to the forum producing Nashi's narrated rituals, that is, the level of mis en scène, as the table partially illustrates. See below about

this event, which reports the beginning of the event, explicitly draws a picture of the participants as being unified and ageless:

41
The national anthem of the Russian Federation echoed and united in an extraordinary way all those who were gathered on the square. Those who were barely 14, those who were already more than 60 years old, those who were just starting their life as well as those who have seen many things in their lives—we all are a single command, citizens of the wonderful, unique country, citizens of Russia.
The cycle marathon started, 1,000 kilometers of the "Road of freedom" ("Doroga svobody": velomarafon startuet 2007).

Nashi clearly aims to re-fuse different generations into a common sense of national unity and identification. That is, people from 14 up to 60 years old, "citizens of this great, unique country", who start their "Road of Freedom" with the national hymn.

*The representation*: This level is essential as it opens interpretations in different directions, or, in terms of this study, other discourses and fields. Thus, I treat representation here as particular discourse. In this text three major discourses are to be re-fused: the historical, modernist-present, and heroic. The historical discourse becomes apparent in a specific historical event, "the first victory of the Home Guard in 1612 against Polish Lithuanian intruders," historical figures Minin and Pozharskii, and the history in the present (historical places on the cyclists' route). In general, the ritualistic value of this historical event is especially important in terms of national identity formation. The Home Guard organized by Minin and Pozharskii against Polish Lithuanian intruders in 1612 symbolized Russia's victory during the so called "Time of Troubles" (Smutnoe vremia),[59] and thus Nashi's action in the present obviously aims to re-fuse this historical cornerstone with the current nation-building process. That is, to create a symbolic victory over the post-Soviet "smutnoe vremia" by visiting places connected to the historical victory.

---

the mis en scène of this text. Of course, it is worth noting that I along with other viewers of these texts definitely belong to the third-order audience, but this viewing definitely takes place in the mis en scène called the Internet.

[59] Historically this period was between 1598-1613 when Russia was occupied by the Polish-Lithuanian commonwealth, and suffered from large-scale social and political restlessness. For a more detailed discussion about this period, see Dunning (2001).

Various emblems of the Orthodox religion, as a unifying factor of the nation, are presented through a historical discourse as they show their presence and ageless nature, and thus aim to bridge the gap between the past and the present. The modernist-present discourse is related to how this historical discourse comes about; by traveling the historical route with contemporary bicycles and with contemporary facilities.[60] In addition, the modernist-present discourse is mostly represented by contemporary forms of sports entertainment, a sort of contemporary version of the historical multithlon: "shooting with bow and air rifle, rafting, and orienteering with the satellite navigation." These all obviously figure as important symbolic devices for the restricted cultural production of "youth" within the framework of the large-scale cultural production of "adults." They are "non-political" aspects of youth culture which are offered by Nashi. The following phrase intensifies the supposedly cogent combination between official patriotic history, the excitement of this sports adventure, as well as technological modernization: "The patriotic route was planned with the help of the Russian navigation system GLONASS."[61]

This modernist-sports discourse activates a particular heroic discourse as well, focusing on the physical challenges of the event, for example, by stating that cyclists "travelled more than 1150 kilometers, slept in tents, and ate in open-air circumstances." Interestingly, in relation to the mentioned modern facilities and activities during the route—especially the mention of "GLONASS"—the heroic discourse shifts the national pride (historical places, nouns of activities, for example, the attribute "patriotic") to the pride of heroic action. In this action the actors are heroically struggling with those conditions which were hardly suitable for the national pride described by nouns and at-

---

[60] In the photos which concern this event, all the bicycles are modern mountain bikes, and many cyclists carry seemingly professional equipment: cycling suits, headgear, sunglasses, and gloves (see Doroga svobody 2007).

[61] This Soviet-Russian satellite navigation system (derives from GLObal'naia NAvigatsionnaia Sputnikovaia Sistema) is mainly used by the Russian Space Forces as an alternative and complementary system for the US based Global Positioning System (GPS). The first GLONASS satellite was launched in 1982, and in 1993 the system received global coverage. Despite several financial problems and almost total decay of the system, particularily in the 1990s, Russia has constantly developed the system. In October 2011, the full orbital constellation of 24 satellites was restored, enabling full global coverage (see Glonass 2014).

tributes. The following headline and the fragment of another text dedicated to the same event finely illustrate this:

> 42
> **"The Road of Freedom": Heat and Bad Roads of the Kostroma Region Excited Participants of the Cycle Marathon**
> Today participants of the patriotic cycle marathon "the Road of freedom" overcame more than one hundred kilometers on roads of the Kostroma region. According to the press-secretary of the "Road of freedom" Irina Borisova, "the route was extremely heavy, roads of the Kostroma region were broken, and temperature reached more than 35 degrees Celsius under the blistering sun." However, everyone gets through "excellently" ("Doroga svobody": Zhara i plokhie 2007).

Along with the extreme weather conditions, the bad, or even horrible, conditions of the roads are also converted into symbolic capital for the heroic discourse. However, the explication of the poor Russian infrastructure especially outside big cities clearly contradicts the modernist-driven accounts, such as "GLONASS," or other modern and high-tech equipments, to say nothing of the general national dignity which Nashi enthusiastically wants to exhibit.

*The means of symbolic production*: As samples in the previous chapter showed, here the reporting is also produced by indirect narration in the past tense. This type of narration allows Nashi to inform about its own activities harmonically, and especially in the sense that all possible flaws of the event are somehow regulated into the presupposed form: The event was accomplished in the way intended. Although in sample 42 "a visiting voice" is allowed to be represented, it is completely internal, and thus a specious example of multivocality: The movement cites its own press-secretary who provides information about the event. An important means in this symbolic production is its diverse vocabulary which activates different discourses (historical, modernist-present, and heroic) but which are not further elaborated upon. They are just presented as particular "cues" in the frames of an official sounding announcement. I shall come to this point below.

*The social powers*: In the framework of this study, these powers are didactics and stimulation framed as Bourdieu's fields of large-scale and restricted cultural productions. In this event Nashi's ambition to bridge the tension between these two powers becomes apparent in its use of emblems of the Orthodox Church as topical cornerstones of the event as they orient the reader to official cultural values, and the positive reputation of the Church

among Russian youth.[62] Furthermore, the modernist-pr(
with the heroic discourse, through these sports-related
produce the official cultural and historical canon with it
ness to the present nation building process. Conseque
via "heroic" cycling, with other sports activities, seem
with youth culture activities.

The mis en scène: The actual forum where this description takes place is Nashi's official website. In this respect, this level could be regarded as a "third-order audience" (see the footnote in the audience-section above). However, my interest is on the features which may inform us about the role of the "mis en scène," that is, the Internet. While the Internet allows real-time, or on-line, information, the aspect which makes Nashi's reports interesting is their particular "off-line" nature. There is no option for immediate comments from potential readers. In general, the past-tense-one-voice-reporting implies the prevalence of traditional newspaper reporting in the sense of the Soviet "newsworthiness" of events without using the interactional possibilities of the Internet. In the previous chapter Oleg in particular drew a clear barrier between the internal, and external, or closed, communication of the movement. Nevertheless, the episodic character of "The Road of Freedom" has been produced by instant reporting easily allowed by the Internet.

This event contains 18 reports published between 8 August and 25 2007, which means that there is one report per day. Frequent reports create a kind of specious on-line reporting which allows readers to follow this event "on line." However, as I pointed out, the distant and monotonic reporting without an option for readers' comments leaves the "mis en scène" rather as a façade of openness than an open forum of "re-fused experience" between Nashi and potential readers/viewers of the website. Kirill Postoutenko (2011) points out that Nashi's use of the Internet in this regard tries to conserve the speaker's (Nashi's) privileges by emulating the traditional mass media with the delayed

---

62 The church is one of those few institutions (within the president and partially the army) among young Russians which are trusted (Omel'chenko 2006: 18-19). In 2008, according to the survey by FOM, 62 % of Russians trusted in the Orthodox Church (in 1999 this figure was 53 %). Among the age-group 18-35, 56 % trusted in the Church. Moreover, 47 % of Russians considered that the Church should take more visible role in the society than it currently does (FOM 2008b).

se while simulating its nominal "spontaneity." In this sense, Nashi's soon is compatible with the particular "monumentalism" of the Internet which
downplays the web's plural and multiple communication possibilities (Schmidt
and Teubener 2006).

The closed mis en scène (website) of Nashi's "Road of Freedom" implies
the role of social powers, didactics and stimulation, for the movement. While
the Internet as such is strongly orientated towards contemporary youth culture, Nashi's communication as a whole reveals a rather strong devotion to it
by producing thousands of web-page reports, photos, as well as video clips.
However, in terms of quality, the true utilization of various voices, namely,
voices from the public, are excluded. Rather, Nashi mimics the multiple voices of youth culture instead of allowing their true presence. This is explicitly
manifested through a formal discourse which, in a manner of speaking, activates cues of a youth culture but regulate these cues into a formal and controlled form. Again, such cues are compatible with Bourdieu's anticipation of
symbolic capital which does not guarantee the success as symbolic capital.
Next I examine these anticipations within the help of a short historical comparison.

**Nashi's Ritualistic Cues**

Mabel Berezin argues that political ritual is a form of "making" political love, or
"reordering the hierarchies of identity," by using examples from Fascist Italy
(2001: 87). According to her, the Italian fascists imagined their political identity as a fusion of public and private conceptions of the self which sharply di-
verged from the style in which Italian citizens constructed their identities (ibid.:
89).[63] These "common" (or in Berezin's terms, non-contingent) identities were
tied to family, region, and religion (the Catholic Church) in the sense of cultural communities. These communities provided cultural repertoires, modes of

---

[63] Berezin emphasizes that national cultures were created at the expense of local and regional cultures (ibid.: 86): Modern nation-states require a cultural infrastructure to en-
sure that commitment to a national polity (in Russia's case, national policy as well, J.L.)
is salient among the "hierarchy" (Berezin's emphasis) of felt identities. This is not only
the case in Fascist Italy, or in societies whose cultural and political practices more or
less resemble totalitarian practices. She points out that all political regimes engage in
some form of symbolic politics (national language, literature, museums, monuments,
etc).

thought and behavior by functioning as the sources of the Italian self and the loci of emotional attachment (ibid.). As a pre-condition for the emergence of Fascist Italy, Berezin sees an empty symbolic space left by democratic political practices, which is consequently open for potential totalitarian forms (ibid.: 87). Pre-liberal forms of government, which monarchy symbolizes, are rejected in a democracy which then leads to certain desacralization of politics. This desacralization is actually an open space for the potential re-sacralization of politics sought by totalitarian initiatives (ibid.). The emotional commitment connected with felt (cultural) identities is central here. Since liberalism and democracy relegate emotion to the private sphere, this means that the denial of emotion embodied in democracy's refusal to incorporate the sacred into its institutions threatens to derail democratic ideals (ibid.: 87-88).

I am not suggesting that my data and its general political context—Putin's Russia—with its centralizing, and thus partially undemocratic measures can be interpreted as analogous with Fascist Italy. The point I am arguing is, that Nashi's web-page reports include a similar attempt to reorder various discourses into a specific new wholeness, a new discourse for national identity. Marlene Laruelle points out that in terms of promoting Russia's need for modernization along with national identity discourse, "Nashi (and Young Guard, the youth section of the United Russia, as well) encourages Russian society to reunify around the advocacy of consensual symbolic referents: that is, a continuous process of manipulating contradictions and toying with multiple identity strategies" (2009c). In this respect Berezin's examples from Fascist Italy are very illuminating. The concept of "open symbolic space" as the precondition for potential "fascist fillings" can easily be found in the studies concerning post-Soviet nationalism and national identity formation. By aiming to combine largely autonomous youth culture practices and a positively valued common space (official policies and polity), Nashi produces similar combinations to those found by Berezin in writing about Fascist Italy (ibid.: 84): That is, blurring the boundary between self and other, self and nation-state, and hence dramatizing the political identity or membership felt in the national polity. Berezin actually supports her own theoretical view in the same way that I am here suggesting when she says that (ibid.: 94):

Identity formation under conditions of antiliberalism provides an extreme case that allows us to place more standard conceptions of political identity formation under the microscope ... I am not suggesting that we are about to witness a resurgence of anti-liberal regimes similar to those of the early 20th century, nor am I suggesting a resurgence of public ritual as a way of political life [although in the light of Nashi this seems to be partially true in Russia, J.L.]. Indeed other technologies of political communication, from television to Internet, compete with ritual. However, I do argue that an analysis of the formal properties of ritual and anti-liberalism has much to contribute to current theoretical discussions of identity as well as to the formulation of hypotheses regarding the emergence of new or unstable political identities.

I would add that in my case the Internet is not a competitor of ritual but an essential contemporary arena of performing rituals (ritual-like strategies), in Alexander's terms, a "mis en scène." In terms of political communication, Nashi aims to harmonize evident ideological tensions and controversies of its own activities within repetitive online writings which, however, potentially narrow the space for the stimulative potential. At the same time, from the viewpoint of the writings' repetitiveness, they finely serve a ritualistic purpose concerning the discursive production of ideal youth along the national identity formation. Berezin points out that (ibid.: 93):

Public political rituals serve as arenas of identity, bounded spaces, where collective national selfhood is enacted. Ritual action communicates familiarity with form, and this familiarity may be as simple as the recognition that one is required to be present at an event. Familiarity and identity are coterminous. The repeated experience of ritual participation produces a feeling of solidarity—"we are all here together, we must share something"; and lastly, it produces collective memory—"we were all there together" [Berezin's emphases]. What is experienced and what is remembered is the act of participating in the ritual event in the name of polity.

These notions are very insightful for understanding Nashi's communication. First, Nashi's intensive use of the name of the movement in its reports strongly explicates the "we" as an identity manifestation. More importantly, the way of using "Nashi" (ours), as some previously discussed samples have shown, explicitly blurs the boundary between the meaning the "we/our" in Russian.[64]

---

64 This is first of all possible by conjugating the name of the movement according to the rules of the Russian grammar when the proper noun Nashi becomes the possessive pronoun "our, ours." Robert E. Moore has analyzed this sort of phenomena in the framework of late-modern brand marketing (2003: 340-343). According to him there are three types of brand as commodities in late modern societies, occurring in the ways these types are promoted: "genericide" (Moore's term for generalization), "ingredient"

Second, the narration with multiple links to familiar events, episodes and figures certainly aims to guarantee the aspect of "familiarity with form," pointed out by Berezin. This familiarity helps to explain the identities and emotions in question (pride, joy, hatred, patriotism, etc).[65] And the third point, which partially sheds light on Nashi's aptitude to create "harmonious reports conducted as intended," is the collective memory; "we were there, we conducted this action, and we did it successfully." In this respect, repetitive reports in the past tense are actually pointing to the need to produce similar reports in the future in order to strengthen and maintain that memory: "Let us do more, and then we can say again we were there and did that". In brief, particular "communities of feeling" are profoundly created by public political rituals (ibid.: 93).

The further point by Berezin, which concerns the controlled or uncontrolled meanings of public political ritual, fits the framework of the tension between didactics and stimulation. Although ritual eliminates indeterminacy in social space through the carefully staged crowding of bodies in public spaces, this does not presume that ritual eliminates indeterminacy as to meaning (ibid.: 94). I argue that this point is particularly suitable for the narrated descriptions (i.e. online writings) of Nashi's actions as well. They are carefully written in the sense of the anticipation of symbolic capital from a dual audience; the political elite, and Russian youth. This indeterminacy is principally linked to the challenge of re-fusing basically de-fused components of social performance (Alexander 2006). Thus, solidarities and memories—the identities of subjects who have gathered together under similar circumstances—may be extremely fluid (Berezin 2001: 94). In this regard, harmonious reports, as cultural products of didactic-driven large-scale cultural production with controlled cues of "stimulative youth culture," can be seen in a central role of regulating narrated ritual's indeterminacy. Let us examine how this appears in the following sam-

---

and "viral" (ibid.). The play with the Nashi is a sort of genericide which means the purpose is to dissipate the division between the proper noun (or, brand) and common noun (possessive pronoun). A good example in Russian of naturalized linguistic practice is the word "Xerox" (kseroks), which means copying machine in general, originated from this particular brand name.

[65] Alexander points out that many contemporary political speechwriters strongly rely on "the greatness" of simplicity (2006: 60). According to Peggy Noonan, the speechwriter of Ronald Reagan and George Bush," simplification is the key to achieving the fusion among speaker, audience, and background culture" (ibid.).

ple (exceptionally I use here the original headline to show up the non-Cyrillic use):

43

**Москва: Африка feat. Азия на Уроках Дружбы**[66]

In November 27 two Lessons of Friendship took place at the same time in different auditoriums of the Moscow Institute of Automatics and Radio-electronics
One of the lessons was held by Floko from Mauritius. An African showed clips (mini-films)[67] about his country in which were seen the everyday life and habits of people on the Black Continent. Students could hear African music and saw how African national musical instruments look like.
The quest talked about the 1941-45 war, and thanked OUR Veterans for that they preserved the normal life not only in his Motherland but also helped other countries, and pointed out, that without the veterans there could be colonies in Africa in these days.
Tajik Lola, who held another Lesson, showed some national wedding habits and costumes for students. A woman invited students to visit Tajikistan and promised to give an excursion for one of the students if he goes to visit her (Moskva: Africa feat. Azia 2006).

One of the most active sections in the framework of Nashi's antifascist activity has been the "Lessons of Friendship" *(Uroki Druzhby)*.[68] The basic idea of this section is to spread interethnic tolerance among Russian youth, mainly in schools and universities. This can be seen as an obvious response to the alarming increase in racist crimes in Russia during the last ten years, especially in early 2000s.[69] What we see in Nashi's role along with the general setting of these lessons is that they are overly official, formal, and didactic. Within a deeper observation this very discourse reproduces essentialist and potentially racist categorizations. A very similar discourse with this one is present in the report Friendly desánt (Vladimir: Druzhestvennyi desant 2007).

---

66 Moscow: Africa feat. Asia in Lessons of Friendship
67 Clarification in brackets (mini-fil'my) is in the original.
68 Actually the "Lessons of Friendship" is not Nashi's invention as this designation was largely used in the Soviet Union. For example, in Soviet Estonia during perestroika when the Estonian independence movement emerged, a visible response to this movement was made in the form of officially organized "Lessons of Friendship." The Communist Party organized these lessons in order to reassure the inevitable ethnic and sociolinguistic tension between Estonian and Russian-speaking people which became apparent at the end of the 1980s (for more, see Lassila 2002).
69 About racism and xenophobia in contemporary Russia, see Kozhevnikova (2006). See also the monitoring site of these crimes by the SOVA center (SOVA 2014).

Foreign cultures—African and/or Asian—are represented in terms of museum pieces. Persons representing these cultures are brought by Nashi in front of students, or pupils, along with their cultural stereotypes (national costumes, musical instruments, and listings of their common habits). Also in these texts, all the possible dialogues, questions, or contingencies have been put into a formal narration which underscores the successful accomplishment of the event. In terms of ritual-like action, and its de-fused starting point, Nashi's solution for the re-fusion of didactics and stimulation in sample 43 is manifest in specific linguistic cues which are typically particular lexicalizations. In the headline, an English abbreviation *feat* (from *featuring*) explicitly anticipates imaginary settings of youth culture.[70]

In the Russian- Cyrillic context the use of English in this way has a strong distinctive function which indexes to the assumptive hierarchical pinnacle of contemporary youth cultures, that is, Anglo-American popular culture. Following Bourdieu's notions of symbolic capital, this explicit use of an English abbreviation in the highly formal and normative orthographic (Cyrillic) context can be interpreted as a heretical departure from orthodox practice (Ryazanova-Clarke 2008; Bourdieu 1991: 128-129). Such variation partially reveals a struggle in the formation of legitimate expressions linked to post-Soviet nation building (Ryazanova-Clarke 2008). Nashi anticipates a felicitious ritual by adding a peculiar English abbreviation from the repertoire of stimulation to a highly didactic interethnic edification. Asian and African cultures are thus "coolly" combined with the official discourse. Similar cues can be seen in the use of "clips" (*roliki*) in the third sentence, followed by the immediate "adult" translation "mini-films" in brackets. A more conceptual than lexical cue is used in the middle of the report in which the cornerstone of Russian patriotism, the war of 1941-45 (though not explicating the "Great Patriotic War"), is shifted into the "mouths" of the foreign cultures in question. This occurs along with the typical blurring of the movement's proper noun with the possessive pronoun, "OUR veterans" (NASHI *Veterany*). This obviously anticipates the possibility of diminishing potential xenophobic attitudes of youth towards African and Asian peoples by using the relatively high value youth attaches to patriot-

---

[70] When I was writing this, an immediate example among several options from Google was the following: "Madonna remix band feat. Dara Rollins."

ism (Russkii natsionalism 2006; Omel'chenko & Goncharova, 2009). In the sense, "when a foreigner sees the value of our patriotism, s/he is a good foreigner."

The previous sample shows how Nashi aims include contemporary forms and symbols of globally driven youth culture into its political and ideological agenda. Hemment has also made similar observations based on her fieldwork on Nashi in the city of Tver (2007; 2009; 2012; 2014). According to her, these "creolizations" of hybrid imagery include globalized icons and images mixed with Soviet, or Russian national symbols (ibid. 2007: 18; see also Wilson 2005: 63 in the framework of general post-Soviet "virtual democracies"). One of Hemment's noteworthy examples concerns a Nashi action in December 2006 in Moscow which she attended: Young people danced and sang along to Soviet wartime songs mixed to a techno beat (ibid.: 19; Hemment 2014: chapter on Nashi). These original music items were actually downloadable from the main website of the pre-November 2009 version. In the latest website version, there was a special music-section as well which included various pop music related news but without any explicit ritual-like connection to the movement's ideological position. For instance, the title *Rihanna, promo dlia "Rated R"* consisted of the artist's revealing promo pictures. Such a change in the movement's information practices intensifies the notion of tension between the ideological contests and forms used for these contents.

Nashi's antifascist agenda represents itself as a coherent combination of present-day social problem (racism and racist crimes), and the official national narrative concerning "the victory over fascists" in "The Great Patriotic War." Moreover, variations between formal and non-formal expressions reveal a poising between the communicative demands of didactics and stimulation. For instance, the immediate translation of "clips" as "mini-films" in brackets shows an uncertainty about legitimate expressions. In the case of the pro-governmental youth movement, this elaboration reveals that potential readers might include people who are not necessarily well-informed about modern tools used in youth culture, presumably those who are strongly positioned as "non-youth" adult elite. A report of Nashi's "Lessons of Friendship," titled as *Рязань: Black & White party*, follows an exactly similar deployment from the globally driven youth cultural repertoire in the general official framework (Ryazan: Black & White party 2006). In spite of the report's explicitly informal or, "youth-driven" headline, the conclusion of the report describes the event as follows: "Everything happened under the electrifying contemporary music." This music obviously refers to hip-hop, techno, and other genres of music listened widely among young people (in Russia, and elsewhere). However, in terms of youth's own voice, these genres are, in all probability, described simply as hip-hop, techno, house, etc., rather than "electrifying contemporary music." In other words, the language of the reports may start with the tone of youth's voice but finally it lapses into a rather "adult" voice in the depiction of young people's world. In addition to the report's Soviet-resonating designation of "friendship of nations" (*druzhba narodov*), the attribute "antifascist" figures in it in the way it was largely used in Soviet authoritative discourse (Yurchak 2006: 63-70): A particular ideological and political denominator (antifascism) is constantly repeated and "multiplied" by attaching it to every possible activity somehow related to this denominator (e.g. "antifascist hairstyle," "antifascist evening party").[71]

Youth cultural cues (e.g. *feat, Black & White party,* as well as the use of English in many other reports of Nashi)[72] figure as symbolic components in re-fusing de-fused real life into a socially and politically distinctive wholeness, into a "community of feeling." A similar combination of concepts from different eras (and hence different fields) is to be found in the following report from Nashi's large-scale summer camp "Seliger 2008":

---

[71] Nashi's harnessing of non-official cultural practices and signifiers to its official-related activities reveals historical connection to perestroika-era practices of the Komsomol. During the last years of the Soviet Union the Komsomol tried to increase its popularity (and consequently downplay the appeal of alternative or the so-called "neformaly"-activities) by selectively picking influences from the "neformaly" (see Pilkington 1994: 126-161).

[72] For example, the report "Ryazan: Voyna s estonskoy produktsiey must go on," is about the boycotting of Estonian products as a protest against the removal of the Bronze Soldier in Tallinn. The report, completely titled in English as "Truth about NATO," is about the photo exhibition criticizing NATO held by Nashi in Romania. The report titled as "Vive la resistance!" is about Nashi's protest against the independence of Kosovo held in Paris. This choice of headline obviously harnesses the "French sensitivity" of social and political protesting, a kind of revolutionary romance. For instance, Igor clearly pointed out in the interview that he admires French political activism. These last two examples, which concern Nashi's activities abroad, reflect "the language spoken abroad", that is, English in the case of NATO, and French in the case of Paris.

44
### Innovative Battle of the Times of The Great Patriotic War
Organizers of the exhibition "Selinn" arranged a real show for participants and quests of the Forum. Battles by miniature models of airplanes, tanks and infantry of the times of The Great Patriotic War dazzled the audience with their trembling and authenticity. Attacks of the Soviet air force to German-Fascist occupiers sent observers to the past of more than a half- century (Innovatsionnyi boy vremen 2008).

What is noteworthy here is that this sample which concerns the strengthening of the memory and value of "The Great Patriotic War" is not labeled, for instance, simply as "simulating a battle of the Great Patriotic War." Instead, the issue is about "the innovative battle of the times of The Great Patriotic War." Large-scale and seemingly professional utilization of contemporary miniature models is regarded as a creative and progressive, that is, "innovative," devotion to the value of the memory of that war. This short report follows the already familiar harmonic and one-voice-past-tense depiction of successful action, and it leaves open the role of Nashi's activists in this performance (see journalism samples above). It is mentioned that the organizers of the camp built this simulated battle for the quests and participants of the camp. While guests of the Seliger have included top-level politicians, participants, as well organizers, actually refer to Nashi. Thus, the didactic position is clearly blurred here with the "stimulative" performance. The ritual-like strategy of the depiction becomes apparent in the combination of "innovative" and "The Great Patriotic War." The use of the term deployed from globally driven business practices, or "knowledge economy,"[73] is attached to the sacred emblem of Russian national identity. In this way, the memory of "The Great Patriotic War" ("our national identity") is conducted "innovatively" by Nashi, although this innovativeness is purely "tokenistic," a one-word mention without any further elaboration. Next I focus on these "tokenistic" cues and their ritualistic role in more detail.

---

[73] An illuminating example of the extensive role of innovation as a global discourse is the "Report of Innovation Policy by the Council of State of Finland for the Finnish Parliament" in 2008 (Valtioneuvoston innovaatiopoliittinen selonteko eduskunnalle 2008). In this 38-page report the word "innovative" with its derivates is repeated more than 300 times.

## Harnessing the "Wild" for an Ideal Youth

In his study of English language tourist discourse and its representations of non-English speaking cultures, Crispin Thurlow points out that the use and depiction of the language of a particular target culture is strikingly brief and tokenistic (2009: 9). English is presented as the "global language" while local people's ways of speaking are invariably deployed as "little more than an exoticizing resource for linguascaping"—that is, as a backdrop for added local flavor or authenticity (ibid).[74] Thurlow points out that within the tokenistic use of a foreign language the presenters and role models of the tourist discourse invite tourists (i.e. the audience of this tourist discourse) to take up a performance of the cosmopolitan traveler (ibid.): "Here's how to be a (British) tourist," or "here's an appropriate way to interact with local people." Leaving aside the aspect of tourism and intercultural communication between particular nations and their mother tongues (e.g. Russian and English), Nashi's deployment of "foreign" semiotic-linguistic elements follows a similar tokenistic linguistic practice. A connection to Althusser's interpellation can also be found since such a controlled and "ready-made" exchange on the part of the sender requires subject-images into which the subjects can be interpellated (transformed). Consequently, interpellation requires an ideology (in my interpretation, socio-political position) which legitimates the sender's power to interpellate the subjects. And, as I have pointed out, for Nashi this is principally "supposed legitimacy," potentially resulting as failed action. From the viewpoint of Nashi's ritual-like strategy the above shown youth cultural cues are seen as sufficiently distinctive and symbolically profitable for the supposed rules of youth cultures but not to such an extent that they could challenge the basic discourse of state-driven didactics. While the barrier between these two fields is uncertain for Nashi, the solution appears as tokenistic cues (single words or symbols): They are believed to have that cultural value which could re-fuse separate realms into a new single and coherent discourse. Let us take a look at how this balancing act appears in the following sample including the photo:

---

[74] Similar decontextualized, tokenistic, and generic representations are typical of the visual settings in the discourses of luxury tourism, see Thurlow & Jaworski 2009.

45
Yaroslavl': "Sanitarians of The Russian Language"
Unfortunately many of us do not avoid swearing in different situations. People's ex-
cuse is that it is the supposed expression of feelings and there is nothing bad in it.
Today the commissars of the Movement "NASHI" were alarmed. Today the commissars conducted a flash mob in which the participants taped their mouths with the
labels "no swearing". The young people went to the city centre and tried to transmit
to Yaroslavlians that cussing is the regress of the population. Everyone must respect themselves, and a person who respects himself, won't swear.
People's reactions varied: some people frowned and said that this is useless and
fixes nothing, while others, on the contrary, expressed a willingness in the fight for
the purity of Russian language. We'll hope that these were not only words, and the
conducted event left its own mark in the hearts of Yaroslavlians (Iaroslavl': Sanitary
russkogo iazyka 2007).

In this report Nashi demonstrates in favor of official cultural and linguistic values by showing its disapproval of bad language which principally means cursing. In this respect, Nashi partially continues Idushchie Vmeste's campaigns
and ideals of cultural purity, highlighted especially in its Moral Codex. These
ideals rather explicitly reproduce the Soviet era's ideals of kul'turnost. The
topic of Sample 45 is probably one of the most essential aspects of it, having
its legacy well before Soviet times: The ideal of the Russian literary language
which is rooted in the nineteenth-century Russian culture built on the basis of

European examples (Gorham 2000; 2003; Figes 2002). In Nashi's time, Putin's policy of "normative national ideals," the State Law of Russian Language in 2005 is an illuminating manifestation of this ideal.[75] Nonetheless, as the photo partially visualizes, the report's discourse draws heavily on practices of unofficial youth cultures which typically stand against official state policies and conformist cultural values. In this sense the practice of this action and its discursive (re)production is, from Nashi's viewpoint, compatible with the rules of a youth culture.[76] Interestingly, this contradiction is deepened by the fact that the very language of the report is rather colloquial.[77] After all, from the viewpoint of particular youth slangs used in the Internet[78] the text represents rather common Russian colloquial speech (*razgovornaia rech*). Furthermore, the term "Sanitarians" in the headline is an explicit cue to Soviet

---

[75] For example the sixth section of the Law's first article is the following: "In the use of the Russian language as the state language of the Russian Federation the use of such words and expressions which do not correspond to the norms of contemporary Russian literary language, with the exception of foreign words which do not have generally used equivalents in Russian, are not allowed" (The State Law 2005). Lara Ryazanova-Clarke (2006: 41) points out that the discussion of the law in the Russian Duma has clearly shown the role of normatively controlled Russian language as a political resource, which is also manifested in the Law itself (see the first article of the State Law, 2005).

[76] An original practice of performative art, developed in underground circles in the Soviet Union, especially in Leningrad in the late 1970s and early 1980s was the so called *stëb* (Yurchak 2006; 2008). In short, the idea of *stëb* was an absolute dissolving of the boundaries between the normal and abnormal, correct and incorrect. It was a sort of performative carnival which heavily drew on ridiculing official practices and discourses, combining them with totally socially exceptional forms of behavior (ibid). However, this had more to do with forms of "just having fun" rather than conscious political statements (ibid). For more, see below concerning Nashi's Bronze Soldier episode.

[77] In helping to scrutinize the colloquial expressions of this particular example, I thank Marjatta Vanhala-Aniszewski and Alexei Lobskii at the Russian Section of the Department of Languages of the University of Jyväskylä.

[78] In the Russian web-context, the most vivid example of "youth anti-language" is the so-called "mob language" (padonskiy iazyk), relatively often used in Russian Live Journal which is the most famous web-forum in Russia (Gorny 2006). The language of "padonkies" is full of the systematic breaking of orthographic rules of normative Russian, partially motivated by the challenges in producing Cyrillic text in a "Latin" dominated web-space. In addition, "padonkies" use all types of creative abbreviations, curse words, and other emotional expressions, which are produced according to specific "grammar." Interestingly, these systematic deviations from official linguistic norms are also related to discussions which can be defined as "intellectual." In this respect, Russian sociolinguist Gazan Guseinov calls "padonkies" the "aristocracy of underground" (2005).

era Komsomol practices, now transformed by Nashi into a presumably distinctive and profitable manifestation of the relative popularity of Soviet nostalgia in Russian society during this decade (Nadkarni & Shevchenko 2004; Levada 2004; Dubin 2004; Gudkov 2002).

The idea of flash mobs is to draw the attention of people in a public space by organizing an unusual action by a large group of people (See Flashmob 2010). This relatively new form of performance art (first appeared less than ten years ago) was originally an apolitical act (ibid.). In Nashi's case this is an explicit adoption of practices of Western counter-culture for Nashi's culture political actions.[79] The attribute "Western" in particular is often perceived as harmful or dangerous to "indigenous Russian culture," although the other side of this "indigenousness" often relies on "Western" ideals (Dubin 2001; 2011). However, in its demonstrations in support of "correct" cultural and linguistic values, Nashi principally deploys the practice of using flash mobs.

Here Nashi anticipates the symbolic capital related to a unique and profitable distinction in the attention space which is crowded by various globally driven cultural impacts as well as other, often non-conformist or oppositional, youth formations. Moreover, in relation to the demand to avoid cursing and "non-Russian" expressions mentioned in the State Law of Language (the State Law 2005, 1/6) as well as in other "language reports" by Nashi,[80] a loan "flash mob" from the repertoire of youth cultures is controversial. The report suggests that a foreign expression works separately ("just a foreign expression") in strengthening the main message (the promotion of a pure Russian

---

[79] In addition, Nashi's harnessing of the flash mob tactic also carries an explicit adoption of youth movement practices used by various oppositional political formations in Russia. According to oner of the main oppositional media representatives in Russia, the newspaper Novaia Gazeta, officialdom considers flash mobs principally as expressions of oppositional activities (Flesh-mob protiv flesh-mobov 2008).

[80] For example, in the report "Nizhny Novgorod: Velikii i moguchii" (the great and magnificent), which is well known patriotic-nationalistic expression for the Russian language (first mentioned by the Russian writer Ivan Turgenev, 1818-1883), Nashi emphasizes the importance to follow the norms of the Russian language as follows: "It is not justified that we often forget that by using non-normative lexicon, we mutilate Russian words, and try to replace them with foreign ones." Almost identical use of "flash mob" is present in the report "Kaluga: FOR the classical literature" in which the movement informs about gathering in the main square of the town to read classical works of Russian literature.

language and culture). This is precisely the situation in which a particular cultural production clashes with habitus's sense of producing it: The ideal of a pure language, which is targeted at youth, is produced by using devices which actually stand against this very ideal. In terms of linguistic-semiotic variations, the following sample is probably the most illuminating of Nashi's reports in this sense. Here I present the original text in the body text in order to highlight the non-cyrillic use:

46
Калуга: Экстрим «по-НАШЕМУ»
Масштабная sport-party состоялась в Калуге 25 ноября по инициативе молодежной организации «FRO» и Движения «НАШИ». «FRO», «Free Riders Organisations» — в вольном переводе—«сообщество свободно катающихся» — новая спортивная организация, созданная по инициативе и при поддержке Движения «НАШИ». Калужские любители BMX, ROLLERBLAIDING, SKATEBORDING и прочих спортивных изысков полтора часа соревновались в своем необычном мастерстве на глазах у сотен восторженных зрителей. Одно слово — экстремалы, не им бояться погоды и ссадин.
Среди участников есть и «профи», и «чайники», и просто зрители, только мечтающие покорить спортивные высоты. «FRO» — молодая организация с большими перспективами. Ее создатели и участники, вдохновленные возможностью почувствовать себя «официальной» командой, будут оттачивать мастерство на созданных своими силами спортивных площадках, радовать калужан спортивными шоу и обучать новичков, которых после сегодняшней «церемонии открытия» появилось несколько десятков. «Новеньким», по словам спортсменов, всегда рады в спортивной «тусовке». Были бы силы и желание научиться. Ребята не скрывают, что их спорт бывает опасен. Но не опаснее, чем ежевечерние прогулки с сигаретой и пивом, к которым так привыкли многие. Спортсмены в этом не нуждаются. Их допинг—адреналин, самый полезный для молодого растущего организма (Kaluga: Ekstrim 2006) [81]

---

[81] **Kaluga: Extreme in "OUR style"**
A large-scale sport-party took place in Kaluga on November 25th by the initiative of the youth movements "FRO" and the Movement "NASHI". The "FRO", "Free Riders Organisations"– in its free translation—society of free bikers—is the new sport organization, established by the initiative and the support of the Movement "NASHI". Kalugian admirers of BMX, ROLLER-BLAIDING, SKATEBORDING and other sport searchers competed in their original mastery one and a half hours in the front of hundreds of delirious spectators. In a word, they are extremists who are not afraid of weather and scratches. Among the participants are "pros" as well as "freshmen" and other spectators who only dream of conquering sporty heights. "FRO" is a young organization of great perspectives. Its founders and participants are inspired by possibility to feel themselves as "offi-

As was seen in the previous samples, also here too the content of the report follows the ideals the state youth policy (Strategiia 2007: 137 in which support for a healthy way of life for Russian youth is expressed as "the need for propaganda for the healthy way of life"). The important point here in terms of the cues of ritual-like strategy is that the aim is to stylize the general didactic underpinning of the text by using supposedly youth language. Nevertheless, following the official framework the most colloquial, or "unsuitable," expressions are regulated by putting them in quotation marks (*"профи"* (pros), *"чайники"* (greenohorns), *"тусовка"* (bunch)). In addition, expressions which lend a sort of formality to the event are put in quotation marks as well ("official," the opening ceremony"), which implies that Nashi wants to orientate the reader to the playful, and presumably youthful, nature of the event. The clearest distinctions are made by using single English words, partially with faulty writing, showing Nashi's desire to be "glocally" up to date.[82] The use of block letters in the words BMX and orthographically faulty written SKATEBORDING and ROLLERBLAIDING reveal the movement's willingness to highlight symbolically profitable forms of the "imaginary West"[83] for local political purposes. In short, with these particular tokenistic cues, supposedly having currency among youth, Nashi aims to re-fuse youth with the negatively valued official didactics to be found, in all probability, among youth.

To elaborate this interpretation in terms of Bourdieu's fields, I suggest that the field of youth politics as part of the larger field of nation building is strongly challenged by the "field" of this social movement's image construction which is the concrete facet of distinctively expressing that very field. What follows is that Nashi aims to manage its communicative demands by using clearly con-

---

cial" team. They will wield their mastery within the attainments from sport fields, entertain Kalugians within their sport show, and teach novices, who appeared a couple of tens after today's "opening ceremony". In the words of the sportsmen, "new guys" always have fun in a sporty "get-together". There were strength and willingness to learn. Guys don't hide that the sport's dangerous. But it's not more dangerous than nightly walks with cigarettes and beer, which are so familiar to many youngsters. Sportsmen do not need them. Their doping is adrenalin: the most useful for the growing young organism.

82 About similar functions of English in the case of Cosmopolitan magazine's non-English versions, see Machin & Van Leeuwen 2005.

83 About the elements and practices of the "imaginery West" in the Soviet context, see Yurchak 2006: 161-164.

trolled and tokenistic expressions of potentially dangerous youth cultures, and deploying these for the general ethos of didactics. The following two examples with the photos illustrate this practice:

47
**Vladimir: Hairstyle as civic position**
The international antifascist-barbershop was opened today in the city center. Loud music was played throughout the day at the theatre square and young people with red and white t-shirts provided special color for everyday life of passers-by. Activists of the program "Lessons of Friendship" from the movement "NASHI" make the outlook of Vladimirian youth brighter, more colorful, happier, and, at the same time, remind them that peace, friendship and cooperation between different people in territories of the multinational Russia is the guarantee of basic and positive change in life (Vladimir: Pricheska kak grazhdanskaia 2007).

48
**Smolensk: A clean street**
OUR antifascists "saved" the wall of the house, located at the address Bakunin Street 22, from a swastika. This house locates just behind the Smolensk State University, which is regarded one of the most prestigious institutes of higher education in the city. Commissars destroyed shameful writings and replaced them by flowers, a heart and a huge writing "I love Russia." After the work antifascists checked the whole street to the end, and after seeing swastikas in other walls, made still few paintings. Now the Bakunin Street is completely cleaned of symbols of the "Brown plague" (Smolensk: Chistaia ulitsa 2007).

In Sample 47 we see an emphatically stereotypical condensation of the "wild" associations linked to youth cultures. In the context of global as well as Russian antifascism a noteworthy point is the connection of this hairstyle to antifascist, or "antifa"-movements in general. According to Vladimir Kozlov, the Russian antifa-movement is closely linked with the punk-rock scene, formed in the 1990s, along with its DIY-practices,[84] which ideologically resonate with anti-consumerism, non-conformism, anti-militarism, the promotion of the rights of social and cultural minorities, ecological consciousness, for example, vegetarianism, as well as animal rights (Aksiutina 2002: 318-319; Kozlov 2008: 37-38).

---

[84] The abbreviation DIY is derived from the words "Do It Yourself," which can be considered a kind of ideological motto of punk-culture, which in the post-Soviet space, has a more restricted role than in its original Western contexts (Aksiutina 2002: 318-319). In this regard, DIY-related political activism in the post-Soviet space is more endangered in relation to civil society practices—mainly because of its relatively young history—and because of its more alien nature from the viewpoint of political power in comparison with Western societies (ibid.).

In this respect, Nashi's antifascist activity clearly recognizes the general global and local parameters of antifa-culture. It is thus an explicit anticipation of symbolic capital with regard to youth cultures, which, from Nashi's viewpoint, can then be smoothly attached to the framework of didactics. In this case, to the ideals of the official youth policy which itself resonates with the Soviet legacy of the term "active civic position" (*aktivnaia grazhdanskaia pozitsiia*, Strategiia 2007; Piattoeva 2005). Consequently, the arrangement of the hairstyle within the Orthodox Church building in the photo is hardly a coincidence. It is a clear attempt to re-fuse temporally, culturally, and discursively de-fused components into one discourse as part of the image of ideal youth, and hence part of an ideal national identity. The most explicit element of this ritual-like strategy is the "antifascist hairstyle" (made by the "antifa-barber") along with its linguistic reproduction. In some other reports Nashi uses various elements of body visualization that are not just restricted to its anti-fascist activity. For instance, face paintings and manicures with the symbols and colors of the movement which are often linked to the repetitive use of particular attributes; for example, along with Nashi's "patriotic" activities the movement produces "patriotic" manicures, etc. (*Briansk: Tochka kreativa* 2007; *Vladimir: Patriot do konchikov nogtey* 2007; Yurchak 2006: 63-70)

In comparison with Idushchie Vmeste's animal rights campaigns (see the discussion related to Samples 1 and 2) Nashi's antifascist activity and its symbolic production reveals a much more explicit and systematic harnessing of elements of restricted cultural production to serve state-driven didactics. Whereas Idushchie Vmeste campaigned for animal rights rather in the way it could be identified as any animal rights movement, Nashi, instead, explicitly makes apparent its engagement in official politics and cultural norms with a systematic and explicit anticipation towards youth culture-driven practices.

The sample *Smolensk: A clean street* is a good example of this. One important symbolic practice of antifa-activity is the use of graffiti in the sense of filling public space with its own ideological messages (Kozlov 2008: 41). In addition, the uses of graffiti are not only restricted to antifa-practices as their use is a countercultural practice in the youth scene in general, in Russia and elsewhere. For example, in the case of Russian neo-Nazi and skinhead movements, a typical practice is the painting of swastikas and other related symbols and slogans onto the public space. In relation to these culturally marginal youth activities—conducted for example by antifa or neo-Nazi groups—the use of graffiti by the pro-Kremlin and pro-official Nashi in its anti-fascist activities is highly revealing. The controlled and tokenistic nature of the report's main photo partially "speaks" in the sense of antifa-graffiti with its potential anarchist and DIY references (see the footnote above). More importantly, it shows the adoption of global (and Western) youth culture practice within particular visual settings. First, as the photo shows, four of "our antifascists" with black-and-white jackets are posing in a way that is familiar to posters and photos of hip-hop and rap-music artists. These are typically presented, as in the photo, in a more or less dirty and peripheral urban environment. In this sense, the photo's visual environment is very compatible with those peripheral frames (or discourses) of rappers, hip-hoppers and their culture, which are contrasted against the bourgeois cleanness of middle-class suburbs or the sterility of city-centers. However, the reality of Russian cities and towns is rather different from that of the US or Western Europe. Dirty concrete and brick walls are a much more "central" reality in several Russian towns, probably including the city in question here, Smolensk. Besides many Russian cities and towns have clean and repaired central areas, there are no large-scale American type middle-class suburbs. Thus, the implicit "counter-referent" of the photo, namely, a clean, sterile urban environment is generally lacking in Russia.

Although these peculiarities of Russian urban contexts are relevant in taking into account hip-hop and graffiti culture, they are not exceptional in the general "evolution" of these subcultures. Indeed, this originally Afro-American peripheral youth culture with its criminal connections has become an important center of global youth cultures, to say nothing of its commercial dimensions not only in the music business but in youth fashion in general. In short, what was originally a protest by an Afro-American urban periphery in the US towards the white elite has been transformed into a mainstream of global youth culture whose performers can be almost anyone in terms of habitus. Nevertheless, the use of graffiti to mark public space derived from this youth culture has remained marginal, and definitely a counterculture practice (For more about nationalist graffiti in Russia in the early 1990s, see Bushnell 1999). Vivid discussions in different countries, especially in cities, have occurred around "the fight against graffiti,"[85] and Russia is no exception.[86] In this respect, it is especially noteworthy that Nashi—as part of the political establishment relying on official values—is not washing away the paintings of fascists and condemning them, for example, as "enemies of our common space." Instead, Nashi is harnessing an aspect of a politically peripheral but culturally visible and thus partially central form of youth culture to its conformist message.

In short, Nashi's attempt to re-fuse explicitly de-fused components between didactics and stimulation is not only about the explicit blurring of the distinction between official and unofficial cultural practices as such but also shows how a globally conventionalized visual framing ("hip-hop" posing under the graffiti in the peripheral urban environment), can be attached to local official and non-peripheral frames (didactics) in a supposedly distinctive way. This "dirty" and "peripheral" environment is actually worthy of official respect. As the report states, "this house locates just behind the Smolensk State University which is regarded one of the most prestigious institutes of higher education in the city." Moreover, Nashi's graffiti itself is a form of harnessing elements from restricted cultural production to serve large-scale cultural production. It essentially follows the stylistic conventions of "global" graffiti, not in the sense of producing subcultural statements which would be understandable only for "insiders" of this subculture. Instead, Nashi produces graffiti which is readable and understandable for all those who read the "mainstream cultural script," that is, the Russian language: "I ♥ Russia" *(Я ♥ Россию)*.

Nashi's report *Kursk: The black square instead of a swastika* is worth adding here in terms of Nashi's antifascist symbolic politics. Probably the most negatively valued types of graffiti in the public space are principally those

---

85 For example in Helsinki there was a special campaign against illegal (i.e. spontaneous) graffiti called "Stop Smudging" (Stop Töhryille) founded in 1998 by the city council of Helsinki. Since then there has been a vivid discussion for and against the campaign as well as graffiti-culture and its nature in general. In general, the main motivation for this campaign was adopted from the zero-tolerance-attitude towards various criminal and criminally related activities in the urban space (Stop töhryille 2014).

86 Although I could not find many media examples condemning graffiti by using the search words "Udalenie graffiti" in Google and Yandex, there were several companies in the Internet which provided their services to clean them. So, in this respect it is obvious that there is a clear demand for cleaning graffiti away in Russia, although so far this has not caused a visible public discussion about "graffiti."

which are just esoteric "licks" by various actors without any sort of larger attempt to extend the readability, or "artistic value" of these public marks. By covering swastikas with black squares, as this report informs, Nashi definitely hides these widely known symbols of racism and fascism, but this sort of action leaves seemingly esoteric marks—just black squares or spots—in the public space. However, here the large-scale cultural production becomes into the picture. The black square has a remarkable symbolic role as a Russian contribution to the world's art history; Kazimier Malevich's constructivist works. The Russian artistic avant-garde hardly carries such value in Russian official culture as, for example, Russian classical literature, but Nashi's harnessing of Malevich as a "civilized" attack against fascist symbols aims to conduct a felicitous ritual-like strategy. This is done by blurring at least two de-fused visual practices—subcultural graffiti and a landmark of art history—into one, supposedly creative, discourse. In addition, here the blurring partially goes on inside the restricted cultural production, that is, the historical avant-garde (see Bourdieu 1993) although in Nashi's repertoire the black square is inevitably linked to the symbolic and cultural capital of today's national cultural conformism, that is, the large-scale cultural production.

The concept of ritual (ritual-like strategy) reveals the key nature of Nashi's political communication. The movement explicitly figures as a "re-fuser" of various de-fused elements of Russian, and in general, contemporary society. In the light of Mabel Berezin's points concerning Fascist Italy, Nashi produces similar combinations between largely autonomous youth cultural practices and positively valued common space with official policies and polity. These combinations highlight Nashi's challenges in contributing to national identity formation and the construction of ideal youth from its socio-political position. Furthermore, these combinations highlight Nashi's devotion to systematically designed production of ideal youth. This raises the question of image which the next chapter examines.

# VII Struggling with Image

## Views from Activists

A possible explanation for the concomitant presence of controversial symbolic choices in the light of Nashi's samples previously discussed could be that they are considered as "pure instruments" in the service of some higher goals. This interpretation gains a particular strength in relation to the Soviet legacy of information practices. However, if this is the case, the crucial challenge which remains for Nashi is, how to communicate its own actions onwards if "the main point" beyond its symbolic production is the only thing that matters. In other words, the coexistence of contradictory symbolic choices could be explained by the phrase "don't follow my words but my thoughts." In this case the question of the movement's image[87] becomes the crucial issue. For instance, Igor sees the issue of the movement's image as crucially important but as yet somehow unarticulated:

> 49
> Jussi: What do you think about image, is it important for the movement, or not?
> Igor: It is extremely important, because for a person who would like to join, there must be something interesting, and it is also important to understand that when our image…ideas which…look like the Putin Jugend, as we are sometimes accused, to forget that, that's not the case. For us, support for Putin based on his personality doesn't exist. For us the important thing is support for his course, and yes, we support that…we're not interested in Putin's personality, or anyone's personality, we're interested in the fate of Russia.
> Jussi: Well, how does image relate to the fate of Russia?
> Igor: Within the frames of this image, we are those who think about the fate of Russia, which leads her to strong, magnificent… and… yes, we are for the great Russia but without fascism.

So, for Igor, image is the thing which actually tempts people to join the movement. It is also something through which people could understand the true meaning of the movement, instead of understanding it wrongly, for example, as the "Putin-Jugend," as he points out. He seemingly regards my

---

[87] In general, I treat image as a term which is linked to political communication (see McNair's definition of political communication in Introduction). In more specific terms, image figures here as an emic-concept; it is a description which is consciously or unconsciously meaningful to a respondent.

question in a way which activates this wrong image of the "Putin-Jugend." Owing to this potential wrong connotation, he elaborates on the movement's relation to Putin by formulating the movement's image as "the interest in the fate of Russia" in the sense of its greatness. Moreover, from Igor's viewpoint, his own talk of Russia's greatness might prompt me to think that Nashi is an extremely nationalist, or even fascist, organization as his addition "without fascism" implies. Without specifying what these "image frames" actually are, Igor's views draw a clear line between the ideological content and communicative forms of this content. This was already apparent in his views above concerning stylistic issues of Nashi's website which he regarded as a "natural journalistic practice."

This view is similar to the controversy over national identity formation in relation to political communication which, according to Irina Semenenko, prevails between "outer" *(vneshnyi obraz)* and "inner images" *(vnutrennyi obraz)* (2008: 10): While the outer image principally concerns how "others" think about "us," the inner image with own preferences—that is, what we actually want and regard as important to tell "others" about "us"—often works beyond the supposed ideals of the outer image. Semenenko's point principally concerns the image work of nations', especially of Russia's, national identity. Nevertheless, this tension can be detected in the inarticulate definition of image that Igor reveals. In other words, his sense of the importance of image (inner image) is not articulated vis-à-vis its potential perceptions (outer image). This situation is to some extent compatible with Soviet-era communication ideals; a message is perceived in the sense that the sender has intended it to be perceived. However, as Nashi's reports have illustrated so far, the aspect of stylization is clearly present in the movement's political communication which suggests that there is also some reflection on the role of image as well. Oleg partially touches on the potential pitfalls in this regard but interprets these problems as "a general rule of the game:"

50
Jussi: How do you see the role and function of image or form *(obraz)* for the movement, in a general sense, as well as from the viewpoint of Nashi?
Oleg: Well...it is necessary to reason logically, too ...a social movement, on the one hand, represents...interests of part of society. On the other hand, it aims to be recognizable and appealing in order to gain trust from society...and in this respect, image plays the key role...It must be said that not everyone understands that and very

often social movements, we, others, social movements, adults, are accused for that their distinct events are only carried in terms of PR.. "you're just doing PR!" It's strange to hear these accusations because…we don't curse producers when they talk about their products. It's a normal relationship. It is thus normal when a social movement within its influence tries to explain about itself and recruit support-ers…have to say that we distinguish ourselves from other organizations because we have always considered our expressions very carefully, how we express our real things in the information field …We should never forget to tell about ourselves. I hope we're moving more or less toward that, although, of course, there are negative moments…but they are necessary…because you cannot please all. The more you tell about yourself, the more people like you, but, automatically (laugh), the more people start to ask…well, not so nice questions…well, that's a normal thing.

Oleg sees that a youth movement's task is, on the one hand, to represent particular interests (official policies in Nashi's case) but, on the other, this must be done "stimulatively." This is related to a movement's task of being trusted (or cogent) in society in general, which implies the presence of one common audience. In other words, he does not see any difference in expec-tation between different audiences, namely, between the official political side, and the side of "apolitical" youth. The expression "interests by part of society," nevertheless, implies that there might be other parts as well, that is, various expectations in society. Furthermore, he speaks in the name of all social movements (as my question partially orientated him to do), or in his words, "it is necessary to reason logically, too," although it is hardly clear that all social organizations would work in such socio-political position as Nashi does.

In terms of the difficulties it has in marketing itself, and in having a reputa-tion of "just doing pr," Oleg's view is definitely true, and this reputation is a challenging task for any political actor. Semenenko argues that lobbying among many Russians is perceived as a strongly corrupt practice which gen-erally reflects Russians' weak trust in society's institutions (2008: 9). In this respect, political (or any) communication in terms of marketing yourself is perceived ultimately as a negative phenomenon, no matter what you say. This dimension of Russia's weak institutions offers one explanation for the relatively unresponsive attitudes to existing political actors, especially among young Russians. Oleg's answer shows that this general communicative situa-tion linked to the issue of image is defined fatalistically, "it is what it is;" there are felicitous and less felicitous actions, and that is a fact you have to accept. At the same time, Oleg regards Nashi as distinct from other movements in that it thinks seriously about the movement's role in the information space. However, no deeper specifications of these "accurate considerations" are given. Instead of describing the movement's image work in terms of quality, Oleg sees the solution for Nashi (and seemingly for other social movements as well) on the basis of quantity. That is, the more you act the more supporters you will get, despite the potential disadvantages of such strategy. As he points out, "that's the normal thing".

In light of Oleg's account which partially follows Igor's views it can be stated that Nashi's image is seen as independent from the actual expressions of it. Although Oleg describes the "necessary" conditions of marketing oneself with Nashi's willingness to talk about itself in its actions, image is seen as a natural element, not only of Nashi's, but presumably of any movement's activities. It is this naturalness which seemingly downplays all potential specifications of image, for example, in the case of a particular project. This unarticulatedness can also be detected in Vadim's views. In the following quote Vadim mentions that an image of a social movement can be corrected, but this correction is not linked to possible problems in communication. Instead, it is linked to problems with the inner engagement of the activists with whom Vadim exhibits some disappointment:

51
After all image (*obraz*) [Vadim corrects my word *imidzh* as *obraz*] is more important than content in today's world. If…there is simply no content, no real content, it is rather difficult to create an image. However, after all, it can be corrected. I can say this because we have…maybe not 80 but about 60% of those who are called activists although in reality it is difficult to call them activists. Well, that's the case if you see it strictly…in "Vadim's" way[88] (laugh).

Vadim's account continues his earlier view which concerned a contrast between true activity and internet-activity. In this case, the latter can be termed "image-activity". Consequently, for Vadim, a "true image" is linked to the elite-level commitment that he himself presumably represents. Let us now take a closer look at this unarticulated element in Nashi's communication. The next two sections illustrate Nashi's contributions to the movement's image in terms of fashion.

---

[88] Here Vadim humorously refers to his own surname as a true example of an activist. For ethical reasons I use here his pseudonym.

## Struggle with Fashion

Before discussing Nashi's special fashion project Shapovalova, let me briefly examine how Nashi's predecessor, Idushchie Vmeste, defined the relationship between the inner and external aspects of an ideal young person in its Moral Codex:

> 52
> A member of the organization "Idushchie Vmeste" must not only strive to be better but also to create an atmosphere of culture, of mutual understanding and respect everywhere s/he is. It is in order to strive to be better, not with the help of clothes and make-up, but with capabilities and intellect. Remember: make-up and clothes can only be respected if there is something behind them. Strive to broaden your knowledge of everything. If you are impressed by the ideology of hippies and rockers, try not only dress the way they do but to learn everything about their ideology, its history and origins. If you are a devotee of works of a musician, artist, writer, do not stop at sleeveless shirt with idols' portraits. Become a true connoisseur of their work with a complete recognition that either you like this or, by contrast, this is something which is truly not worthy of spending time (Moral Codex, *Stremlenie "byt' luche" vezde i vo vsem*).

Idushchie Vmeste defines the position of an ideal young person as a sort of "intellectual educator" against "superficial mimicry." The movement demands that potential members adopt different cultural trends in terms of their "content" instead of their "forms." For example, by pointing out that "Remember: any make-up and clothes can only be respected if there is something behind them."[89] An orientation towards youth is made in the part in which Idushchie Vmeste explicates hippies and rockers by demanding that these youth culture figures must be perceived in terms of their "ideology," not only through their looks. This is again an illuminating manifestation of the movement's sense of following the Soviet era's ideals of kul'turnost: the movement dictates princi-

---

[89] It is worth mentioning that in Bourdieu's analysis of artistic production in capitalist contexts (especially in France) intellectually demanding products, for example, experimental art, are initially products of the field of restricted production, while less demanding (e.g. middle-brow art) works are typical products of the field of large-scale production. However, as Bourdieu continues, "in order to renew its own popular agenda "middle-brow art" (a key representative of large-scale production) needs to adopt the more venerable themes, or subjects, of "high art" (restricted production), or those most amenable to the traditional laws of composition in the popular arts (for example, a particular division of roles)" (1993: 129).

ples for young Russian in terms of correct cultural practices (see, for example, about the Soviet advice literature in this respect in Kelly 2001). As distinct from these views, Nashi has clearly recognized the importance of "superficial forms" and has made a visible step towards them in its own political communication. However, an obvious struggle is apparent in the movement's image-work as the following two samples illustrate:

53
**The metropolitan Kirill warned liberals of the flames of the apocalypse (12 November 2007, 13:43)**
The contemporary world might be destroyed if the liberal concept of human rights gains the upper hand, the head of external relations of the Moscow Patriarchate, the Metropolitan of Smolensk and Kaliningrad, Kirill announced at the meeting with students of the Moscow State Technical University of Bauman. His words were informed by Interfax.

"Today we live the postmodern epoch and the key feature of this epoch is a very dangerous idea: the postmodern epoch does not invoke the concept of truth—truth is relative, there are as many truths as there are heads. Instead of truth there is a concept of freedom of opinions," the orthodox head (*pravoslavnyi ierarkh*) warned the student youth.

According to Kirill, it was not a long time ago that an idea of legalizing homosexual marriages was impossible. "15 years ago it was impossible but today it is not only possible, but there is a struggle against it at level of legislation in order to enclose the people (*narod*) from the enforcement of such practice".

"The next frills (*vitok*) will be pedophilia because liberation from homosexuality is understood untruthfully, as a result of vast distribution of ideas of human rights," the Metropolitan drew conclusions.

He pointed out that "if those criteria—which are offered us by liberal philosophy related to rights and freedoms—become the only criteria for values of human deeds, pedophilia will be legalized among us."

"There is no end for that process because the end is in hell, in the flames of the apocalypse", the Metropolitan Kirill concluded.

He also touched the orthodox view of geopolitics. The Metropolitan said that "one civilizational model cannot strive to the global domination by claiming that it is the holder of the ultimate truth, and the rest of the world must twine unto this model."

That is why we stand for the multipolar world which we understand not only as poles of political power, as many politicians think, but as an existence of civilizational models," the representative of the church said.

"We suggest that the world would be built up on the combination of civilizational models, not on the influential basis of unification of certain concrete, in this case, Western liberal model," the Metropolitan Kirill added. IA REGNUM (Mitropol Kirill predupredil 2007).

54
**A Nizhny-Novgorodian has been acknowledged as the most stylish English-woman** (12 November 2007, 14:28)
Russian model, Nizhni-Novgorodian by birth, Natalia Vodianova has been acknowledged as the most stylish woman of Great Britain, RIA Rosbalt informs.

The experts of the British journal Harper's Bazaar conducted the ranking of those 25 inhabitants of Great Britain who have been acknowledged in the art of dressing in 2007.

This time the best of the best was the wife of Lord Justin Portman, model Natalia Vodianova, Nizhni-Novgorodian by birth. In addition to her, there were two more foreigners in the top ten: Belgian top model Anuk Leper and her Romanian colleague Irina Lazarenu.

Natalia Vodianova is one of the most exacting models of the world. Once, she was an ordinary girl from a poor family who lived in a small khrushchevka,[90] and sold fruits in a marquee. Today, the top model from Russia, Natalia Vodyanova, resides in an 800 square meter apartment in Manhattan and is regarded as one of the wealthiest women in Britain.

---

[90] This is a designation for the apartment houses that were built throughout the territories of the former Eastern Bloc during the era of the Communist Party Secretary Nikita Khrushchev (1953-1964).

In spite of all this, the model does not flatter herself. She properly visits her parents in Nizhny Novgorod. Besides, Natalia bought a commodious four-room apartment in Nizhny for her mother, and the best doctors are now taking care for the health of her lovely little sister, who suffers from cerebral palsy (Samoy stil'noy anglichankoy 2007).

As the dates and times of the headlines show, these texts were published one after the other on the main website of Nashi. In all probability, the same webmaster, or webmasters, posted these texts on the site. At that time the main website included a section "Our news" where these texts were located (since then this section disappeared, but the items were still available after that). The coexistent publication of the reports shows that both texts were considered worth publishing, that is, they were considered important for Nashi's public image during a certain "micro" period (12 November 2007). From the viewpoint of a young person, the Vodianova-text might be more contributive in terms of stimulation than the Kirill-text but not necessarily. The Orthodox Church has been one of Nashi's important agendas, and this sort of citing of religious authority may easily work stimulatively for young people who consider the Church's moral principles important. For instance, explicitly used biblical metaphors and the moralistic discourse in the Kirill-text indicate a sort of "religious and moral stimulation." Indeed, Kirill's message, warning against "dangerous Western liberty" finely resonates with the values of those Orthodox Church believers whom Olga Sibireva calls the "Orthodox subculture." These values include salvation of the soul, patriotism, patriarchal traditionalism including an explicit rejection of the West and Western culture as the domain of the antichrist (2009: 10).

Nonetheless, in terms of the images that these reports mediate it is worth asking to what extent Kirill's world view and the image of "paternal clergyman" match the explicit orientation towards the particular and rather stereotypic representations of "Western success" mentioned in the Vodianova text: the cult of this sexualized supermodel beauty, which is finely expressed by the photo of her attached, consumption, fashion, richness, and individualism? Or, we may ask, to what extent would potential admirers of Vodianova follow Kirill's moral instructions? This evident contradiction and its management can be partially detected in the reports. In the Kirill-report Nashi exhaustively cites Kirill's words, and thus it is actually Kirill who is speaking and warning students of the dangers of Western liberalism. Such quotation allows Nashi to distance its view from the views of the person quoted. In this case, the attached photo of Kirill even underscores his autonomic and authoritative position. This distancing from Nashi's views comes about by explicitly mentioning that this news item was originally produced by the news agency Interfax. It is also worth pointing that Kirill's major concern is sexuality, more profoundly the moral panic about homosexuality, which is lacking in Nashi's web site, except the reports concerning abortion.[91] So, while the issues of sexuality for Nashi are more or less "non-topic", the distancing in question allows Nashi to make its point by supporting Kirill's views without making its own views explicit. Consequently, in the Vodianova report the main character itself is a young

---

[91] On Nashi's website I found 45 reports using the search word "abort" which all condemn them. In general, in all these reports abort are viewed either in the sense of harming traditional values (mainly in relation to religious values), or as an important obstacle for improving the bad demographics of the country. However, in relation to the total amount of Nashi's reports (more than 30, 000) explicit condemnation of abort is relatively marginal.

Russian, and presumably an ideal one who has made her way from "rags to riches." In addition, despite her overwhelming material success "she properly visits her parents." In short, Vodianova is "a good young Russian," successful and morally dutiful.

In the Kirill report the anticipation within the didactic message towards "autonomous" youth is clear, since the Church has been one of those few institutions (with the president and the army) among young Russians that is trusted (Omel'chenko 2006: 18-19).[92] In this respect, the Orthodox Church is an important link between didactics and stimulation, and thus presumably allows Nashi profitably to re-fuse through an overly moralistic message with youth.[93] In the Vodianova text this re-fusion works in the opposite way; from western-global individualistic ideals (stimulation) to "Russian ideals" (i.e. the didactics of a person behaving correctly). After all, the ideological controversy between these reports is clear. In terms of mediated image as parts of Nashi's contribution to its own public image, these two coexistent reports suggest that Western-global signifiers of fashion and individual success are promoted along with views which are strongly against these signifiers. In general terms, the reports' coexistence fits Nashi's eclectic patriotic optimism as distinct from Iduschie Vmeste's moral emphasis and its overall legacy of the Soviet kul'turnost. In other words, for Nashi all those features which supposedly serve "the success of Russianness" are worth mentioning.

The Vodianova-report as Nashi's symbolic product has a wider resonance in Russian society during the last ten years. Larissa Rudova and Birgit Menzel argue that the culture of glamour owes its origins to the politics introduced by Putin to extract Russia from the situation it had found itself in the 1990s (2008: 2): economic disaster, political instability, crime and poverty. In this respect, the image of the rich "new Russians" of the 1990s wearing brightly colored jackets and gold necklaces, often connected with criminal activities, has been transformed into "a hard-working, educated and stylish haute bourgeois

---

92 In 2008, according to a survey by FOM, 62 % of Russians trusted the Orthodox Church (in 1999 this figure was 53 %). Among the age-group 18-35, 56 % trusted the Church. Moreover, 47 % of Russians considered that the Church should have a more visible role in society than it currently does (FOM 2008b).

93 In the Nasha armiia video a combination of the Orthodox Church and youth culture elements was presented by linking a picture of an orthodox priest to a sharp and distorted synthesizor sound (see "The Didactics and Stimulation of "Our Army"").

under the regime of Putin" (ibid.). Menzel continues by arguing that during the Putin era glamour and its "life-style centeredness" (my emphasis and formulation) has become an official ideology in Russia, not just a tactic of "bread and circuses" (2008: 4): Glamour plays a decisive role in the competition for jobs and is promoted by the political elite, especially by the Putin-administration, and as a whole, glamour has become a matter of national pride.

Nashi's devotion to stylization and image is compatible with these larger socio-cultural as well as political trends although it is difficult to say how decisive role glamour plays in Russian politics. Nevertheless, explicit traces of this trend can be found in Nashi's report related to high level domestic politics. In June 2008 Nashi reported on a round-table session held in the Russian Duma on the theme "intellectual youth" and titled "The intellect youth must be fashionable" (Umnaia molodezh dolzhna byt' modnoi 2008). Except for the headline, the text of the report does not mention anything concrete about this up-to-dateness but focuses on the need to pay attention to talented youth in terms of a political reserve. Photos in the report, by contrast, obviously illustrate the "look" and pose of some participants of the round-table session that Nashi considers natural combination of talent and up-to-dateness; fine suits, glasses with light frames or rimless, female beauty as well as self confident faces. In this report, the themes of the round-table session listed are orientated to a more effective utilization of intellectual and talented youth in society than was seemingly the case earlier. From this viewpoint it appears that the association of "intellectual and talent" should become fashionable as such. The devotion to fashion, unarticulated in the report, except in the headline, is similar to the narrated ritual-like strategy in terms of its tokenistic harnessing of the "other" in the service of the "self": Single words, expressions, and concepts which are traditionally regarded as alien to the main (in this case official) discourse are brought in but in a way which relegates these alien elements to a static and stereotypical role. Consequently, this relegation can be seen as an effect of social powers in a ritual-like strategy. In other words, today official politics presumably must include the notion of fashion, which is obviously becoming more important in Russian society than before. At the same time, besides the point that stylishness is intrinsically seen among youth as important it must be attached to "true", that is, official cultural values dictated by "adult"-driven didactic practices. Nashi's special program Shapovalova in the field of fashion is a tangible case in point.

## Shapovalova

In the spring 2008 a young designer and Nashi activist Antonina Shapovalova presented her first collection of youth clothes as part of Nashi's activities.[94] This special fashion section of Nashi was labeled as Shapovalova, and it was described on the website of Shapovalova collections as follows:

55
Despite the point that the collections of Shapovalova are appealing foremost by their rebellious and staggering look, attention should also be paid to the point that T-shirts and design clothes of "SHAPOVALO-VA" are distinct in terms of their original, intellectual, patriotic and socio-politically useful design. In addition, their quality and manufacturing technology are fully capable to compete with the best foreign examples. The familiar writings have already become the most distinguished features. For instance, (these include) the mini-bikinis "Vova, I'm with you!," which were recognized as a hit of the year 2008, or the men's underwear "Russia is not under Entente," topicality of certain themes (the collection of demographic T-shirts "Breeding is nice and useful," "I want three!," "I was told by....mother and father"), as well as a broad and versatile technology used: to print t-shirts the designer uses glitter, thick layers, flocking, boiling, crystal, folio, lens effect, phosphorus, and other less familiar techniques.
The theme of unity and a strong state with a rich and original culture is extremely important in the period of the global crisis. The collections of the designer are trenchant, brash and thus, patriotic.
A real discovery for those who are not afraid of provocations: t-shirts. Some distinguish themselves though their witty figures and writings, others, in contrast, express a sense of pride in the country.
There are many well-known devotees of the brand SHAPOVALOVA who own her clothes in their wardrobes. For example, President of the Russian Federation Dmitry Medvedev, Vladimir Putin, Vladislav Surkov, Sergey Ivanov, governors of different oblasts, business magnates, sev-

---

[94] I am grateful to Maria Petterson for giving me interesting accounts concerning her interview with Antonina Shapovalova.

eral famous performers as well as hundreds of young people from all around Russia (Shapovalova 2010).

These last five paragraphs of the introduction and the promo-text of Shapovalova's fashion project reveal how Nashi's narrated ritual-like strategy sought to handle the inevitable tension which this fashion project creates. A repetitive alternation between didactics and stimulation becomes apparent; by emphasizing, on the one hand, points of the official youth policy with the cultural conformism related to it, and on the other, a sort of "youth culture avant-garde" which this collection supposedly represents. The first paragraph directs the reader towards "deeper" accounts of Shapovalova despite its "rebellious" and "staggering" presentation and look. This shift is justified by labeling these "rebellious" clothes simply as "patriotic" and "original" along with references to their quality, which is compatible with the best of foreign fashion.

In the second paragraph this "true meaning" is elaborated by describing the garments' designations in relation to their function. For example, "demographic t-shirts" with "soft" sexual connotations ("Reproduction is nice and useful" and "I want three")[95], and mini-bikinis with a much more explicit sexual connotation: The text, "Vova, I'm with you!" *(Vova, ia s toboy!)*,[96] is printed on the front of the bikini's bottom half. I interpret this sort of representation as a clear attempt to create "rebellious" and "staggering" associations within a didactic message. It seems that the tokenistic labeling of the clothes as "original" and "patriotic" is nothing more than the adding of certain words to these clothes, whose symbolic (and in all probability economic) value is to be guaranteed by their "shocking" nature.

---

[95] These writings were intensified by using the exact typographic and linguistic adoption with a different verb from the warnings printed, for instance, in Russian cigarette boxes: "Ministry of Health recommends: Reproduction is nice and useful." In general, the visual setting in the catalogue in which this t-shirt was promoted underlined heterosexual normativity, see Appendix 1. Accordingly, this was linked to the official demographic wish (or implicit demand) to increase birthrate also mentioned in the youth policy (Strategiia 2007). The slogan "I want three" refers to the ideal of three children per family, see Appendix 2.

[96] "Vova" is a colloquial name for Vladimir, here referring to the popularity of Vladimir Putin among Russians, especially over his second presidential term, and more profoundly in this context it refers to the reputation of Putin as a sex symbol among Russian women. For more sexual and gendered aspects of Nashi's activities, see Sperling 2012.

In terms of tokenistic labeling, there is an explicit orientation towards the English language which so dominates Western and indeed global advertising and brand promotion, in the very term Shapovalova. It is almost always written in Latin letters and block capitals. A similar textual practice is present in the use of the global trademark sign™ with Shapovalova's brand name (Shapovalova 2010). This aims to re-fuse national identity policy with the valuable global practices in question, and more interestingly, with "Russia" when it is written in Russian. These garments of patriotic fashion are then to be refused, not only with a patriotic position as such, but also, for example, with charity actions on behalf of children (Blagotvoritel'nost segodnia v mode 2008). Nashi presumably recognizes the hierarchies of capitalism's global semiotic practices by using a Western logo, or in Ron Scollon's (2001) terms, "commodity/sign" with the Cyrillic and "indigenous" version of the name *Россия*. Indeed, there is an alphabetical symmetry between the English *Trademark* and the Russian *Торговая Марка*. Shapovalova's "originality" is principally to be found in Western-global youth fashion with its conventions and practices (about "sociolinguistic traveling", see Blommaert 2003). The combination *Россия™* in global youth culture's visual practices (e.g. trendy t-shirts) is believed to have a distinctive ability to conduct a profitable orientation towards both Nashi's communicative demands (didactics and stimulation), and thus to work as a successful ritual-like strategy.

Furthermore, the orientation towards a restricted field of production—and purely in Bourdieu's (1993) sense as communication between producers—is found in the second paragraph of the sample: the special and unusual materials and techniques used in manufacturing clothes are mentioned. For ordinary consumers of textiles as well as followers of fashion this discourse on textile manufacturing does not necessarily say anything. However, this discourse indicates symbolic capital in the field of fashion and clothes. In short, Shapovalova seems to be a professional. Consequently, for other professionals in textiles or "true representatives" of this field of production, in addition to symbolic capital, these words may indicate professional capital and cogency in this field. Shapovalova is a professional, or even an extraordinary producer of clothes (or she is not, depending on the value of these materials among other textile specialists).

In the third paragraph the shift towards didactics is made again, now by brief-ly mentioning the importance of national unity, especially in the context of the global financial crisis.[97] A closure of the sentence with a tokenistic labeling is made by mentioning that the collections of the designer are "trenchant, brash, and thus, patriotic." Following the inevitable tension which this sentence aims to tackle by considering "trenchant" and "brash" clothes as naturally "patriot-ic," in the fourth paragraph it is deemed necessary to admit that these clothes cannot please all: "A real discovery for those who are not afraid of provoca-tions." Here the distinction follows the barrier between "the great ones" and "the small ones" (Chiapello & Fairclough 2002) which was present in Nashi's recruitment video for the army. The final paragraph aims then to prove Shapovalova's importance and brilliance by listing well known contemporary celebrities who have become fans of Shapovalova's clothes. Quite unexcep-tionally, these people are, on the one hand, well known representatives of the didactic framework (including the president and the prime minister) and, on the other, "ordinary" Russian youth.

The point which matters in this promo-text of the designer is the way by which Nashi aims to manage the tension that the aspect of fashion (or image at large) causes for its political communication. This management can be captured in terms of a ritual-like strategy between de-fused representations (youth fashion and official state policies) under the force of social powers (Nashi's socio-political position between the demands of didactics and stimu-lation). A good example of this strategy is the beauty contest under the title "Miss Constitution 2008" organized by Nashi in Vassil'ev square in Moscow in December 2008. The basic idea of the event was to attach female beauty with the "brand" of the Constitution of the Russian Federation. Nashi itself de-fines this attachment as follows in the report dedicated to this event:

56
Each brand has its own face. The movement "NASHI" thinks that the Constitution of Russia, as a state brand, must have its own face, a real image (*obraz*). "Miss Con-stitution" is the embodiment of the best qualities of the state's main law and epoch (Obraz Rossii 2008).

---

[97] This account reveals that the text is written at the turn of 2008-2009 when the global financial crisis hit Russia.

The sample suggests that the constitution did not have its form or "image," and this implicit need is recognized by the nature of the "Miss Constitution" event. The federal commissar Nikita Borovikov, the leader of Nashi after Vassili Iakemenko, elaborates this combination of the constitution and female beauty as follows:

57
"Big global brands are familiar to everyone...each brand has its own face; Sportsmen, models, actors, successful people in general. You see them, and you immediately recognize them. However, there is a brand in which, like in mirror, the state is reflected. This is the Constitution, a state brand. And, today we want to choose a girl who is worth its image. Correct as the letter of the law, clear as the language of the law's chapters, perfect as the formulation of the law's clauses. We want that this competition would become an annual, beautiful tradition of Russia" (Obraz Rossii 2008).

Noteworthy remarks of Borovikov here are "familiar to everyone" and "each brand has," which exhibit the sort of essentialist understanding of global brands and their promotion strategies. This essentialism allows Nashi to adopt the same "natural" practice for the field of state institutions; in this case for the "branding" of the Constitution. Consequently, the given branding follows didactic conditions with the metaphors that, from Nashi's viewpoint, describe both, the winning girl and the law. A singer of a music group who performed at the contest put this as follows:

58
"Russia's youth must have an understanding of state holidays: Victory Day, Day of Russia, Constitution Day...organizers of the event chose a precise format for this event: it is beautiful and informative, it appeals young people and reminds them (of it) and it may become a good tradition" (Obraz Rossii 2008).

Hence, the issue is about the stimulation of a state element which must be known among Russian youth just like other well known national and state holidays.[98] Accordingly, as Borovikov's quote revealed, this stimulation is justified by Western, indeed global, models of branding. Here we see a phenom-

---

[98] The date of the contest is the Day of the Constitution which is one of the new national days in post-Soviet Russia. The first post-Soviet constitution was passed on December 12, 1993, and since 1994 due to the ukase of Boris Yeltsin, it was decided that 12 December would be national holiday. The popularity and importance of this holiday has remained relatively weak among Russians (Den' Konstitutsii 2010).

enon in a Russian local context, which Arjun Appadurai would define as a "scape," in this case a "mediascape" or "ideoscape" (1996): A profitable and valuable practice which is adopted and transformed in different places of the globe. Such adoptions are basically understandable vis-à-vis global trends, but it is definitely worth asking how the actual content of the constitution can be promoted by activities, mentioned in the report, that have hardly anything to do with sections of the constitution; for example, female beauty in the sense of bikinis, cat walks, dancing, or singing? Only exception might be the "intellectual competition" organized in the contest, and probably related to the law (Obraz Rossii 2008).

Ideological and political manipulation could be a possible answer here. In other words, Nashi entertainingly legitimizes the current constitution by directing young Russians away from any potentially dangerous understandings of the constitution which could lead to potential demands from its implementation. Indeed, this has been a repetive agenda for Russia's non-parliamentary opposition over the course of Putin's rule. According to this view, Nashi simply gives "circuses besides bread" in the sense of legitimizing the current political and ideological regime. However, this sort of simplistic interpretation of ideological manipulation is overly restricted, and I think quite distant from the truth. Within this interpretation we should assume that Nashi prefers to downplay the existence of the Constitution since, from the regime's viewpoint, it mentions various "problematic" rights of citizens. Although Nashi certainly aims to legitimize existing state structures, institutions, and symbols among Russian youth, the issue is not just about keeping young Russians "happy" at the expense of the Constitution's dry contents. As a member of the jury of beauty content puts in the report:

59
The image of the Constitution must be slender, dainty and informative, as these girls are. It is necessary to be familiar with the main law of the state, and when the Constitution is as beautiful as here, to become familiar with it is very nice as well (Obraz Rossii 2008).

The issue is about the political socialization of youth via particular communicative choices vis-à-vis global as well as local socio-cultural and political practices. In other words, Nashi recognizes the "cultural necessity" of harnessing practices of youth-driven global cultures to the service of the state-driven didactics in the sense of conducting a ritual-like strategy. However, the outcome of this combination is problematic, and thus potentially "misrecognized" and unsuccessful. In addition to a potential gap among the audience concerning the "natural" combination of female beauty and the constitution, there seems to be a gap in articulating the issue of fashion among the interviewed Nashi activists. The next section examines this issue starting with a short discussion on style among young Russians.

### Shapovalova from Activists' Viewpoint

In a study of young Russians' perceptions of style in the framework of consumption, Serguei Oushakine points out that, in the 1990s, Russian students' discursive construction of the rich new Russian man seemed to follow the cultural logic of Soviet consumption patterns, rooted in the experience of Soviet era shortages (2000a: 115). This means—according to Oushakine's adoption of Bourdieu's concepts of "taste of luxury" and "taste of necessity"[99]—that students could not find a discourse which could follow adequate cultural signifiers, and consequently, which could homologically represent the distinctive economic location of the new rich. As a result, students chose to follow the path of quantitative rather than qualitative representation, that is, "they chose to express the taste of luxury in terms of taste of necessity" (ibid.). Oushakine argues that this feature reflects a bigger socio-cultural situation: The absence of a developed field of post-Soviet cultural production shifts the accent from symbolic production to symbolic consumption (ibid.).

Following Bourdieu's fields of cultural production Oushakine calls the manifestation of this shift "restricted large-scale production" whose "Russian prototype" can be seen in a new Russian man of the 1990s (ibid: 113); the crimson

---

[99] "The taste of luxury" is a feature of the social elite in general (and more specifically, of the particular elites of particular fields), which means more or less absolute domination and capability to conduct felicitous distinctions in relation to one's own habitus. These distinctions are often characterized by various, and at first sight, trivial and qualitatively related distinctions (tastes in design, accents in speech, colors in clothing, etc). At the other end of this classification, among the working class, these distinctions of the elite remain more or less unclear principally due to the lack of economic capital leading to the lack of particular cultural capital related to these elite distinctions. It follows that the ideal way of making distinctions among the working class can be termed "the taste of necessity." That is, to consume what you can consume, and in the event you consume more, this is done in terms of quantity instead of quality (For more, see Bourdieu 1984).

suit with a huge gold-neck chain and a cellular phone in his hand. This original formation of "restricted large-scale" becomes apparent in the highly exclusive position of the new rich of the 1990s in Russia. The goods that this new Russian man consumed were not special, or restricted, in terms of their larger cultural recognition. All Russians knew about the products that the new Russians were consuming but their seemingly endless economic capability to consume these "common" goods of large-scale cultural production was meant to distinguish them from ordinary people (ibid.). In this respect, as Oushakine (ibid.) continues, "students' accent on quantity in their descriptions of the new Russians has its roots in the missing link of the culturally productive field," that is, such forms of communication which could register these features in terms of quality.

This discussion has a certain explanatory force in relation to Nashi's political communication, especially to the missing link between the image and its actual communicative components in the articulation. This missing link became partially apparent in Oleg's, Igor's, and Vadim's views about the Internet, as well as in their views on image. However, it is important to make certain reservations with regard to the concept of "restricted large-scale production" concerning the perceptions of a distinctive style, in the 1990s, in Russia, mentioned by Oushakine. As distinct from the 1990s, during the first decade of 2000s the gulf between new Russians and ordinary, or "poor," Russians, has become more complex among the Russian elite with its know-how of "true glamor" and its brands (Gusarova 2008: 16). In order to keep a distance between it and a growingly "fashion-conscious" (my emphasis and formulation) Russian middle class, the elite has developed new attempts to bolster its status: For example, by searching constantly for luxury brands not yet known to the broader public in order to preserve the system of stratification (ibid.). However, as I pointed out above, despite these attempts by the new "new Russians" and despite the growing gap between rich and poor, in Putin's Russia glamor has become a more common and more middle-class habitual element in general, and is also attached to the issue of national pride (Menzel 2008: 4). Birgit Menzel argues that in addition to the point that "managers have become the designers of the New Russian Patriotism," actual manifestations of this new glamour-driven ideology are "mixtures of the patriotic cult of Russia's past, the glorification of the current post-imperial renaissance, in

which even the Orthodox Church participates in glamorous media performances, and the global Western cult of celebrity" (ibid.).

When I urged Oleg to elaborate on the role of Shapovalova in relation to
Nashi's image, he emphasized its independence from the movement by
pointing out that "Shapovalova is not a special project, we don't have special
projects that would be targeted at organizing the movement's image." Yet, he
added with a laugh that this could be the case. In a more serious vein, for
Oleg Shapovalova is something which is superficial, and not related to "the
true" content of the movement. Nonetheless, a connection between the
movement and Shapovalova was apparent in relation to patriotism, although
Oleg articulated this connection with a slight hesitation: "Shapovalova is the
project for...for the attempt to produce...well, patriotic clothes." This is related
to an attempt to "modify" the militant association which Oleg defined as a typical stereotype of a person wearing patriotic clothes.

Given that Oleg wants to define Shapovalova as an attempt to produce patriotic clothes of good quality which was separate from Nashi, it is worth asking why he did not want this attempt, or project, to be considered part of the
movement's public image. A plausible answer lies in the incompatibility that
Nashi sees between the explicit "look" of fashion, and thus its superficiality,
and the movement's political "content." One strategy which is revealed in
Oleg's elaboration of the relationship between Nashi and Shapovalova, is to
see it as a natural practice used globally. As an example Oleg mentioned a
habit to wear the flag of Great Britain on one's back.[100] In this vein he suggests that Shapovalova is only about putting various state symbols and draw-
ings onto garments of good quality in a fashionable way and nothing more.
Nevertheless, from the viewpoint of the Miss Constitution report, fashion has

---

[100] The origins of using the British flag (or, the Union flag) as a trendy patriotic garment
can be found in the British mod-culture which was a crucial part of the pop-culture in
the second half of the 1960s. Although its use had patriotic dimensions (related, for
example, to the home victory of England in football's World Cup in 1966) various
mocking and non-conformist uses were related to its use as well (see, for example,
Swinging London). Later, for example, British pop-icon, and definite non-conformist
David Bowie has used it in his visual repertoire (See the front cover of his album
*Earthling*). In this regard, Oleg's implicit wish to see the Russian flag in similar connections is rather different, since in Nashi's case this attempt is tightly linked not with pop-
culture and non-conformist practices but with official and highly conformist ideas.

the explicit function to develop national and official political values among youth. For Oleg the connection between these two remains unarticulated.

Igor actually expressed this gap between the form and content with regard to Shapovalova. In addition, he did not try to avoid his negative attitude towards the fashion project, when he mentioned that "he doesn't understand how it is related to our goals and tasks." Moreover, he stressed that he would never wear any clothes of Shapovalova. Vadim, instead, saw Shapovalova within an essentialist framework in which form (image) and content are conflated. For him image is something which essentially strives upwards: "In practice, everyone must have an image, in order to plan, to be, or to become somehow significant," as he pointed out in his interview. He also contrasted this image to an image of each individual (*obraz kazhdogo otdel'nogo cheloveka*) which implies that for him this personal image of everyone is somehow subordinate. In terms of Russia's national image, Vadim mentioned traditional symbols of Russianness—matrioshka, vodka, Kalashnikov, ballet and bears—in an overly critical manner. He pointed out that this situation needs to be changed, and Nashi is linked to this change, or in any event Nashi has not stopped dreaming of a new Russia with its new image. In this regard, it is interesting how positively Vadim saw Shapovalova,[101] since the designer uses exactly these same stereotypic symbols, for example matrioshki and Gagarin.[102]

Vadim also justified the initial function of Shapovalova by referring to foreign examples. In this discussion he wandered rather far from the actual topic. He pointed out that Russians are ashamed to be Russians abroad for no reason since Russia is a great country with a great history with no more, or even less, sins than, for example, Germany and the UK. On the one hand, this implies that matrioshki and other symbols of Russianness printed on Shapovalova's garments are acceptable because Russia is a great country.

---

[101] See Appendides 3 and 4. In his interview Vadim briefly mentioned one of Shapovalova's t-shirts which especially appealed to him. For him this shirt was "one of the coolest" (odin is samykh krutikh) in Shapovalova's shop in the famous department store GUM in Moscow, where it existed up till end of 2008.

[102] Many t-shirts of Shapovalova illustrate an explicit orientation towards Western driven youth fashion by modifying various national symbols into different forms: For instance, in Appendix 3 a half-naked woman in matrioshka with the text "Love Russian" (Liubi russkoe 2010), and Appendix 4, the portrait of Iuri Gagarin drawn by pearl like figures with a phrase "Iura, thanks! Space is OURS" (Spasibo Iura! Kosmos NASH 2010).

And, these symbols are acceptable because of the numerous foreign examples of such practice, on the other. Vadim referred to his (real or imagined) walks in Paris or New York and has a positive view of valued national symbols by mentioning: "And, for me it would be nice if people, after seeing these kinds of clothes from other countries, would like to wear such clothes."

In this light, Shapovalova's clothes are linked to the message that Russia has something more than just those features which construct its supposedly negative image. As Vadim said, "I think this proves that Russia is not just a world power with its planes, tanks, diplomatically, that is with its diplomatic missions takes everything using its oil, gas pipelines, or gold by its currency reserves." Instead, there is, in his words, "culture" and "active and proud youth," and this is where Vadim locates Shapovalova. Finally he framed it by saying that "fashion is for that it lives its own life." This implies that Shapovalova does not have such negative associations as Russia's natural resources seemingly have. Nevertheless, by framing Shapovalova as a thing which lives its own life, Vadim puts fashion into its "autonomous" position which reveals that he does not articulate the difference between fashions as such, and fashions in their actual use. In the case of the latter, Shapovalova is no doubt an explicit example of the political use of fashion.

In sum, Nashi's clear intention to be a part of the recently emerged fashion-driven tendency in Russian political communication has not led it to abandon views which are compatible with Idushchie Vmeste's "true Russian contents" contrasted with, presumably "Western", superficial mimicry. In light of Shapovalova, Nashi harnesses this general and relatively central youth culture tendency (i.e. fashion) but when the movement wants to be a part of this large-scale tendency, it wants to be seen as a separate and restricted sphere. This is tangibly present in the interviewed activists' views concerning image and Shapovalova in particular. This wish to maintain these two as independent from each other but similarly to see combinations between them—that is, a particular fashionable patriotism—as distinctive is a big challenge for Nashi's discursive production of ideal youth. Shapovalova definitely runs the risk identified by Bourdieu when he writes that "original experimentation entering the field of large-scale production almost always comes up against the breakdown in communication liable to arise from the use of codes inaccessible to the "mass public" (1993: 129)." This argument also works vice versa.

An original experimentation entering the field of restricted production (that is youth fashion from the viewpoint of dominating adults' politics) with the aims of state-didactics almost always comes up against the breakdown in communication liable to arise from the use of codes inaccessible to those who want to keep youth culture and its communicative forms away from political and other similar maneuverings. In the next chapter I examine an episode from Nashi's history which illustrates the movement's most intensive attempt to be a distinctive and appealing youth formation, which, however, resulted in an infelicitous way.

# VIII How to be a Distinctive Conformist?

## Emotions as a Communicative Problem

In Chapter four I examined Nashi's and Nashi's predecessor's, Idushchie Vmeste's, central texts which showed the development from Idushchie Vmeste's exhaustive moral panic to Nashi's eclectic patriotic optimism. Nashi's different and more positively valued understanding of the need for a new Russia, and its ideal youth, not only shows a shift away from Idushchie Vmeste's explicit didactics to a more stimulative strategy but that this is also a different discursive strategy seeking to produce emotions. Randall Collins points out that emotions' external effects are particularly important for determining the appeal of social movements to their potential supporters (Collins calls them "conscience constituencies"), which may have preexisting sympathies which emotionally correlate with the movement's aims (2001: 31). In addition, Nashi's ritual-like actions are compatible with Beverly Skeggs's notions of emotional capital in relation to nationalism (2004: 19). She asserts that the aim of accumulating particular "national capital" (my emphasis) is precisely to convert it into a national belonging, to have this accumulated national cultural capital recognized as legitimately national by the dominant cultural grouping. I sketched in section "Values and youth policy in Putin era" that it is rather obvious that many Russians including youth have views similar to those of Nashi concerning national dignity, patriotism, and social and political order, which is manifested, for example, in the support for Putin. However, the fact that these views and their emotions are compatible does not guarantee Nashi's success. Quite contrary, Nashi's repetitive scandals, and the very formation after the failure of Idushchie Vmeste, inform that the pro-Kremlin youth's political communication results in the formations constantly having to balance between various officially related themes (e.g. according to the official youth policy) and, in light of Nashi's examples, relatively controlled hints of youth culture.

Mabel Berezin writes in her discussion of emotions and politics, that what is interesting from a social science perspective is not that we have emotions but the mechanisms that transpose these emotions into some sort of action or institutional arrangement (2002: 37); that is the moments in which we do and do not act emotionally. Hence, from this viewpoint, there is a difference between the moment of emotion (cognitive, private) and the expression of that emotion (social and potentially political). In terms of the latter, Berezin asserts that "codifying, managing, mobilizing emotions transforms them into culturally accepted behaviors, situates them in time and space and, depending upon the context, adds a political dimension to the emotion" (ibid.: 35). This is the central point of this chapter. Instead of focusing on what emotions Nashi produces, my special concern is on how various feelings must be communicated from a particular social position in order to maximize the symbolic capital for one's own activity. It follows that due to Nashi's social and political position its expressions of emotions seemingly be inappropriate for producing a politically correct feeling of national identity.

The previous chapters demonstrated how the balancing between didactics and stimulation appears in selected online writings of Nashi, and how it produces ideal youth within this balancing act. In order to frame Nashi's Bronze Soldier as a central case of the movement's infelicitous communication, let me sketch briefly the most well known—and fatal—action of Idushchie Vmeste.

### Idushchie Vmeste's Book Campaign

In 2002 Idushchie Vmeste organized a campaign "The Exchange of Books" (Obmen knig) whose purpose was to collect "harmful literature" from people and to give various canonical works of Russian classical literature for exchange. The movement's official announcement dedicated to this campaign in March 2002 shows that an important element in Idushchie Vmeste's expression and management of its own emotions—and obvious work for stimulation—was a humorous and carnivalistic exaggeration of its enemies. The earnest description of the supremacy, problem, and moral harmfulness of commercial mass literature for the heritage of the Russian literary tradition at the beginning of the announcement was elaborated piecemeal with taunting details. It was pointed out, for example, that the (harmful) books collected will be not used for commercial purposes but will be returned to the authors. The climax of this mockery could be found in the announcement's footnotes, whose use mimics official-academic style. The footnotes added that the list of harmful authors is formulated "according to the degree of social damage that these writers have upon our society and culture in general." It was also added that there is a reversed coefficient in the case of (Viktor) Pelevin (one book per two of Pelevin's books). Pelevin was one of the main targets of the movements in terms of immoral writers. It was also informed in the footnotes that "tales of Marx" (sochineniia Marksa) will be sent to his "Motherland," to the city of Karl Marx-Stadt (which was the DDR-era designation for the city of Chemnitz). This humorous addition also reveals Idushchie Vmeste's strategy to re-fuse different literary genres—"bad" literary fiction, and "bad" political-economy—both useless to Idushchie Vmeste's Russia.

These trivialities are worth mentioning since the aspect which intensifies the carnivalistic nature of the announcement is that it was related to the cam-paign's official press conference that the movement organized for the media (Obmen knig 2002). This carnivalistic and humorous discourse of the action continued, and the official closure of the action was made by announcing that the books collected have been returned to the authors in sacks with the stamp "To be returned to the author." These included Pelevin and Vladimir Sorokin, probably the best known contemporary writer in Russia in early 2000s. In addition, the movement announced that books from Marx will be sent to any departments of Marxism-Leninism left in the Russian educational system.

"The Exchange of Books" received wide attention in the Russian media, and partially abroad, but clearly in terms which did not meet the move-ment's expectations (Räsänen 2006; Simons 2003). The first scandal appeared when the writer Boris Vassil'ev—who the movement regarded as a good and correct contemporary writer and whose books it offered in the exchange—contracted out of the action. Then the minister of culture, Mikhail Shvydkoi announced in public that "Idushchie Vmeste has no right to define what is good or bad in literature and art, and represent-atives of the political elite must not only contract out of this action but also define it as a provocation against the constitutional rights of the citizens of Russia as well as freedom of speech and expression" ("Idushchie Vmeste" zashli 2002; Pisateli 2002; for a more detailed discussion of this episode in Finnish, see Räsänen 2006).

However, soon after the official condemnation of the action by the minister of culture, the movement made public its open letter to Shvydkoy in which the movement justified its action (Otkrytoe pis'mo 2002). In this letter Iduschie Vmeste asked, "should the state, according to Your view, save its own citizens (especially its youth) and their spiritual world from any encroachment from the "margins"? If this is not the case, then why does the state save citizens from criminals, hooligans, and cursing?" In other words, by equating these qualities Idushchie Vmeste demanded that the state be systematic in fighting against pernicious elements in Russian society and culture. This fighting should not only be the case with criminals and hooligans, but also with these pernicious writers as far as the deeds of criminals, hooligans, and cursing are hardly regarded in terms of freedom of expression. This document partially proved that the movement's emotional commitment seemingly goes beyond official political and cultural sentiments, and this appeared to be harmful for the reputation of the political establishment (See Andreev 2006). In this sense, it is relevant to point out that the general content of Idushchie Vmeste's didactic discourse—its moral concern about youth—largely corresponded with the general conservative tendencies of Putin's regime, as well as Russian society. However, in communicating this conservatism the movement totally failed.

Regardless of the condemnation of the action by the political authorities, Idushchie Vmeste continued its war against "pernicious writers." The main target became Vladimir Sorokin, whose "pornographic" novel "Light blue grease" (*Goluboe salo*),[103] and especially his libretto for the play "Rosenthal's children" (*Deti Rozentalia*)—which it was announced would be performed in the most sacred place of Russian theatre, the *Bolshoi*, in Moscow, in the summer 2002—were too much for the movement. Idushchie Vmeste's reaction included the already familiar mockery, but even more intensively: Activists of the movement threw torn up works of the writer into a huge toilet made of pasteboard in front of the Bolshoy Theatre (Debutatov vozbudilo 2002; Bol'shoi teatr 2005; Räsänen 2006; Simons 2003). After this incident, Putin's advisor at that time, Sergei Iarzhemskii announced that "Sorokin can be compared to those depressed writers, Mandelshtam, Solzhenitsyn, Pasternak, Brodsky, and there is no need to go back to those times" (Räsänen 2006: 43). Perhaps an even more harsh defeat for the movement than explicit distancing

---

103 The word "light blue" is a generally used designation for homosexuals in Russian.

of the Kremlin from the action was that during the episode the sale of Sorokin's books rose dramatically (ibid.).

Idushchie Vmeste's book campaign can be termed as a sort of "emotional didactics," an instructionally driven demand for correct values and norms in which various negative emotions are constantly expressed. In other words, the key strategy in the description of these harmful, amoral, pernicious, pornographic, etc. features (e.g. events or figures) is the vilification of "the other" instead of the elaboration of the supremacy of "us." Its supposedly stimulative value is based on the assumption of the effectiveness of exaggerating "the other" in highly negative terms. The action was definitely compatible with the need to create enemies through the use of negative examples (see "Our Army"- video above), as Andreev defined the features of the movements' passionarity (2006). Nashi's most well known action exhibits clear similarities with Idushchie Vmeste's book campaign. Before moving to examples from Nashi's Bronze Soldier, I briefly discuss the important origins of this communicat-ive practice.

During the late 1970s and early 1980s in the underground artistic circles of Leningrad, a special cultural and communicative practice was created which is known by the Russian slang term *stëb*; a peculiar form of irony that differed from sarcasm, cynicism, derision, or any of the more familiar genres of absurd humor (Yurchak 2006: 249-250; Yurchak 2008). Alexei Yurchak writes that stëb "required such a degree of overidentification with the object, person, or idea at which this stëb was directed that it was often impossible to tell whether it was a form of sincere support, subtle ridicule, or a peculiar mixture of the two" (2006: ibid.). He asserts that this original artistic practice developed due to, and in the context of late socialism when the whole of Soviet society with its authoritative discourse had become immutable, ubiquitous, and highly normalized, or "hypernormalized" (ibid.: 252) In addition to the "overidentification"[104] with a particular symbol (or object), that is the precise and slightly grotesque reproduction of the authoritative form (e.g. slogan, official

---

[104] According to Parker the concept of "overidentification" is a concept drawn from the armoury of psychoanalysis but forged by cultural activists in the political art collective Neue Slowenische Kunst into a weapon against Tito Stalinism, and contemporary neo-liberalism. Overidentification works because it draws attention to the way the overt message in art, ideology, and day-dreaming is supplemented by an obscene element, the hidden reverse of the message that contains the illicit charge of enjoyment. Slavoj Zhizhek in particular has applied the concept of overidentification in his works (Parker 2005).

speech, visual image etc), the stëb procedure involved the "decontextualisation" of that symbol; placing this form in a context that is unintended and un-
expected for it (ibid.). A noteworthy point in the use of stëb was that its practi-
tioners refused to define stëb as a protest against the official regime (ibid.:
250-251). Instead, "the aesthetic of stëb avoided any political or social concerns or straightforward affiliation with support or opposition of anything"
(ibid.). For example, the famous underground artistic and cultural movement
in Leningrad that time, Mit'ki, turned their whole lifestyle into a grotesque socialist-realist representation of Soviet life with its official optimism which
turned into a complete lack of problems, concerns, and goals (ibid.: 253). Another group, the so-called "necrorealists," went further by adapting the raw bi-
ological vitality of the socialist-realist hero but dissociating it from meaning,
speech, and personhood (ibid; Yurchak 2008).

One might ask how these esoteric underground artistic formations of the
late Soviet era can be related to Nashi and its predecessor (principally pursu-
ing conservative and conformist ideology). The first important point is that the
aesthetics of stëb practices was not limited to these esoteric artistic groups
but, according to Yurchak, became truly wide-spread among the young people of that time, that is, among "the last Soviet generation" (Yurchak's definition) (2006: 259). This point alone hardly explains the use of stëb-like features in the communication of the post-Soviet Idushchie Vmeste and Nashi as
a potential recent historical relic. Nevertheless, its familiarity beyond restricted
and marginalized circles gives grounds to assume that stëb-like features re-
appeared after the hypernormalized and authoritative Soviet framework had
disappeared, although now with new functions. The second point is linked to
stëb's ambiguity. One general difficulty is in defining whether it is a protest, a
form of support, or both. For example, even among the various peer-groups
of Komsomol activists—despite their position as official representatives and
"guardians" of official political and cultural practices—the use of stëb was a
common practice during the 1980s (Yurchak 2006: 259).[105]

---

[105] The example that Yurchak offers here is a birthday congratulation to a Komsomol activist by his colleagues written according to the discursive elements of the official Soviet directive (ukazanie) but which is actually full of carnivalistic and humorous elements (2006: 259-264). Without knowing the Komsomol context of this practice, this
could be read as a creative mockery against the political authorities. Yurchak's interpretation of this fun is that this "directive" did not simply ridicule authoritative discourse
but rather decontextualize authoritative forms—showing the general performative shift

Furthermore it is reasonable to take into account the role of the actor in the case of public political communication as distinct from the publicity of certain artistic groups or the internal meetings of political groups (e.g. the Komsomol in the footnote above). As Idushchie Vmeste's book campaign illustrated with its carnivalistic, or "stëb-like," elements, they were definitely meant to function as protests which would vilify the movement's enemies. With this strategy Idushchie Vmeste definitely aimed to receive symbolic capital in the attention space in which it acted. However, the perception of the movement's symbolic production was indeed ambiguous, as is typically the case with the use of stëb. Thus, the use of stëb as an anticipation of symbolic capital was seen by Idushchie Vmeste as an advantageous choice to demonstrate its emotional commitment, but due to the movement's socio-political position this strategy failed. Let me now examine how Nashi reacted to the decision of the Estonian authorities to remove the Soviet era Bronze Soldier statue from the central Tallinn district of Tônismäe to Tallinn's military cemetery in late April 2007. See also Mijnssen's (2012) valuable contribution to this theme as well.

### Nashi's Bronze Soldier

The relocation of the Soviet-era statue "The Bronze Soldier" from the central Tallinn district Tônismägi to the Tallinn's military cemetery by Estonian authorities in late April 2007 offered, from Nashi's viewpoint, a brilliant platform to demonstrate the importance of, and its emotional commitment to, this event.[106] Within its larger context, the episode activated simmered memory politics disputes between Russia and the former Soviet republics and satellites (notably Estonia, Latvia, Ukraine and Poland) in the most dramatic form since the re-independence of the Baltic States in 1991. The central focus in

---

in official discourse which occurred during late socialism—with unanticipated meanings whose initial value lay in their creativity (ibid.: 264).

[106] The Bronze Soldier is the informal name of this highly controversial Soviet World War II war memorial in Tallinn. Originally the statue was named "Monument to the Liberators of Tallinn" which was unveiled on September 22, 1947, three years after the Red Army reached Tallinn on September 22, 1944 during the Second World War. Its original location, a small park on Tônismägi in central Tallinn (during the Soviet years the place was called Liberators' Square), consisted of a burial site of thirteen Red Army soldiers' which were reburied there in April 1945. For more, see "Bronze Soldier of Tallinn"; a detailed discussion of this episode with regard to Nashi, see Mijnssen (2012).

these debates has been inter-pretations of the Second World War and its consequences for Eastern Europe. In the case of the Bronze Soldier in Estonia, a notable addition to this memory politics background was played by Estonia's Russian speaking population whose attitudes toward Soviet era have been much warmer than Estonian speakers' (See, for example, Laitin 1998). In this regard, Russia's patriotic response to the removal of the statue generally regarded Russian speakers in Estonia as compatriots in this episode.

In terms of expressing particular emotions for political purposes, Mabel Berezin's point, "codifying, managing, mobilizing emotions transforms them into culturally accepted behaviors, situates them in time and space, and depending upon the context, adds a political dimension to the emotion," conforms perfectly to Nashi's Bronze Soldier (2002: 35). The injustice that official Russia expressed toward the removal appeared to Nashi as a chance to make possible the re-fusion of the domestic concern with "fascism," and historical and nationally relevant external fascists. That is, a combination of the concern about growing domestic ethnic crimes and their political implications, Russians' generally growing engagement with national dignity over the last fifteen years, and the outrage against the violation of a symbol of the most consensual and important pillar of Russian national identity, "The Great Patriotic War" (Kozhevnikova 2006: 87; Dubin 2001; 2004; 2011; Gudkov 2002; Gudkov & Dubin 2006). In short, the fight against contemporary fascism as a social problem shows its legitimacy through one of the nation's major historical achievements, namely the "Great Victory" over fascism in 1945. In order to refuse this value with the present on the basis of a commonly shared threat, it follows that contemporary "fascists"—all those who call this victory into the question—aim to tarnish this value, in this case "Estonian fascists." Despite seemingly weak coherence between these two—the national patriotic policies of the Baltic States and violent attacks against those who do not look like Russians in Russia—Nashi seemingly believed that this would work as a strategy to distinguish itself within the nation's anger against Estonian history and memory policies. The Bronze Soldier became the most intensive activity of the movement. The archive section of Nashi's website before the version of November 2009 (the last one before the movement's demise in 2012) included more than 1,300 reports in which Estonia was mentioned, principally in negative terms (these items were available in the new version, as well).

Nashi's official response, the "ultimatum," to the statue's removal began as follows:

60
**The date for the demolition of the Estonian embassy building in Moscow has been decided**
The federal commissar of the Movement Nashi, Vassili Iakemenko announced the date of the demolition of the Estonian embassy building in Moscow: June 12, 2007. As it was pointed out in the official announcement of the Movement Nashi, "it is necessary to find out possibility to remove the embassy of the fascist Estonia into another, more suitable place according to the law (*imenno v ramkakh zakona*) (Opredelena data 2007; Ofitsial'noe zaiavlenie 2007).

Such an account of a social movement, expressed with explicitly official language but whose content is deeply absurd, raises a question of its seriousness. The headline of this report followed by the announcement of the movement's leader Vassili Iakemenko mimics the stëb-like overidentification and decontextualization of the object. The Estonian authorities had announced a few days earlier—obviously with official bureaucratic language—that the statue would be demolished /removed from its original location.[107] Nashi then shows its own moral outrage by overidentifying the object. At the same time, the goal of the action for which this official language informs definitely decontextualizes the object: "the date of the demolition of the Estonian embassy building is June 12, 2007." In terms of political ritual, this date explicitly illustrates Nashi's attempt to attach a particularly patriotic and supposedly unifying element to the Independence Day of Russia (currently *Den' Rossii*), which is celebrated on June 12. This recently established holiday has remained relatively strange to many Russians (as the Day of Constitution, see samples 56-59 above), and the usage of the date here exhibits Nashi's willingness to promote its weak reputation.

---

[107] These terms clearly illustrate the struggle over meanings and their interpret-tations between the official Estonian and Russian sides during, and after, the episode. The Estonian side systematically emphasized the verb "to carry" (viima), largely used in the passive (See Pronkssôdur 2014). The Russian side, instead, interpreted this as a violent action, not only in symbolic, but concrete terms as well. This is because the use of the term "demolition" is intrinsically seen as the preceding stage of removal. In other words, the statue must be first demolished, only then can it be removed. For example, the Russian version of the Bronze Soldier in Wikipedia used exclusively the term demontazh (See Bronzovyi soldat 2014).

However, while the use of stёb could be an effective strategy in terms of mocking a particular political establishment and its practices, in the case of a pro-state movement that promotes official patriotic policies, stёb seems to be a highly tentative strategy. In terms of protesting, it is evident that Nashi is against the Estonian official interpretation of the Second World War and its consequences (the Soviet-era as an occupation), resulting in a particular history politics toward the statue. Yet, Nashi's response suggests that the movement's commitment to the theme is so intense that the communicative forms used in this protest risk the content of their political message. In this case, it is in order to ask whether Nashi truly believes that it can demolish and remove the embassy building, or if it is sufficient that the audience believe it can accomplish such a goal.

This announcement was related to Nashi's major anti-Estonian rally. The one-week blockade of the Estonian embassy in Moscow in late April and early May 2007 was followed by hundreds of anti-Estonian rallies in different parts of Russia over the course of that year. These rallies illustrate Nashi's obvious willingness to identify itself as a true defender of Russia's national values, especially patriotism and the official narrative of Russia's "great history." From the viewpoint of the tension between didactics and stimulation, this "anti-Estonian intensity" explicitly challenges the balance between Nashi's communicative demands. While the emotional commitment of the rallies was often expressed via stёb- like elements (explicit stimulation), this pursuit challenges the limits of correctness linked to didactics. This balancing within the attempt to distinguish itself from official instances is present in the "ultimatum" from Nashi's leader Vassili Iakemenko (the sample above is the first paragraph of it). What follows that slightly grotesque decontextualisation of the demolition/ removal action is the emotionally loaded request from all (citizens of Russia) to comment on and pay attention to this issue:

61
Each citizen, no matter his or her position must answer the question: Has he or she done everything so that historical justice has been redressed. We must remember that if this [removal of the embassy] will be done, it will be an unconditional victory over neo-fascism, victory over trampling on memory. This act of political will by particular citizens, the leadership of the country as a whole, shall be the most important step for the further political and moral rebirth of Russia (Opredelena data 2007).

While Iakemenko's vision of Nashi appears to be a re-fused community based upon Russia's national dignity, he clearly reserves a vanguard role for Nashi in this potential re-fusion by mentioning "certain citizens" (Nashi) before "the leadership of the country as a whole," and by demonstrating the movement's sacrificing position in relation to the political regime, as the rest of the report reveals:

62
Collecting signatures for the support of OUR decision to demolish the embassy goes on. More than 100,000 Muscovites and guests of the capital have signed the ultimatum. Hundreds of thousands of Russians in tens of cities of the country—in Nizhny Novgorod, St. Petersburg, Penza, Volgograd, Krasnodar, and in many others—have joined the action.

Today at approximately 4 pm, the commissar of the movement Nashi, Alexander Salikov, tore down the Estonian flag from the embassy building. This was a single initiative by Alexander, the appearance of his civic position and demonstration of his attitudes against the activities of the Estonian authorities. Alexander Salikov and also two of ours, Dmitry Olenin and Aleksei Smirnov, were arrested by the officers of the OMON and carried to the Presnenski militia department (Presnenskoe OVD). Ours were held in the militia department for more than three hours, and after that they were released. Each commissar received a 500-rouble fine due to the violation of administrative law. After three hours, more than 200 activists of the movements Nashi and Young Russia arrived, and after the release of the activists they all went back to demonstrate in the front of the embassy.

The demonstration around the Estonian embassy has continued for five days around the clock. At the moment more than 250 activists from the movements Nashi, Young Russia, and Locals are attending the demonstration in the Malyi Kislovskiy Lane (Opredelena data 2007).

The grotesque, stëb- like headline of Iakemenko's ultimatum is strength-ened by this description of Nashi's persistence in collecting signatures for the ultimatum. The description follows Nashi's common practice of its online-writings described in previous chapters: to blur its name ("ours") with the playing of the Russian possessive pronoun; the task of "Ours" is our (Russia's) task. In the second paragraph, the description of the arrest of the activists clearly draws its social and political value from the practice and discourse of the field of restricted cultural production—that is, a culture of practices that stand against official conformism. The civic position (*grazhdanskaia pozitsiia*) that the movement generally represents according to the framework of the large-scale cultural production (respect toward law and order) is now contrasted with the self-denial of an activist. In other words, a true civic position is contrasted to formal laws. Nashi's willingness to report on this incident in detail explicitly shows how it potentially risks its own status as a pro-government and conformist movement. In the following excerpt, the movement wants to remind the reader about this legal and conformist side of its activities:

63
**Unknown people threw stones at the Estonian embassy building**
Last night an unknown person threw stones at the Estonian embassy building. As a result the glass of one window was damaged and two windows were cracked. According to participants, the stones were thrown by few people from the neighboring house. After seeing the hooligans, our commissars with activists from Young Russia and the Locals tried to catch them. However, the provocateurs could not be caught. The movement Nashi officially announces that our activists have nothing to do with this incident. We are not announcing the first time that we act according to the law exclusively (Neizvestnye zabrosali 2007).

This report is strikingly different from the purposefulness of explaining the moral obligation to break laws in the name of protesting the violation of sacred national values (tearing down the Estonian flag on the territory of the embassy). In all probability, the reporting of a stereotypical act of hooliganism (throwing stones)—no matter by whom—offers Nashi an opportunity to compensate its relatively unrestrained, and presumably stimulative, nationalistic sentiments by making a reminder of its engagement on the official side of society. It follows that in this episode Nashi's highly emphasized symbolism seemingly causes effects that risk its own position as a movement loyal to the Kremlin and official policies. In addition, it risks its position as a serious movement, as "the ultimatum of the demolition/removal of the Estonian embassy building according to the law" illustrates. The intention to keep this ultimatum alive is realized through stëb- like activities, for example, by erecting stands for posters in various areas onto which local people can write or draw their anti-Estonian comments. These stands were guarded by Nashi "commissars" wearing World War II-era Red Army uniforms (Vladimir: Liudi gotovy 2007). In probably the clearest example of full parody, Nashi urged local people in the town of Kovrov to ask whether they were infected by "the horrible virus called eSStonian fascism," and then cordially announced that "the majority of Kovrovians were not infected, and did not need antifascist vaccination" (Kovrov: Spasatel'nyi ukol 2007).

The first big challenge for Nashi's persistent interest in the Bronze Soldier theme was to redeem the explicitly emotion-laden ultimatum to demolish/remove the Estonian embassy building from its current location. At the deadline of the ultimatum, Russia's Independence Day on June 12, 2007, Nashi made public the following report:

> 64
> **Let it stand. So far...**
> More than a month ago the statue of the Soviet soldier-liberator was removed in Tallinn. A part of Estonian society—only a part—stood against this by active protests. Defenders of the statue were killed and thrown into jail, but still fascist Estonian authorities managed to receive victory. The statue was destroyed and the grave of the fallen buried under the monument defamed.
> During protests around the Estonian embassy, we suggested to demolish the Estonian embassy building and to remove it to a distant district of Moscow in order that it will not disfigure the historical outlook of the capital. We approached authorities of all levels. We asked thousands of people. However, it seems only few people in the society are ready to forcefully defend the memory of the fallen as well as stand against reinterpretations of the Second World War. And, in order to avoid even deeper division in the society, it was decided not to start the demolition on the date that was announced.
> Fascist authorities in Estonia decided to remove the statue—and they removed it. In Moscow, however, the fascist embassy still stands; so far. As a symbol of not-readiness, many people agree that the memory of the fallen is sacred. As a warning of our indecision and inconsistence in many things concerning our country and the great pages of its history, due to the 1990s, that will disturb us in the future, as well, when we defend our Motherland not only in big things, but in small things, too. And it necessarily becomes the guarantee of defeats in the future, not only of our conscience but of our memory, as well. Let it stand. So far (Pust' stoit 2007).

Despite the serious international consequences of this episode, not only between Russia and Estonia but also between Russia and the European Union (Haukkala 2007), nothing as absurd as demolishing and removing the Estonian embassy was likely to happen. Especially in terms of the original ultimatum, in which the issue was not only about the demolition and removal of the embassy in metaphorical terms, but principally the demolition/removal of the embassy building. Furthermore, although the European Union largely condemned Russia's official reaction, during the peak of the episode one can find critique toward Nashi from instances of Russia's official voices, as well. On May 7, 2007, the Russian analytical pro-governmental journal *Ekspert* explicitly criticized Russia's "unsystematic," "pathetic," and "ineffective" response to

Estonia's defamation of "our sacred values" and attempts "to demolish the Yalta world order by turning Russia the liberator into Russia the aggressor" (Novaia Ialta 2007). "Hooligan activities by the representatives of Nashi" were mentioned as a concrete example of this failed response. That is no wonder since no matter what Nashi's ultimate goals in its ultimatum were, the fact that the embassy remained where it was (an outcome that was more than predictable) meant Nashi suffered a symbolic loss.[108] Consequently, this loss must be redeemed somehow. This redemption was done by showing Nashi's self-denial and persistence in setting a goal of organizing hundreds of rallies. Although this goal was not achieved, Nashi's failure was projected onto others by using a blatantly Soviet sounding account, according to which only a part of the Estonian society[109] actively protested the removal, and then by accusing all of Russian society. Thus, Nashi first wanted to highlight its intention to defy the "conformist integration" of society by bravely protesting against the defamation of society's memory. However, the actual symbolic loss (the failure of the ultimatum) is redeemed by pointing out that Nashi did not conduct this ultimatum because it did not want society to become even more fragmented. In the last paragraph Nashi moves back to showing the experienced injustice and "imbalance" by repeating the bluster of the headline but also reminding Nashi's consciousness of potential, subsequent violations of Russia's values. Now Nashi clearly speaks from its "independently constructed didactic position" that presumably allows warning society regarding its passivity, as a

---

108 Interestingly, despite "the official voice of the Kremlin," the newspaper Rossiiskaya Gazeta (RG), wrote intensively about the Bronze Soldier from a highly patriotic point of view during the peak of the episode (119 articles in which the word "Estonia" was mentioned between April 15 and June 15, 2007), it referred to Nashi's activities only twice. The first was an article about Nashi's ultimatum and "patriotic persistence" ("Nashi" fakty na ikh argument," May 3, 2007 and the second was an article about Nashi's demonstration for the release of its activist Mark Siryk "Nash Mark—Aktsiia," May 5, 2007. There were no mentions after the deadline of the ultimatum. Thus, although RG's rare mentions of Nashi show its clear support, the small number of overall mentions suggests that Nashi did not have a special role in the general patriotic response that this episode launched.

109 This view implies that Estonia would be still part of Russia without mentioning Estonia's demographic division between Estonian and Russian-speaking people, and without specifying who was actually for and against the removal of the Bronze Soldier in Estonia.

legacy of the 1990s, in terms of the witnessed and potentially forthcoming defamations of "our Motherland."

The important aspect in this redemption of symbolic loss, as well as in later anti-Estonian rallies and reports, is the use of innocent victims. According to Randall Collins, these victims must not only be innocent, but must also be emblems of the movement's dedication or be quickly converted into such emblematic material (2001: 33). This is vividly present in the beginning of the sample above, in which Nashi blatantly inflates the consequences for the part of Estonia that defended the statue by arguing in the past tense passive that "the defenders of the statue were killed and thrown into jail." The latter statement is more or less true despite its propagandistic tone. The Estonian authorities did arrest hundreds of people during "the Bronze night," but only one confirmed human loss took place, the death of a Russian-speaking Estonian student, Dmitry Ganin (Bronze Night 2010; Dmitri Ganin 2010). Ganin's death received wide publicity in the Russian media, but Nashi was the vanguard in terms of his martyrdom. By September 2009, 150 reports could be found on Nashi's website using the search word *Ganin*. In many of these reports— following the ritual-like strategy—Dmitry Ganin was explicitly re-fused with victims of the Great Patriotic War. The following report from the city of Tula, published on the first anniversary of Ganin's death, is an example of this:

65
**Tula: Commemoration Day of Dmitry Ganin**
Today commissars of the movement Nashi gathered on Victory Square to lay flowers at the statue for the fallen in the wars. Exactly a year ago, Dmitry Ganin was killed in Tallinn when he was defending the honor of Russia and the memory of the heroes who fought in the Great Patriotic War. Youth gathered on the square to take part in the mourning event dedicated to the anniversary of his death.
We have not forgotten the events in Estonia. We continue to collect signatures for the "Bronze book" against the "black lists." We won't surrender but, on the contrary, will become more confident day by day of our justness. History cannot be rewritten. The Bronze Soldier, despite standing no more in Tônismägi Square, will always remind of the country that beat fascism (Tula: Den' pamiati 2008).

Ganin's death brilliantly illustrates the importance that innocent victims have for many social movements, and how these victims become martyrs. This occurs because the victims are taken to represent the moral power of the movement. They symbolize the feeling that the movement will ultimately win out (Collins 2001: 32-33). For Nashi, actively protesting for Mark Siryk,[110] one of Nashi's Estonian–Russian activists, who was arrested and charged in the Bronze Night riot, illustrated this power of being right. However, Ganin intensifies this feeling because for Nashi, he proved the justness of its cause by his death, and thus he functions as an ideal martyr. In this regard, the important dimension in Ganin's martyrdom is its link to Nashi's platform of emotional commitment and ritual-like re-fusion. From Nashi's view-point Ganin's death can be naturally re-fused with the sacred memory of the fallen of "The Great Patriotic War" and the honor of the country, as well as the Russian youth. One also sees a change in Nashi's persistence on this theme after the failed ultimatum for the removal of embassy—and Nashi's reorganization. Now Nashi collects signatures for a special "Bronze book" that is somewhat the counterpart for Estonia's black lists for Nashi activists travelling to the Schengen area (Molodezh: sub'ekt ili ob'ekt 2008).

**Aftermath**

At the end of January 2008 the newspaper *Kommersant* wrote that Nashi would cease to exist in its current form and would be radically re-organized. In addition to the Moscow central office only of Nashi's fifty regional sections five (seemingly the most active) were allowed to continue their work (Vladimir, Ivanov, Tula, Voronezh, and Iaroslavl') while the rest will be shut down. According to the *Kommersant*, one reason for this reorganization was the negative attitude of the forthcoming president Dmitri Medvedev (Medvedev had been elected as the candidate for the presidency of the party United Russia in December 2007) towards the movement, and even Putin had begun to consider that Nashi had become a problem for Russia's relations with the West. An important role in this explanation is the fact that several of Nashi's activists had received a travel ban to the Schengen area (actually to the countries of the EU) as a result of an initiative of the Estonian authorities after the Bronze Night riot. Another possible reason for the reorganization concerned the loss of charismatic and central leaders of the movement: Vassili Iakemenko had been nominated to the head of the State youth committee, and Sergei

---

[110] In the latest version of Nashi's website, one could find eighteen reports about the case of Mark Siryk.

Belokonev, became a member of the State Duma, and later the Duma representative on youth issues. A third view underlines Nashi's irrelevance: The acute threat of the "Orange Revolution" was over (see Stanovaia's points in Chapter 3; about the "Orange Revolution" and Russia, see Umland 2010; Mijnssen 2012), and Nashi was no longer needed. Finally, from the viewpoint of the closed regional sections (e.g. Saint Petersburg) the Kremlin was not satisfied with their ineffectiveness at mobilization ("Nashisty" ukhodiat tikho 2008; "Nashi" stali chuzhimi 2008).

Although *Kommersant* was definitely right concerning the reorganization—it really took place—it is not worth speculating further what was, or were, the actual reasons for it in terms of political decisions. In light of this book, I suggest that the aspect of political communication can reasonably be seen as the central reason for Nashi's failure. In relation to Idushchie Vmeste's book campaign Nashi's key episode show similarities that can be conceptualized as the incapability to conduct symbolic production that would be felicitous in, and from, their social-political position. An illuminating example in relation to Nashi's attempt to consolidate, as well as prove its importance, in the changed situation, is present in a report, given in January 2008 (Molodëzh: sub'ekt ili ob'ekt 2008). It begins with a formal and official description of the session and its participants with a description of the topics discussed. When Nashi, the Bronze Soldier episode and its consequences (travel ban to the Schengen zone) come into the picture, the description changes into an "our" description, that is, a positioning against those, who are labeled simply as "adults." The report states that "adult politicians attempted to stonewall this issue but youth did not allow this, the commissars of the Movement "NASHI" demonstrated around the Estonian embassy almost one month, not allowing society to forget this problem" (ibid.). Nonetheless, in terms of the discussion's forum mentioned in the report (the Public Chamber of the Russian Federation) as well as the key participants of the session, it is obvious that former key members of Nashi, Iakemenko and Belokonev, are, in their current position, more than close to those Nashi describes here as "passive nonyouth," that is, adult politicians. Within the tension between Nashi's new position (after the reorganization in January 2008) and the new position of its former key members, Nashi presumably aims to identify itself with the whole of youth, as if Nashi is Russian youth. In relation to other "progressive" youth movements (i.e. those who attended the embassy blockade), the movement defines its own position as the vanguard of the movements (with the typical language game between the brand name and possessive pronoun): "After OURS the movements Young Guard, Young Russia, and Locals supported this initiative" (ibid.).

The relevance of Nashi's Bronze Soldier is principally in those communicative practices that it used in producing its own model contribution to this particular event. Moreover, it represents a clear continuation from Idushchie Vmeste's Book Campaign, not only in terms of communicative practices, but of their consequences as well. Both episodes also have interesting connections to the perestroika-era discussion on the democratization of socialism, and in general, the limits of glasnost. While perestroika was a centralized plan of the Communist Party to rebuild the socialist system with the help of glasnost—which eventually made the system's ideological crisis apparent—the grass-roots "glasnost" of Idushchie Vmeste and Nashi on the basis of the official framework (state supported conservatism and patriotism) had effects that the Kremlin regarded harmful for its own "perestroika" (Lassila 2010; see the comprehensive discussion on youth during perestroika in Pilkington 1994). Of course, the socio-political context between Idushchie Vmeste and Nashi, and the last years of the Soviet Union, and the scope of the consequences of the actions involved are crucially different. Nevertheless, in terms of political communication the issue of appropriate limits regarding youth's political role show certain similarities. In addition, here the political and ideological positions are reversed in comparison with perestroika: While it can be argued that during perestroika the democratization of socialism was not enough for the Soviet people, Idushchie Vmeste's and Nashi's "passionate" engagement with official values seems to be too radical for the officially sanctioned, or politically correct, patriotism (See Lassila 2011b). This relatively narrow and imaginery comparison shows, after all, the incompatibility between those who possess power and those who want to be involved in this power but cannot convey the themes of power (e.g. official ideas) appropriately.

In terms of Bourdieu's symbolic/cultural production the movements' challenge in expressing politically correct emotions in its socio-political position can be illustrated as a challenge of converting particular, subjectively perceived emotions into profitable "objective" emotions. A good example is given by Sara Ahmed in her discussion of "affective economies" (2004). Analyzing an example picked from the Aryan Nations website, she points out that "it is "love" for the nation that makes white Aryans "hate" those whom they consider as strangers, as the ones who are taking away the nation and the role of the Aryans in its history, as well as their future" (ibid.: 117-118). Although Ahmed's example is relatively extreme, it is far from extraordinary in how it produces a sort of "fantasy of ordinary through particular emotional work" (ibid.).

From this standpoint the question is what kind of communicative and symbolic conversion is socio-culturally legitimate? In terms of Nashi's role as an anti-Orange political formation, the movement's political discourse can be approached in terms of challenges that arise when a state-conformist and regime-maintaining social movement tries to conduct a "ritual-like strategy à l'Orange" in the context of post-Orange Russia. That is, the creation of a community that was able to accomplish its ultimate goal: changing the regime. For Nashi, the central challenge is how to transform the political glory of an oppositional force into a political glory of existing political conformism around official policies. In this respect, a relevant Russian counterpart for Nashi is one of its major opponents, the National Bolshevik Party (NBP), during Nashi's early years. The NBP has appeared as one of the most scandalous, controversial, but also aesthetically well-known youth movements in post-Soviet Russia. The National Bolsheviks have largely received their reputation—not least by the creativity of their leader, writer Eduard Limonov—through various theatrical performances and actions, and this is partially due to the fact that there is no ideological or "substantive" catechism that would explain the political guidelines of the NBP (Sokolov 2006: 147). In terms of political style, this means that the NBP's sovereign position in the oppositional field, that is the field of restricted cultural production, allows almost any kind of combination for the sake of symbolic capital. Whereas NBP's activities appear in the periphery in relation to the conformist center, it can be assumed that the accumulation of the NBP's symbolic capital can be strengthened by its illegitimacy in the field of large-scale cultural production. As Mikhail Sokolov writes, "politics for the NBP is principally a form of creative self-expression that allows simultaneous and effective use, for instance, of Nazi-officer Ernst Röhm or Che Guevara in terms of maintaining old, and mobilizing new supporters" (ibid.). In short, the whole political style and image of the NBP can be seen as an emphatic mockery of its enemies and exaggeration of goals by "overidentifying" and "decontextualizing" them. Although such stëb- like strategy risks the reputation of the movement as well, the NBP's position guarantees its success for the movement. While there is an explicit link to the Kremlin policies in Nashi's political position—totally unlike the NBP—it seems that it is Nashi's didactic position that is "water" for the potential "fire" of youth culture resonating political aesthetization (stimulation).

The Bronze Soldier is an illuminating case of these challenges. Regarding the growing patriotic and nationalistic sentiments in Russia's public opinion during the last ten years (Dubin 2001; 2004; 2011; Gudkov 2002; Gudkov & Dubin 2006), along with the large-scale apoliticalness of youth, it becomes partially understandable why Nashi uses so much energy for promoting patriotism. There is a clear patriotic potential in the population, among youth in particular, and this potential must be utilized. For Nashi, however, as a conductor of official policies, the main problem is how this potential could be utilized within the creation a cogent public image for the movement.

Nashi's supposedly profitable communicative strategy to re-fuse these defused social powers is an adaptation of stëb, seen as ultimately independent in relation to political contents. Stëb appears purely as an expressive tool, a form of "political technology," on the basis of models that have been used in totally different political positions (the Orange side in Ukraine, or NBP's carnivalistic fascism in Russia). Regarding the potential effects that stëb- like strategies have caused for the public image of pro-Kremlin groups, and partially for the conditions of their sustainability, there seems to be a lack of self-reflection in their political communication. Stëb-like activities of Idushchie Vmeste, within its book campaign in the name of freedom of expression and for the sake of "correct moral values" led to consequences that were opposite to those desired and intended. They included disassociation by the Kremlin and the growing popularity of the accused writers. Consequently, Nashi's outrage toward the demolition/ removal of the Bronze Soldier was converted into an absurd ultimatum for the demolition of the Estonian embassy, as well as for creating new emblems of Russian patriotism and nationalism, celebrating the martyrs linked to the event, and later suggesting various officials rename streets for these martyrs (Uvekovechim pamiat' 2007). It is obvious that

Nashi's stëb- like activities around the Bronze Soldier were not valued arguments against the political elite's decision to reorganize Nashi in early 2008. Or, these activities were one of the central reasons for the reorganization, since Nashi's bad image had become, in part and from an international perspective, Russia's bad image.

# IX Discussion

In 2002, the Russian sociologist and current director of the Levada Center, Lev Gudkov, argued that there is no process of true development in Russia in terms of functional differentiation in society, social networks, or new mechanisms of institutionalization (2002: 6). Instead, he identified the process in Russia as the "disintegration of the previous (i.e. Soviet) institutional system in which various quasi-traditional structures and formations figure as compensatory mechanisms to this disintegration," and labeled this process as "traditionalizing modernization" (traditsionaliziruiushchaia modernizatsiia). Gudkov argued that the issue is about the adoption of the new (in this case Western), which in turn fulfills the aims of the traditional and routine ideology (ibid.: 6-7). In terms of national identity, this process is manifested as a "contradictory structure of identification" on two levels. The first level contains values from the Soviet era (superpower-oriented mobilization and nationalism), while the second contains views of peaceful and normal life, "a vague prototype of civil society" (ibid.: 7).

Though one should avoid taking Gudkov's notion of the contradictory structure of identification too literally, his views are nevertheless not outdated in early 2014. Today Gudkov's argument sounds perhaps too generalizing, or at least too premature, in judging the Russian society as a society which lacks true development and constructive social networks. Rather, the emerged distrust of the regime since late 2011 shows that political expectations are becoming more pluralistic in Russia. Yet, this plurality does not prove that the society has become less conservative, or less reliant on traditions than it was in 2002. What it shows, however, is that the political supply on the basis unity, state patriotism, or societal stability in a sense of "competitive alternativelessness" faces growing difficulties in satisfying multiple societal demands. As a pro-regime representative of Gudkov's "traditionalizing modernization," Nashi can be seen in a double role. On the one hand, Nashi's political communication has pointed at general challenges of the Kremlin's symbolic politics well before the movement's main patron was forced to take up the gauntlet in late 2011. On the other hand, the movement's communication has shown how a political performance in the situation of citizens'—particularly the youth's—non-compulsory political engagement comes about under the compulsory need of societal and political distinction. In other words, although Putin's Russia has been anything but politically free, at least the citizens have had the freedom to be politically indifferent, and Russia's youth has certainly been "active" in this regard. Whereas political apathy and indifference at large has certainly helped the Kremlin to sustain its electoral authoritarian rule (see e.g. Gel'man 2013), the citizens' political indifference has hindered any symbolic support to the regime as well. Nashi's symbolic production of ideal youth has been at the core of this dilemma; to activate youth socially and politically but not to stimulate them beyond the pre-determined pro-regime track.

The controversy between progressivity and conservatism makes a notable addition to Nashi's rocky and often scandalous search for its "distinctive conformism" between state didactics and youth's stimulation. Conservatism became hallmark for Idushchie Vmeste, whose progressivity largely relied on the Soviet-type of moral enlightenment against pernicious influences in youth culture. If there were any attempts to update the Soviet legacy of kul'turnost for Russia's youth of early 2000s, they vanished in the movement's moral didactics. Nashi, instead, has paid much deeper attention to its communication by actively harnessing these "pernicious" elements for the movement's conservative, and didactic, basis. As this book has shown, Nashi's symbolic investment to a progressive and vanguard image has resulted in anything coherent or clear-cut. Furthermore, along with the protests in 2011-12, core supporters of Putin manifested themselves as those who are against any progressivity in terms of political changes. A tangible case in point is an interview of a young female supporter of Putin in the documentary film "Winter, Go Away!", which depicts protest activities from a grass-root perspective in Moscow in that winter: She justifies her support to Putin and the regime by mentioning her modest, "non-progressive," position, and unlike the opponents of Putin, "whose life is completely perfect," she does not know how her life might become "more difficult if there will be another president"; that is why she cannot oppose Putin (Zima, ukhodi!, 2012). Although the range of political and societal views among Putin's supporters is certainly wide, this comment illustrates how a major division between progressivity and conservatism came to the fore in Russia's sudden political activation in 2011-12. Within this activation, the symbolic pro-regime progressivity, headed by Nashi and other pro-Putin youth formations years before the winter, became quickly associated as the most desperate guardians of the stagnant regime.

Nashi's ultimately counter-productive communication prompts to ponder peculiarities that the study has raised in relation to larger post-Soviet socio-symbolic practices. In his study of post-Soviet Russian nostalgia Serguei Oushakine extends Roman Jakobson's views regarding linguistic aphasia (2007; 2000b). According to Oushakine, difficulty in finding adequate signifiers for new situations in Russia—similar to what Jakobson describes in terms of "expressive aphasia"—is compensated for through "the use of extensive manipulations with the elements available within adopted visual or textual borders" (2007: 467). In addition, "elaborate rituals of the combination of borrowed signs become the main condition and the main content of symbolic production, but, at the same time, the open-ended selection of new tools and materials is drastically diminished" (ibid.). In this vein, through their reliance on Soviet-era "harmonious reports," Nashi's repetitive online writings fit Oushakine's definition: the usage of various symbolic combinations occurs within a narrow range of discursive tools. In short, it seems that almost anything can be combined, but these combinations strongly rely on socio-culturally familiar elements despite various contexts of their use.

For example, a Nashi report on blood donation with a photo of Nashi volunteers in a Russian town in front of a Lenin statue and entitled "Donor-heroes", demonstrates Oushakine's "symbolic aphasia" (Donory-geroi 2007). Both signifiers—the term "donor-heroes" and the statue of Lenin (although only with the text of Lenin in the photo)—activate practices related to the Soviet-era volunteer work. At the same time, because Nashi's ideological position as a post-Soviet modernizer simultaneously espouses a view that downplays Soviet-era political symbols,[111] such symbolic manifestation is clearly contradictory. The "aphatic" aspect in this case comes about in the way of gathering at

---

[111] It seems that for Nashi everything that can be re-articulated as symbols of the Soviet-era geopolitical greatness are actively used, especially, the commemoration of the Great Patriotic War. See Mijnssen's study in this respect (2012). However, Lenin as a purely political symbol of the Soviet Union with its political dead-end is to be avoided. This anti-communist activity was intensively present in many of Idushchie Vmeste's activities.

a place in a town which in all probability still figures in a central role socially (i.e. the familiar meeting place), but this significance is derived from its political meaning in the recent past (the statue of Lenin in a Soviet town). Thus, it seems that culturally familiar and appreciated practice of donating blood, a common practice in the Soviet Union, is symbolically produced in relation to culturally familiar symbols of this practice, that is, Soviet-era volunteerism and Lenin.

Two further aspects in Nashi's political communication illustrate this point: First, the constant use of the term "commissar" for active members of the movement, and second, the Internet-domain *su* (Soviet Union) for Nashi's official website (see also Mijnssen 2012: 58). According to Igor, the principal reason for the *su*-domain for Nashi's web-address was simply due to the fact that the address nashi.ru already existed, and hence a new domain was needed. From the viewpoint of symbolic capital, Igor's explanation for the *su*-domain was more revealing: "First of all, "su" is expensive,"[112] which implies that it is more prestigious than the "cheap" *ru*- domain. This symbolic value obviously redeems the ideological disadvantages related to the *su*- domain. Nashi's obvious intention is to add generally known cultural symbols and discourses to own "unique" projects by labeling different stylistic choices with regard to particular ideological denominators (e.g. antifascist activists use antifascist hairstyles). Thus, from Nashi's viewpoint, a counter-culturally driven choice should provide a stimulative potential for its ideological position, as if this choice would be a freely floating form without any ideological content, and, more precisely, without any ideological-historical constraints. In this case, the hairstyle which is generally related to anti-conformist activities, would automatically become an effective symbol for the ideologically conservative movement.

The Bronze Soldier incident offers a vivid example of Nashi's intention to attach generally known, or widely discussed, symbols and themes, to new contexts—that is, decontextualizing them after they are recontextualized. After the statue was moved to the Tallinn military cemetery, several Nashi activists traveled to Tallinn to stand around Tônismäe—the area where the Bronze

---

112 According to Igor in May 2008 the *ru*-domain cost approximately 8-10 dollars per month, while the price of the *su*-domain was approximately 90 dollars per month for the user.

soldier was located. They labeled themselves "living statues" (i.e. living Bronze Soldiers), wore World War II-era Red Army uniforms, and carried Nashi flags. In addition to these overly emotional and, from Nashi's viewpoint, sacrificial commitments to the theme, Nashi organized highly symbolic welcoming ceremonies for the "living statues" at the Moscow railway station for returning activists expelled by the Estonian authorities (Zhivye pamiatniki 2007).

To frame these "aphatic" features of Nashi's communication with Gudkov's general notion of traditionalizing modernization, Nashi's political communication follows the tension Alexei Yurchak identifies in his work on symbols and brand names in post-Soviet space (2000: 414): "first, in order to break the past they (the semiotic and linguistic choices) must be strikingly new and familiar. Second, to be able to draw on the forms of the symbolic capital from the past and present they must be experienced as recognizable and meaningful" (ibid.). For Nashi and Idushchie Vmeste the result is a kind of "aphatic novelty" in which symbolic components of a message are generally known but the way how these components are brought together within political pro-regime activities is completely new, if anything but successful. Perhaps the most radical case has been the usage of stëb, or stëb-like practices, a particular form of humour that originated from politically indifferent underground circles of the period of the late socialism.

This book has demonstrated that stëb, more commonly associated with oppositional activities (see Lyytikäinen 2014), applies to pro-governmental and conformist Nashi (and Idushchie Vmeste) as well. If the usage of stëb figures as a kind of carnivalistic substitute for the opposition's helplessness under the more or less authoritarian regime, what about Nashi and other pro-regime formations then which are also apt to use similar symbolic practices? Nashi's insurmountable need to be distinctive in youth's attention space has been my primary explanation to this question which is based on Bourdieu's ideas of differently positioned forms of cultural production. In short, in order to receive success for your symbolic choices, and communication in general, these choices must be balanced with the societal expectations defined by various power struggles in the given society. Only true elites can deviate from these expectations and thus define potential future expectations for lower levels (or classes). Nashi has not been an elite in this regard; rather a paradigmatic case of Bourdieu's representative of the middle class who desperately anticipates not only a taste of the elite (Bourdieu 1984), but of youth culture as well.

We may conclude that the inarticulate nature of Nashi's political communication in terms of the relationship between image and political message cannot result in anything but controversy. Yet further research is required to determine why symbolic and semiotic choices in favor of a particular image are not articulated as part of political and social activities. My preliminary explanation for this is twofold. On the one hand, this unarticulatedness stems from the legacy of Soviet information practices which contain belief in a "mathematical" transmission of messages on the basis of the sender's thought. It follows that forms used for the message are seen completely secondary. On the other hand, as the activists' views concerning the Shapovalova project showed, they preferred to see the issue of image in relation to fashion as separate, or "restricted," from the "true" ideological content. In this regard, it is worth asking: is there a sort of lacuna between idealized monolithic political content (as in the Soviet Union) and extremely fluid and dynamic "glocalized" semiotic forms (the post-Soviet space)? Is this fluidity of forms seen as an expressive freedom from the politically dogmatic Soviet past, which is attached to politico-ideological contents that draw from Soviet (hegemonic) political practices? Nashi's political communication suggests that this has been the case. Time will tell to what extent this applies to political activism at large within the decreased legitimacy of Putin's rule.

# Bibliography

## Sources from Nashi

Blagotvoritelnost' segodnia v mode (published 2 June 2008, 15:44), available at http://www.nashi.su/news/25049 (accessed 17 January 2014).

Briansk: Tochka kreativa (published 31.5.2007, 14:12), available at http://nashi.su/news/18540 (accessed 17 January 2014).

Donory-geroi, a photo of Nashi's action, originally available at http://www.na shi33.ru/gal/details.php?image_id=2820 (accessed and printed 15 June 15 2007, not available anymore).

Doroga svobody startuet (published 11 August 2007, 17:20), available at http://nashi.su/news/20046 (accessed 17 January 2014).

Doroga svobody: Velomarafon zavershilsia v Moskve, (published 25 August 2007, 16:52), available at http://nashi.su/news/20093 (accessed 17 January 2014).

Doroga svobody: Zhara i plokhie dorogi Kostromskoy oblasti razzadorili uchastnikov velomarafona (published 15 August, 2007 18:45), available at http://nashi.su/news/20055 (accessed 17 January 2014).

Estonskii gosfashizm (reports found by using this searchword), originally available at http://nashi.su/news/archive/type_rus/search_госфашизм (accessed 2 March, 2010, not available anymore).

Estonskii gosudarstvennyi vandalizm (published 13 January 2007, 15:59), available at http://nashi.su/news/10932 (accessed 17 January 2014).

Iaroslavl': "NASHI" sobiraiut "pampersy" dlia detey-invalidov (published 16 March 2008, 19:53), available at http://nashi.su/news/23474 (accessed 17 January 2014).

Iaroslavl': Neobkhodimoe delo (published 16 March 2008, 19:49), available at http://nashi.su/news/23473 (accessed 17 January 2014).

Iaroslavl': Sanitary russkogo iazyka (published 19 March 2007, 16:35), available at http://nashi.su/news/14796 (accessed 17 January 2014).

Innovatsionnyi boi vremen Velikoi Otechestvennyi voiny (published 21 July 2008, 16:31), available at http://nashi.su/news/25644 (accessed 17 January 2014).

Kaliningrad: Uznaem sami, rasskazhem drugim (published 19 November 2007, 19:18), available at http://nashi.su/news/22492 (accessed 17 January 2014).

Kaluga: Ekstrim "po-NASHEMU" (published 25 November 2006, 17:51), available at http://www.nashi.su/news/9185 (accessed 17 January 2014).

Kaluga: Nashi ZA klassicheskuiu literaturu (published 28 August 2006, 19:46), available at http://nashi.su/news/5054 (accessed 17 January 2014).

Kondopoga: A ty znaesh Kondopogu? (published 16 March 2008, 19:02), available at http://nashi.su/news/23460 (accessed 17 January 2014).

Kovrov: Spasatel'nyi "ukol" esStonskogo fashizma (published 28 May 2007, 18:16), available at http://nashi.su/news/18436 (accessed 17 January 2014).

Kursk: Chernyi kvadrat vmesto svastiki (published 22 September 2007, 16:36), available at http://nashi.su/news/20632 (accessed 17 January 2014).

Livny: urok patriotizma dlia gimnazistov (published 16 March 2008, 18:51), available at http://nashi.su/news/23455 (accessed 17 January 2014).

Liubi russkoe (t-shirt), originally available at http://nashi.su/shop/card/389 (accessed 24 February 2010, not available anymore).

Manifest, originally available at http://nashi.su/manifest (accessed 4 February 2010).

Manifest s kommentariami, originally available at http://nashi.su/manifest/comments (accessed 4 February 2010).

Mitropolit Kirill predupredil liberalov ob ogne apokalipsisa (published 12 November 2007, 13:43), available at http://www.nashi.su/news/22279 (accessed 17 January 2014). Molodëzh: sub'ekt ili ob'ekt, vot v chem vopros (published 31.1.2008, 15:14), originally available at http://www.Nashi.su/news/23216 (accessed and printed February 23, 2010, not available anymore).

Moskva: Afrika feat. Aziya na Urokakh Druzhby (published 27 November 2006, 14:45), available at http://nashi.su/news/9554 (accessed 17 January 2014).

Moskva: Rytsarskoe posviashchenie patriotov (published 16 March 2008, 19:24), available at http://nashi.su/news/23463 (accessed 17 January 2014).

Naryshkino: Chto ty khochesh molodezh? (published 16 March 2008, 18:59), available at http://nashi.su/news/23459 (accessed 17 January 2014).

Nasha armiia video (2007), available at http://www.youtube.com/watch?v= v6AV3zPP9VQ (accessed 17 January 2014).

Natsional'nyi institut Vyshaya Shkola Upravleniia, available at http://www.vshu.ru/ (accessed 17 January 2014).

Neizvestnye zabrosali kamniami zdanie estonskogo posol'stva (published 3 May 2007, 06:46), available at http://nashi.su/news/17142 (accessed 17 January 2014).

Nizhny Novgorod: Velikiy i moguchiy! (published 30 June 2008, 23:36) available at http://www.nashi.su/news/25555 (accessed 17 January 2014).

Obraz Rossii (published 12 Decmeber 2008, 17:07), available at http://www.nashi.su/news/26048 (accessed 17 January 2014).

Ofitsial'noe zaiavlenie Dvizhenie "NASHI" po povodu istecheniia sroka ultimatum Estonskomu pravitel'stvu (published 1 May 2007, 19:22), available at http://nashi.su/news/17063 (accessed 17 January 2014).

Opredelena data demontazha zdanii Estonskogo posol'stva v Moskve (published 1 May 2007, 22:58), available at http://nashi.su/news/17098 (accessed 17 January 2014).

Parizh: Narodnaia partiia s narodnym dvizheniem (published 19 March 2008, 20:14), available at http://nashi.su/news/23478 (accessed 17 January 2014).

Priazha: Davayte znakomitsia (published 16 March 2008, 18:57), available at http://nashi.su/news/23458 (accessed 17 January 2014).

Professiia zhurnalist. Istoriia uspekha (published 16 March 2008, 19:06), available at http://nashi.su/news/23462 (accessed 17 January 2014).

Pust' stoit. Poka... (published 12 June 2007, 23:30), available at http://nashi.su/ news/19015 (accessed 17 January 2014).

Reforma vysshego obrazovaniia Rossii (Nashi activist Makar Vikhliantsev's views on the Russian education at the nashi33.ru-site, 22 March 2006 (printed 5 February 2008, not available anymore).

Riazan: Black & White party (published 29 October 2006, 08:08), available at http://nashi.su/news/7562 (accessed 20 January 2014).

Riazan: Rossiiskoe obrazovanie—luchshee v mire! (published 29 June 2007), available at http://nashi.su/news/19582, (accessed 20 January 2014).

Riazan: Voina s estonskoi produktsiei must go on (published 29 May 2007, 20:00), available at http://www.nashi.su/news/18449 (accessed 20 January 2014).

Rihanna, promo dlia "Rated R," originally available at http://nashi.su/inte resting/28252 (accessed 22 February 2010, not available anymore).

Rybinks: Vmeste—protiv fashizma (published 16 March 2008, 17:55), available at http://nashi.su/news/23469 (accessed 20 January 2014).

Samoi stil'noi anglichankoi priznana urozhenka Nizhnego Novgoroda (published 12 November 2007, 14:28), available at http://www.nashi.su/ news/22285 (accessed 20 January 2014).

Saransk: Zhurnalisty dolzhen umet' manipulirovat' (published 29 November 2007, 17:06), available at http://nashi.su/news/22815 (accessed 20 January 2014).

Shapovalova (2010), originally available at http://www.shapovalova.ru/#/histo ry, in January 2014 the text available at http://www.justfollowme.ru/sha povalova? iframe=true&width=900&height=450 (accessed 20 January 2014).

Smolensk: Chistaia ulitsa (published 22 April 2007, 19:55) available at http://nashi.su/news/16508 (accessed 17 January 2014).

Spasibo, Iura! Kosmos, NASH! (t-shirt), originally available at http://nashi.su/ shop/card/435 (accessed 24 February 2010, not available anymore).

Tula: Bronzovaia kniga kak pamiat' o podvigakh geroev (published 16 March 2008, 18:56), available at http://nashi.su/news/23457 (accessed 17 January 2014).

Truth about Nato, (published 3 April 2008, 13:25), available at http://www.na shi.su/news/23738, 22.2.2010 (accessed 17 January 2014).

Tula: Den' pamiati Dmitriia Ganina (published 26 April 2008, 12:32), available at http://nashi.su/news/24286 (accessed 17 January 2014).

Tver: Zhurnalisty BBC proveli otkrytyi master-klass v Nashei shkole molodykh zhurnalistov (published 30 June 30 2006, 13:34), available at http://nashi. su/news/4781 (accessed 17 January 2014).

Umnaia molodëzh dolzhna byt' modnoi (published 9 June 2008, 19:51), originally available at http://www.nashi.su/news/25218 (accessed 17 January 2014).

Uvekovechim pamiat' o geroe (published 6 June 2007, 13:44), available at http://www.nashi.su/news/18719 (accessed 20 January 2014).

Vive la resistance! (published 5 March 2008, 18:08), available at http://www.nashi.su/news/23416 (accessed 20 January 2014).

Vladimir: Druzhestvennyi desant v Petushkakh (published 31 January 2007, 17:10), available at http://nashi.su/news/11961 (accessed 20 January 2014).

Vladimir: Liudi gotovy k piketirovaniiu (published 1 May 2007, 13:51), available at http://nashi.su/news/17143 (accessed 20 January 2014).

Vladimir: Patriot do konchikov nogtey (published 11 March 2007, 14:07), available at http://nashi.su/news/14394 (accessed 20 January 2014).

Vladimir: Pricheska kak grazhdanskaia pozitsiia (published 18 June 2007, 18:19), available at http://nashi.su/news/19188 (accessed 20 January 2014).

Voronezh: Snova v nashem zale net pustogo mesta (published 16 March 2008, 18:40), available at http://nashi.su/news/23454 (accessed 17 January 2014).

Vorotynsk: "Bronzovye soldaty" na ulitsakh goroda (published 16 March 2008, 19:11), available at http://nashi.su/news/23461 (accessed 17 January 2014).

"Zhivye pamiatniki" dobralis' do Moskvy (published 11 June 2007, 10:28), available at http://nashi.su/news/18945 (accessed 17 January 2014).

"29-ia stat'ia Konstitutsii ne narushena (published 28 July 2010, 23:40), available at http://nashi.su/news/32520 (accessed 20 January 2014).

**Sources from Idushchie Vmeste**

Aktsiia zavershena: Knigi vernulis avtoram (published on March 2002), originally available at http://www.idushie.ru/rus/document/press/books2/fin al/index.php (accessed and printed 9 November 2007, not available anymore).

Generalnaia uborka Rossii (Idushchie Vmeste 2001), originally available at http://www.idushie.ru/rus/about/activity/actions/uborka/index.html (accessed 1 February 2010, not available anymore).

Iduschie Vmeste 7 May 2001, originally available at http://www.idushie.ru/p hotos/actions/7may2001/index.php (accessed 1 February 2010, not available anymore).

Miagkii prigovor za zverskoe ubiistvo (published October 2007), originally available at http://idushie.ru/rus/document/press/surov/index13.php (accessed 15 February 2007, not available anymore).

Moral'niy kodeks chlena organizatsii "Idushchie Vmeste", originally available at http://www.idushie.ru/rus/about/kodeks/index.php (accessed and printed February 15, 2007, not available anymore).

MY PROTIV KORRIDY! (published on September 2001), originally available at http://idushie.ru/rus/document/press/corrida/index.php (accessed 15 February 15 2007, not available anymore).

Obmen knig (Aktsiia po obmenu knig zavershena, published on February 2002), originally available at http://www.idushie.ru/rus/document/ press/books2/index.php (accessed 30 May 2007, not available anymore).

Otkrytoe pis'mo ministerstvu kul'tury (published on January 2002), originally available at http://www.idushie.ru/rus/document/letters/ministru/index.php (accessed 9 June 2007, not available anymore).

Pamiatka "Idushchemu", Idushchie Vmeste 2001, originally available at http:// idushie.ru/rus/about/Pamiatka/ (accessed 12 June 2007, not available anymore).

**Sources from the Media**

Bolshoi teatr: v libretto Sorokina opery "Deti Rozentalya" net pornografii, *Newsru.com*, 3 March 3 2005, available at http://newsru.com/cinema/03 mar2005/opera.html (accessed 15 May 2012).

Deputatov vozbudilo libretto, *Kommersant*, 3 March, 2005, available at http://www.kommersant.ru/doc/551975 (accessed 17 January 2014).

Flesh-mob protiv flesh-mobov?, *Novaia Gazeta*, 1 April 2008, available at http://www.novayagazeta.ru/society/40863.html (accessed 17 January 2014).

"Idushchie Vmeste" zashli slishkom daleko (2002), *Radiomaiak.ru*, originally available at http://old.radiomayak.ru/archive/text?stream=society&item =1361 (accessed 11 August 2009).

Ivanov, Dmitry (2005), "Idushchie Vmeste nastupili na grabli," *Lenta.ru*, 23 February 2005, available at http://www.lenta.ru/articles/2005/02/23 /young/_Printed.htm (accessed 17 January 2014).

Komsomol'skaia Pravda (2005), Lider "Nashikh" Vasili Iakemenko: My za suverennuiu demokratiiu. Za svobodnogo cheloveka v svobodnoi strane, 26 October 2005, available at http://www.ufa.kp.ru/daily/23602/46035/ (accessed 17 January 2014).

Nash Mark, *Rossiiskaia Gazeta*, 5 May 2007, available at http://www.rg.ru/2007/05/ 05/mark.html (accessed 24 January 2014).

"Nashe" inter'viu, Aktsija online (2007), Svetlana Maksimchenko, 31 March 2007, available at http://www.akzia.ru/politics/31-03-2007/1740.html (accessed 17 January 2014).

"Nashi" fakty na ikh argumenty, *Rossiiskaia Gazeta*, 3 May 2007, available at http://www.rg.ru/2007/05/03/nashi.html (accessed 24 January 2014).

"Nashi" stali chuzhimi, *Kommersant*, 29 January 2008, available at http://www.kommersant.ru/doc.aspx?DocsID=846635 (accessed 17 January 2014).

"Nashikh" zakryvaiut, *Gazeta.ru*, 6 April, 2012, available at http://www.gaze ta.ru/politics/2012/04/06_a_4151693.shtml (accessed 17 January 2014).

"Nashisty" ukhodiat tikho, *Fontanka.ru*, 28 January 2008, available at http://www.fontanka.ru/2008/01/28/053/print.html (accessed 17 January 2014).

Novaia Ialta, *Ekspert*, 7 May 2007, available at http://expert.ru/expert/ 2007/17/demontazh_bronzovogo_soldata_editorial/ (accessed 17 January 2014).

Pisateli i Minkul'tury kritikuiut aktsiiu "Idushchikh vmeste" po obmenu "vrednye" knigi na "poleznye," *Newsru.com*, 21 January 2002, available at http://www.newsru.com/russia/21Jan2002/knigi.html (accessed 17 January 2014).

Putin i burundiki, *Lenta.ru*, 28 July, 2011, available at http://lenta.ru/articles/ 2011/ 07/28/seliger/ (accessed 20 January 2014).

Putin ejects Kremlin 'puppet master' after protests, *The Guardian*, 27 December 2011. Available at http://www.guardian.co.uk/world/2011/dec/27/vladi mir-putin-ejects-vladislav-surkov (accessed 20 January 2014).

Putin's Kiss (documentary film by Lise Birk Pedersen, 2011), more information available at http://putinskissmovie.com/index.html (accessed 20 January 2014).

Putin Says U.S. Is Undermining Global Stability, *The New York Times*, 11 February 2007, available at http://www.nytimes.com/2007/02/11/world/europe/11munich.html?pagewanted=all&_r=0 (accessed 23 January 2014).

Russians Plant Flag on the Arctic Seabed, *The New York Times*, 3 August 3 2007, available at http://www.nytimes.com/2007/08/03/world/Europe/03 arctic.html (accessed 23 January 2014).

Savina Ekaterina, Taratuta, Iulia & Shevchuk, Mikhail, Kratkii kurs istorii dvizheniia "Nashi", *Kommersant*, 29 January 2008, available at http://www.kommersant. ru/doc/846750 (accessed 20 January 2014).

Shevchuk, Mikhail & Kamyshev, Dmitry, Obyknovennyi "Nashizm," *Kommersant* 21 February 2005, available at http://www.kommersant.ru/doc/ 549170 (accessed 20 January 2014).

Vladislav Surkov naznachen vitse-premerom, *Lenta.ru*, 27 December 2011, available at http://lenta.ru/news/2011/12/27/surkov/ (accessed 20 January 2014).

Za "Nashu" pobedu, *Moskovskii Komsomolets*, 18 December 2006, available at http://www.pressmon.com/cgi-bin/press_view.cgi?id=1990441 (accessed 20 January 2014).

Zapadnye kompanii otkrestilis' ot foruma "Seliger", *Grani.ru*, 14 September 2010, available at http://www.grani.ru/Politics/Russia/m.181675.html (accessed 20 January 2014).

**Literature**

Aksiutina, Olga (2002), Vlast i kontrkultura v 1980-e-90-e gody. *Kultura i vlast v usloviakh kommunikatsionnoi revoliutsii XX veka*. Forum nemetskikh i rossiiskikh issledovatelei. Moskva: "Airo-XX", 303-334.

Ahmed, Sara (2004), Affective Economies. *Social Text 79*, Vol.22, No. 2: 117-139.

Alexander, Jeffrey C. & Mast, Jason L. (2006), Introduction: symbolic action in theory and practice: the cultural pragmatics of symbolic action. *Social Performance: Symbolic Action, Cultural Pragmatics, and Ritual*. J.C. Alexander, B. Giesen, J.L. Mast (eds.), Cambridge University Press, 1-28.

Alexander, Jeffrey C. (2006), Cultural pragmatics: social performance between ritual and strategy. *Social Performance: Symbolic Action, Cultural Pragmatics, and Ritual*. J.C. Alexander, B. Giesen, J.L. Mast (eds.), Cambridge University Press, 29-90.

Althusser, Louis (1971), Ideology and Ideological State Apparatuses. *"Lenin and Philosophy" and Other Essays*. Monthly Review Press, available at http://www.marxists.org/reference/archive/althusser/1970/ideology.htm (accessed May 15, 2012.

Anderson, Benedict (2006), *Imagined Communities: Reflections on the origin and spread of nationalism*. New Edition. London: Verso.

Andreev, Dmitry (2006), Fenomen molodëzhnoi "upravliaemoi passionarnosti" i vozmozhnye stsenarii ego perspektiv. *Molodëzh i politika*. Moskva: Biblioteka liberalnogo chteniia 17. Moskovskoe biuro fonda Fridrikha Naumanna, 49-61.

Appadurai, Arjun (1996), *Modernity at Large: Cultural Dimensions of Globalization*. Minneapolis, MN: University of Minnesota Press.

Atwal, Maya (2009), Evaluating Nashi's Sustainability: Autonomy, Agency and Activism. *Europe-Asia Studies*, Vol. 61, No. 5: 743–758.

Berezin, Mabel (2001), Emotions and Political Identity: Mobilizing Affec-tion for the Polity. *Passionate Politics: Emotions and Social Movements*. Jeff Goodwin & al, (eds). Chicago & London: The University of Chicago Press, 83-98.

Berezin, Mabel (2002), Secure states: towards a political sociology of emotions. *Emotions and Sociology*. Jack Barbalet (ed), London: Basil Blackwell, 33-52.

Blommaert, Jan (2003), Commentary: A sociolinguistics of globalization. *Journal of Sociolinguistics* 7/4, 2003: 607-623.

Blum, Douglas W. (2006), Russian Youth Policy: Shaping the Nation's State Future. *SAIS Review* vol. XXVI no. 2 (Summer-Fall), 95-108.

Bode, Nicole & Makarychev, Andrey (2013), The New Social Media in Russia: Political Blogging by the Government and the Opposition. *Problems of Post-Communism*, №2 (March/April), 60:2, pp. 53-62.

Bourdieu, Pierre (1984), *Distinction. The Social Critique of the Judge-ment of Taste.* Harvard University Press.

Bourdieu, Pierre (1991), *Language and Symbolic Power.* Polity Press.

Bourdieu, Pierre (1993), *The Field of Cultural Production.* Polity Press.

Bourdieu, Pierre (1996), *The Rules of Art.* Stanford University Press.

Bronze Night (2014), available at http://en.wikipedia.org/wiki/Bronze_Night (accessed 20 January 2014).

Bronzovyi soldat (2014), available at http://ru.wikipedia.org/wiki/Бронзо вый_солдат (accessed 20 January 2014).

Bronze Soldier of Tallinn (2014), available at http://en.wikipedia.org/wiki/Bro nzeSoldier_of_Tallinn (accessed 20 January 2014).

Buchacek, Doug (2006), *Nasha Pravda, Nashe Delo: The Mobilization of the Nashi Generation in Contemporary Russia.* M.A. thesis, University of North Carolina, Chapel Hill.

Bushnell, John (1999), Paranoid Graffiti at Execution Wall: Nationalist Interpretations of Russia's Travail. *Consuming Russia: Popular Culture, Sex, and Society Since Gorbachev.* A.M.Barker (ed.). Durham (N.C.): Duke University Press, 397-413.

Campbell, Elaine (2000), The Rhetorical Language of Numbers: The Politics of Criminal Statistics. *Radical Statistics Journal*, 75, available at http://www.radstats.org.uk/no075/campbell.htm (accessed 20 January 2014).

Cameron, Deborah (1995) *Verbal Hygiene.* London and New York: Routledge.

Chiapello, Eve & Fairclough, Norman (2002), Understanding the new management ideology: a transdisciplinary contribution from critical discourse analysis and new sociology of capitalism. *Discourse & Society.* Vol 13(2):185-208.

Chilton, Paul (2005), Manipulation, Memes and Metaphors: The Case of Mein Kampf. *Manipulation and Ideologies in the Twentieth Century.* Louis de Saussure & Peter Schulz (Eds). John Benjamins Publishing Company, 15-44.

Chouliaraki, Lilie & Fairclough, Norman (1999), *Discourse in Late Modernity. Rethinking Critical Discourse Analysis.* Edinburgh: Edinburgh University Press.

Collins, Randall (2001), Social Movements and the Focus of Emotional Attention. *Passionate Politics: Emotions and Social Movements.* Jeff Goodwin & al, (eds). Chicago & London: The University of Chicago Press, 27-44.

Danilin, Pavel (2006), *Novaia molodëzhnaia politika 2003-2005.* Moskva: Izdatel'stvo "Evropa".

Davno.ru (2014), available at http://www.davno.ru/posters/collections/моор (accessed 20 January 2014).

Den' Konstitutsii (2014), available at http://ru.wikipedia.org/wiki/День_Конст итуцииРоссийской_Федерации (accessed 20 January 2014).

Dmitri Ganin (2014), available at http://fi.wikipedia.org/wiki/Dmitri_Ganin (accessed 20 January 2014).

Douglas, Mary (1966), *Purity and Danger. An analysis of the concepts of pollution and taboo.* London, NY: Routledge.

Dubin, Boris (2001), Zapad, granitsa, osobyi put': simvolika "drugogo" v politicheskoi mifologii Rossii, *Neprikosnovennyi zapas* 3(17), available at http://magazines.russ.ru/nz/2001/3/dub.html (accessed 20 January 2014).

Dubin, Boris (2004), "Krovovaia" voyna i "velikaia" pobeda, *Otechestvennye zapiski* 5(20), available at http://magazines.russ.ru/oz/2004/5/2004_5_5.html (accessed 20 January 2014).

Dubin, Boris (2011), *Rossiia nulevykh: politicheskaia kul'tura, istoricheskaia pamiat,' povsdnevnaia zhizn'.* Moskva: Rosspen.

Dunning, Chester S.L (2001), *A Short History of Russia's First Civil War. The Time of Troubles and the Founding of the Romanov Dynasty.* The Pennsylvania University Press.

Earthling (the album cover), available at http://en.wikipedia.org/wiki/File:Earthling %28album%29.jpg (accessed 20 January 2014).

Ellis, Frank (1998), The Media as Social Engineer. *Russian Cultural Studies: an introduction.* Catriona Kelly & David Shepherd (eds). Oxford University Press, 192-222.

Fairclough, Norman (1992), *Discourse and Social Change.* Cambridge: Polity Press.

Fairclough, Norman (1995), *Media Discourse*. Bloomsbury.

Fairclough, Norman (1997), *Miten media puhuu*. Tampere: Vastapaino.

Fedorov, Valeri (2005), Politizatsiia Molodëzhi, omolozhenie politiki. *VTSIOM*, 17 June 2005, available at http://wciom.ru/index.php?id=266&uid=1379 (accessed 20 January 2014).

Figes, Orlando (2002), *Natasha's Dance—A Cultural History of Russia*. New York:Picador.

Flashmob (2014), available at http://en.wikipedia.org/wiki/Flash_mob (accessed 20 January 2014).

FOM (2005), *Politicheskii potentsial i politicheskaia aktivnost' molodëzhi*, 2 June 2005, available at http://bd.fom.ru/report/ map/dd052222 (accessed 20 January 2014).

FOM (2007), "Nashi" i drugie molodëzhnye dvizheniia, 12 April 2007, available at http://bd.fom.ru/report/map/d071516 (accessed 20 January 2014).

FOM (2008a), *Molodëzh v politike*, 22 May 2008, available at http://bd.fom.ru/ report/%20map/dominant/dom0820/d082024 (accessed 20 January 2014).

FOM (2008b), *Smert' Patriarkha Alekseya II*, 18 December 2008, available at http://bd.fom.ru/report/cat/cult/rel_rel/rel_/d085010 (accessed 20 January 2014).

Gel'man, Vladimir (2013), *Iz ognia da v polymia: Rossiiskaia politika posle SSSR*. Sankt-Peterburg: BKhV-Peterburg.

Gerovitch, Slava (2002), *From Newspeak to Cyberspeak: A History of Soviet Cybernetics*. Cambridge Massachusetts & London: The MIT Press.

Glonass (2014), available at http://en.wikipedia.org/wiki/GLONASS (accessed 20 January 2014).

Golovko, Evgeni & Vakhtin, Nikolai (2004), *Sotsiolingvistika i sotsiologiia iazyka*. SPb: EUSP.

Goodwin, Jeff, Jasper, James M. & Polletta, Francesca (2001), Introduction: Why Emotions Matter? *Passionate Politics: Emotions and Social Movements*. Jeff Goodwin & al, (eds). Chicago & London: The University of Chicago Press, pp. 1-24.

Gorham, Michael S. (2000), Natsiia ili snikerizatsiia? Identity and Perversion in the Language Debates of Late and Post-Soviet Russia, *The Russian Review* 59, pp. 614-629.

Gorham, Michael S. (2003), *Speaking in Soviet Tongues: Language Culture and the Politics of Voice in Revolutionary Russia*. DeKalb, Ill.: Northern Illinois University Press.

Gorham, Michael S. (2005), Putin's Language, *Ab Imperio* (Kazan, Russia) 4: 381-401.

Gorny, Eugene (2006), Russian LiveJournal. The Impact of Cultural Identity on the Development of a Virtual community. *Control + Shift. Public and Private Usages of the Russian Internet*. H. Schmidt, K.Teubener & N. Konradova (eds). Norderstedt: Books on Demand, available at http://www.katy-teubener.de/joomla/images/stories/texts/publikationen/control_shift_01.pdf (accessed 20 January 2014).

Gorsuch, Anne E. (2000), *Youth in Revolutionary Russia*. Bloomington & Indianapolis: Indiana University Press.

Gosudarstvennaia (2005) (Gosudarstvennaia programma "Patrioticheskaia vospitanie grazhdan Rossiiskoi Federatsii na 2006-2010 gody," available at http://www.ed.gov.ru/young_people/gragd_patr_vospit/gosprog_patriot/ (accessed 20 January 2014).

Gudkov, Lev (2002), Russkii neotraditsionalizm i soprotivlenie peremenam. *Otechestvennye zapiski* 3 (4), available at http://magazines.russ.ru/oz/2002/3/2002 _03_09.html (accessed 20 January 2014).

Gudkov, Lev & Dubin, Boris (2006), Est' li perspektiva u russkogo natsionalizma? *Russkiy nacionalizm: ideologiia i nastroenie*. Alexander Verkhovski (ed). Moskva: SOVA.

Gusarova, Kseniia (2008), The Deviant Norm: Glamour in Russian Fashion. *Kultura* 6/2008, available at http://www.kultura-rus.uni-bremen.de/index.php?option=com_content&view=article&id=298%3Anorm-und-abweichung-glamour-in-der-mode&catid=39%3Aautorinnen&Itemid=49&lang=en (accessed 20 January 2014).

Guseinov, Gasan (2005), Berloga vebloga.Vvedenie v erraticheskuiu semantiku, *Speakrus.ru*, available http://speakrus.ru/gg/microprosa_erratica-1.htm (accessed 20 January 2014).

Haukkala, Hiski (2007), Poliittisen ja institutionaalisen solidaarisuuden rooli Viron ja Venäjän välisessä patsaskiistassa. Näkökulma: Pronssisoturin pitkä varjo—muistin politiikkaa ja kansallista uhoa (Marko Lehti, Matti Jutila, Markku Jokisipilä, Jussi Lassila, Hiski Haukkala), *Kosmopolis*

3/2007, 78-86 (59-86) (The role of political and solidarity in the statue-debate between Estonia and Russia. A viewpoint: The long shadow of the Bronze Soldier—Memory politics and national bluster, *Kosmopolis: The Finnish Review of Peace and Conflict Research*).

Heikkinen, Vesa. (1999), *Ideologinen merkitys - kriittisen tekstintutkimuk-sen teoriassa ja käytännössä*. Helsinki: SKS (*Ideological meaning—in the theory and practice of critical text analysis*).

Hemment, Julie (2007), *Youth voluntarism and the restructuring of social assistance in Russia*, paper presented to the Kennan Institute workshop, International Development Assistance in Post-Soviet Space, Woodrow Wilson Center for International Scholars, Washington DC, May 2007 (used by author's permission).

Hemment, Julie (2009), Soviet-Style Neoliberalism?: Nashi, Youth Voluntarism, and the Restructuring Social Welfare in Russia. *Problems of Post-Communism*, vol. 56, no.6, 36-50.

Hemment, Julie (2012), Nashi, Youth Voluntarism, and Potemkin NGOs: Making Sense of Civil Society in Post-Soviet Russia. *Slavic Review*, Vol. 71, No. 2, 234-260.

Hemment, Julie (2014), *Volunteers, Entrepreneurs and Patriots: youth as new subjects of state policy in Putin's Russia*. Indiana University Press (forthcoming).

Hietala, Veijo (1996), *Ruudun hurma. Johdatus TV-kulttuuriin*. Jyväskylä: YLE-opetuspalvelut (*Spell of screen. Introduction to television culture*).

Horvath, Robert (2011), Putin's 'Preventive Counter-Revolution': Post-Soviet Authoritarianism and the Spectre of Velvet Revolution. *Europe-Asia Studies* 63, no. 1 (January 2011): 1–25.

Jasper, James M. (1997), *The Art of Moral Protest. Culture, Biography, and Creativity in Social Movements*. Chicago & London: The Chicago University Press.

Kashin, Oleg (2006), Sezon meteoritnykh dozhdei. *Novaia molodëzhnaia politika 2003-2005*. Pavel Danilin (author). Moskva: Izdatel'stvo "Evropa," 3-7.

Kelly, Catriona, Shepherd, David & White, Stephen (1998), Conclusion: Towards Post-Soviet Pluralism? Postmodernism and Beyond. *Russian Cul-*

*tural Studies: an introduction*. Catriona Kelly & David Shepherd (eds). Oxford University Press, 387-400.

Kelly, Catriona (2001), *Refining Russia: Advice Literature, Polite Culture, and Gender from Catherine to El'tsin*. Oxford University Press.

Kenez, Peter & Shepherd, David (1998), "Revolutionary" Models for High Literature: resisiting Poetics. *Russian Cultural Studies: an introduction*. Catriona Kelly & David Shepherd (eds). Oxford University Press, 21-55.

Korguniuk, Iuri (2000), Molodëzhnaia politika sovremennykh rossiiskikh partii. Teoriia i praktika. *Rossiia na rubezhe vekov: politicheskie partii i molodëzh*. Moskva: MGPU, available at http://www.partinform.ru/articles /molod.htm (accessed 20 January 2014).

Kozhevnikova, Galina (2006), Radikal'nyi natsionalizm i protivodeistvie emu. *Russkii Natsionalizm. Ideologiia i nastroenie*. Aleksandr Verhovskii (ed.). Moskva: SOVA, 8-87.

Kozlov, Vladimir (2008), *Real'naia kul'tura ot Al'ternativy do emo*. Sankt Peterburg: Amfora.

Kratasjuk, Ekaterina (2006), Construction of "Reality" in Russian Mass Media News on Television and on the Internet. *Control + Shift. Public and Private Usages of the Russian Internet*. H. Schmidt, K.Teubener & N. Konradova (eds). Norderstedt: Books on Demand, available at http://www.ka ty-teubener.de/joomla/images/stories/texts/publikationen/control_shift_01 .pdf (accessed 20 January 2014).

Laitin, David D. (1998), *Identity in Formation: The Russian-Speaking Populations in the Near Abroad*. Ithaca&London: Cornell University Press.

Lane, David (2009), "Coloured Revolution" as a Political Phenomenon. *Journal of Communist Studies and Transition Politics* 25, no. 2 (2009): 113-135.

Laruelle, Marlene (2009a), Introduction. *Russian Nationalism and National Reassertion of Russia*. Marlene Laruelle (ed). Routledge.

Laruelle, Marlene (2009b), *Inside and Around the Kremlin's Black Box: The New Nationalist Think Tanks in Russia*. Institute for Security & Development Policy Stockholm Paper, October 2009, available at http://www.isd p.eu/images/stories/isdp-main-pdf/2009_laruelle_inside-and-around-the-kremlins-black-box.pdf (accessed 20 January 2014).

Laruelle, Marlene (2009c), *Youth, Patriotism and Memory in Russia.* Seminar paper held at the Aleksanteri Institute in Helsinki, November 10, 2009 (used by author's permission).

Laruelle, Marlene (2011), Negotiating History: Memory Wars in the Near Abroad and Pro-Kremlin youth movements, *Demokratizatsiia—The Journal of Post-Soviet Democratization* Vol 19, No 3 (Summer): 233-252.

Lassila, Jussi (2002), *Perelom etnicheskoi simvoliki: primenenie semioticheskogo metoda Iu. M. Lotmana pri russkoyazychnom official'nom gazetnom diskurse v Estonii v 1989-90 gg.* Master thesis, University of Jyväskylä, available at https://jyx.jyu.fi/dspace/handle/123456789/12711 (accessed February 22, 2010).

Lassila, Jussi (2007a), Commissars on the market: Discursive commodities of the youth movement NASHI. *Voices and Values of Young People - Representations in Russian Media.* Marjatta Vanhala-Aniszewski & Lea Siilin (eds). Aleksanteri Series 6/2007, pp. 99-136.

Lassila, Jussi (2007b), Ideologisesta tyylistä tyylikkääseen ideologiaan. *Idäntutkimus* 3/2007: 41-52. (From ideological style to stylish ideology, *Finnish Review of Russian and Eastern European Studies*).

Lassila, Jussi (2010), Reading perestroika-era tension into the activity of the pro-Putin youth movements. *Perestroika: Process and Con-sequenses.* Markku Kangaspuro, Jouko Nikula & Ivor Stodolsky (eds). Studia Historica 80. Helsinki: Finnish Literary Society, 262-283.

Lassila, Jussi (2011a) *Anticipating Ideal youth in Putin's Russia: The Web-Texts, Communicative Demands, and Symbolic Capital of the Youth Movements "Nashi" and "Idushchie vmeste."* Unpublished PhD, Dept. of Languages / University of Jyväskylä & Aleksanteri Institute.

Lassila, Jussi (2011b), Making sense of Nashi's Political Style: The Bronze Soldier and the Counter-Orange Community. *Demokratizatsiia—The Journal of Post-Soviet Democratization* Vol 19, No3: 253-276.

Lassila Jussi (2012), *The Quest for an Ideal Youth in Putin's Russia II: The Search for Distinctive Conformism in the Political Communication of Nashi, 2005-2009.* Stuttgart: Ibidem-Verlag.

Leskinen, Virve (2009), *Reprezentatsiia molodëzhnogo dvizheniia "Nashi" v tekstakh "Rossiiskoi gazety" v 2005-2008 gg.* Master thesis, University of Jyväskylä.

Levada (2004), Nostalgiia po proshlomu, 19 March 2004, available at http://www.levada.ru/press/2004031901.html (accessed 20 January 2014).

Levada (2008), Patriotizm i dvizheniia "NASHI", 21 January 2008, available at http://www.levada.ru/press/2008012101.html (accessed 20 January 2014). (accessed 20 January 2014).

Levada centre (2010), *Obshchectvennoe mnenie—2010*, available at http://www. levada.ru/books/obshchestvennoe-mnenie-2010 (accessed 20 January 2014).

Levada (2013), Indeksy odobreniia deiatel'nosti Vladimira Putina i Dmitriia Medvedeva, available at http://www.levada.ru/indeksy (accessed 20 January 2014).

Lonkila, Markku (2008), The Internet and Anti-military Activism in Russia. *Europe-Asia Studies*, Vol. 60, No 7: 1125-1149.

Lonkila, Markku (2012), Russian Protest On- and Offline: The Role of Social Media in the Moscow Opposition Demonstrations in December 2011. *FIIA Briefing Paper* 98. Available at www.fiia.fi/assets/publications/bp98.pdf (accessed 17 January 2014).

Lukov, Valeri (2006), Gosudarstvennaia moledëzhnaia politika: bitva kontseptsii i ozhidanie rezultatov. *Molodëzh i politika*. Moskva: Biblioteka liberalnogo chteniia 17. Moskovskoe biuro fonda Fridrikha Naumanna, 73-88.

Liukshin, Dmitri & Mezhvedilov, Arif (2006), Poiski poteriannogo poko-leniia v utrachennom vremeni. Molodëzh v politicheskom pole sovre-mennoy Rossii: problema instrumental'noy prigodnosti. *Molodëzh i politika*. Moskva: Biblioteka liberalnogo chteniya 17. Moskovskoe biuro fonda Fridrikha Naumanna, 35-48.

Lyytikäinen, Laura (2014), *Performing Political Opposition in Russia. The Case of the Russian Youth Movement "Oborona."* PhD Dissertation, Faculty of Social Sciences, University of Helsinki (forthcoming).

Machin, David & Van Leeuwen, Theo (2005), Language style and lifestyle: the case of a global magazine. *Media, Culture & Society*. Vol 27(4), 577–600.

Markov, Sergey (2006) Vlast' shagaet vperedi. *Goriachaia molodëzh Rossii*. V.A. Savel'ev (ed.), Moskva, Kvanta, 279–280.

McNair, Brian (1995), *An Introduction to Political Communication*. Routledge.

Menzel, Birgit (2008), Russian Discourse on Glamour. *Kultura* 6/2008, available at http://www.academia.edu/3551416/Glamour_Russia_engl._edition _Kultura_6_2008_ed._Birgit_Menzel_Larissa_Rudova (accessed February 23, 2010).

Mijnssen, Ivo (2012), *The Quest for an Ideal Youth in Putin's Russia I. Back to Our Future! History, Modernity and Patriotism according to Nashi, 2005–2012*, Stuttgart: ibidem-Verlag.

Moore, Robert E. (2003), From genericide to viral marketing: on "brand". *Language & Communication*, vol 23, Issues 3–4: 331–357.

Moral Code of the Builder of Communism, available at http://en.wikipedi a.org/wiki/Moral_Code_of_the_Builder_of_Communism (accessed 20 January 2014).

Myles, John 1999, From habitus to mouth: Language and class in Bourdieu's sociology of language, *Theory & Society* 28: 879-901.

Nadkarni, Maya & Shevchenko, Olga (2004), The Politics of Nostalgia. A case for comparative analysis of postsocialist practices. *Ab Imperio* 2: 487-519.

Nafus, Dawn (2003), The Aesthetics of the Internet in St. Petersburg: Why Metaphor Matters? *The Communication Review*, 6: 185-212.

Negrine, Ralph (2012), Professionalizing Dissent: Protest, Political Communication, and the Media. *The Establishment Responds: Power, Politics, and Protest since 1945*. Edited by Kathrin Fahlenbrach, Martin Klimke, Joachim Scharloth & Laura Wong. NY: Palgrave MacMillan.

Omel'chenko, Elena (2004), Subkul'tury i kul'turnye strategii na molodezhnoi stsene kontsa XX veka: kto kogo? *Neprikosnovennyi zapas* 4(36), available at http://magazines.russ.ru/nz/2004/4/om8.html (accessed 20 January 2014).

Omel'chenko, Elena (2005a), Russian Youth Scenes at the Turn of the 21st century, or How the Yobs are Driving out the Informals. *Kultura* 2/2005, pp. 3-7, available at http://www.kultura-rus.uni-brmen.de/index.php?opt ion=com_content& view=article&id=241%3ArussIndische-jugendszenen-um-die-jahrtausend-wende-oder-prolos-gegen-alternative&catid=39%3A autorinnen& Itemid=49& lang=en (accessed 20 January 2014).

Omel'chenko, Elena (2005b), Ritual Battles, or Who are the Yobs? *Kultura* 2/2005, pp. 8-9, available at http://www.kultura-rus.uni-bremen.de/index .php?option=com_content&view=article&id=39%3Arituelle-schlachten-od er-wer-sind-die-prolos&catid=39%3Aautorinnen&Itemid=49&lang=en (accessed 20 January 2014).

Omel'chenko, Elena (2006), Molodëzh dlia politikov vs. molodëzh dlia sebia? Razmyshleniia o tsennostyakh n fobiakh rossiiskoi molodëzhi. *Molodëzh i politika*. Moskovskoe biuro fonda Fridrikha Naumanna. Moskva: Biblioteka liberalnogo chteniia (17), 9-34.

Omel'chenko, Elena & Goncharova, Nataliya (2009), Ksenofobnye nastroeniia na fone novogo rossiiskogo natsionalizma. *Neokonchatel'nyi analiz...Ksenofobnye nastroeniia v molodëzhnoy srede*. Pod red. E. Omel'chenko, E. Luk'yanovoy. Ulyanovsk: Izdatel'stvo Ulyanovskogo gosudarstvennogo universiteta, pp. 83-110.

Open Source Center of the US Director of National Intelligence (2007), *Source Descriptors of Key Russian Media* (6 December 2007), available at http://www.fas.org/irp/dni/osc/russian-media.pdf (accessed 17 January 2014).

Oushakine, Serguei (2000a), The Quantity of Style—Imaginary Consumption in the New Russia. *Theory, Culture & Society*, Vol. 17(5): 97-120.

Oushakine, Serguei (2000b), In the State of Post-Soviet Aphasia: Symbolic Development in Contemporary Russia. *Europe-Asia Studies*, Vol. 52, No. 6: 991-1016.

Oushakine, Serguei (2007), "We're nostalgic but we're not crazy": Retrofitting the Past in Russia. *The Russian Review* 66 (July): 451-82.

Oushakine, Serguei (2009), *The Patriotsim of Despair—Nation, War, and Loss in Russia*. Cornell University Press.

Pajnik, Mojca & Lesjak-Tušek, Petra (2002), Observing Discourses of Advertising: Mobitel's Interpellation of Potential Consumers. *Journal of Communication Inquiry* 26:3: 277-299

Parker, Ian (2005), *Overidentification*. Explanation of the term at the site of the Lancaster University Management School, available at http://www.lums.lancs.ac.uk/events/owt/6455/ (accessed 17 January 2014).

Petukhov, Vladimir (2006), Kumiry rossiiskoi Molodëzhi: vzgliad sotsiologa. *Goriachaya molodëzh Rossii.* V.A Savel'ev (ed.), Kvanta, Moskva, pp. 281–283.

Piattoeva, Nelli (2005), Citizenship Education as an Expression of Democratization and Nation-Building Processes in Russia. *European Education,* vol. 37, no. 3, Fall 2005, 38–52.

Pilkington, Hilary (1994), *Russia's youth and its culture: A nation's constructors and constructed.* London & NY: Routledge.

Pilkington, Hilary (1998), "The Future is Ours": Youth Culture in Russia 1953 to the Present. *Russian Cultural Studies, an introduction.* Catriona Kelly & David Shepherd (eds.) Oxford University Press, 368-386.

Postoutenko, Kirill (2010), Prolegomena to the Study of Totalitarian Communication. *Totalitarian Communication. Hierarchies, Codes and Messages.* Kirill Postoutenko (ed). Bielefeld: Transcript, 11-40.

Postoutenko, Kirill (2011), a personal e-mail response (20 June 2011).

Pro suverennuiu demokratiiu (2007), Poliakov, L.V. (ed). Moskva: Evropa.

Pronkssôdur, available at http://et.wikipedia.org/wiki/Pronkss%C3%B5dur (accessed 20 January 2014).

Rauer, Valentin (2006), Symbols in action: Willy Brandt's kneefall at the Warsaw Memorial. *Social Performance: Symbolic Action, Cultural Pragmatics, and Ritual.* Jeffrey C. Alexander, Bernhard Giesen, Jason L. Mast (eds.), Cambridge University Press, pp. 257-282.

Robertson, Graeme B. (2009), Managing Society: Protest, Civil Society, and Regime in Putin's Russia. *Slavic Review.* Vol 68, No 3, pp. 528-547.

Romanenko, Andrei (2003), *Obraz ritora v sovetskoi slovesnoi kul'ture.* Moskva, Izdatelstvo Flinta, Nauka.

Rudova, Larissa & Menzel, Birgit (2008), Uniting Russia in Glamour. *Kultura* 6, pp. 2-4, available at http://www.kultura-rus.uni-bremen.de/kultura_dokumente/ausgaben/englisch/kultura_6_2008_EN.pdf (accessed 20 January 2014).

Ryazanova-Clarke, Lara (2006), "The State Turning to Language": Power and Identity in Russian Language Policy Today. *Russian Language Journal* Vol. 56: 37-56.

Ryazanova-Clarke, Lara (2008), Re-Creation of the Nation: Orthodox and Heterodox Discourses in Post-Soviet Russia. *Scando-Slavica Tomus* 54: 223-239.

Räsänen, Salla (2006), Kohtauksia eräästä kirjasodasta. *Idäntutkimus* 2/2006 (Episodes from a book war, *Finnish Review of Russian and Eastern European Studies*)

Savage, Jon (2007), *Teenage: The Prehistory of Youth Culture 1875-1945.* Penguin Books.

Savel'ev, Viktor (2006), *Goriachaia Molodëzh Rossii.* Moskva: OOO Kvanta.

Scherrer, Jutta (2009), Kul'turologiia and the "civilisational turn": The culrural and civilizational paradigms in post-Communist Russia. *Keynote paper at a symposium at the Baltic and East European Graduate School,* Södertörn College, Stockholm, May 25, 2009.

Scollon, Ron (2001), Multilingualism and intellectual property: Visual holophrastic discourse and the commodity/sign. *Georgetown University Roundtable on Languages and Linguistics 1999.* James E. Alatis & Ai-Hui Tan (eds.). Washington D.C: Georgetown University Press, pp. 404-417.

Schmid, Ulrich (2006), Nashi—Die Putin-Jugend. Sowjettradition und politische Konzeptkunst. *Osteuropa* 5/2006, pp.5-18.

Schmidt, Henrike & Teubener, Katy (2006), (Counter)Public Sphere(s) on the Russian Internet. *Control + Shift. Public and Private Usages of the Russian Internet.* H. Schmidt, K.Teubener & N. Konradova (eds.) Norderstedt: Books on Demand, available at http://www.katyteubener.de/joomla/images/stories/texts/publikationen/control_shift_01.pdf (accessed 20 January 2014).

Semenenko, Irina (2008), Obrazy i imidzhi v diskurse natsional'noi identichnosti. *Politicheskaia issledovaniia* 5/2008, pp. 7-18.

Sibireva, Olga (2009), Where Satan Still Lives. Orthodox Subculture in Russia. *Kultura* 2: 10-15, available at http://www.kultura-rus.uni-bremen.de/index.php?option=com_content&view=article&id=306%3Awoder-satan-noch-lebendig-ist-orthodoxe-subkultur-in-russland&catid=39%3Aautorinnen&Itemid=49&lang=en (accessed 20 January 2014).

Shnirel'man, Viktor (2006), "Nesovmestimost' kul'tur": ot nauchnykh kontseptsii i shkol'nogo obrazovaniia do real'noi politiki. *Russkii natsion-*

*alizm: ideologiia i nastroeniia*. Moskva: Informatsionno-analiticheskii tsentr "SOVA", pp. 183-222.

Shnirel'man, Viktor (2009), To Make a Bridge: Eurasian Discourse in the Post-Soviet World. *Anthropology of East Europe Review*, 27 (2): 68-85.

Simons, Gregory (2003), Vladimir Putin and the debate of the Emergence of Cult of Personality. *Working Papers, 77*. Department of East European Studies, Uppsala University / University of Canterbury.

Skeggs, Beverly (2004), *Class, Self, Culture*. London & NY: Routledge.

Skinner, Quentin (1974), Some problems in the analysis of political thought and action, *Political Theory* 2: 277.

Smetanina, Svetlana (2002), *Media-tekst v sisteme kultury*. SPb: Izdatelstvo Mihajlova V.A

Smyth, Regina, Sobolev, Anton & Soboleva, Irina (2013), Well-Organized Play: Symbolic Politics and the Effect of the Pro-Putin Rallies. *Problems of Post-Communism*, №2 (March/April), 60:2, 24-39.

SOVA (2014), (Informatsionno-analiticheskiy tsentr), available at http://sova-center.ru/ (accessed 20 January 2014).

Sokolov, Mikhail (2006), Natsional-Bolshevistskaia partiia: ideologicheskaia evoliutsiia i politicheskii stil'. *Russkii Natsionalizm. Ideologiia i nastroenie*, Aleksandr Verhovskii (ed). Moskva: SOVA, pp. 139-164.

Sperling, Valerie (2009), Making the Public Patriotic: Militarism and Anti-Militarism in Russia. *Russian Nationalism and National Reassertion of Russia*. Edited by Marlene Laruelle. Routledge, 218-271.

Sperling, Valerie (2012), Nashi Devushki: Gender and Political Youth Activism in Putin's and Medvedev's Russia, *Post-Soviet Affairs*, 28, 2: 232–261.

Sperling, Valerie (2014), *Sex, Politics, and Putin: Gender, Activism, and Political Legitimacy in Russia* (forthcoming).

SRAS (2014), *The School of Russian and Asian Studies*, available at http://www.sras.org/nashi_russian_youth_movement (accessed 20 January 2014).

Stanovaia, Tat'iana (2005), Molodëzhnye organizatsii v sovremennoi Rossii *Politkom.ru*, available at http://www.politcom.ru/320.html (accessed 20 January 2014).

Stop töhryille (Stop smudging), available at http://fi.wikipedia.org/wiki/Stop_t% C3%B6hryille (accessed 20 January 2014).

State Law of Russian Language (2005), *53-F3 Federal'nyi zakon Rossiiskoi Federatsii "O gosudarstvennom iazyke Rossiiskoi Federatsii"*, available at http://www.gramma.ru/RUS/?id=1.10 (accessed 20 January 2014).

Strategiia 2007 (*Strategiia gosudarstevennoi molodežnoi politiki s kommentariami)*, Gusev, B.B. & Lopukhin, A.M. (eds). Moskva: Izdatel'stvo gosudarsvennogo sotsial'nogo universiteta.

Swinging London (2014), available at http://www.artandpopularculture.com/ Swinging_London (accessed 20 January 2014).

Svynarenko, Arsenyi (2005), Growing to Be a Citizen - Civil Society and Youth Policies in Karelia. *Social structure, Public Space and Civil Society in Karelia.* Harri Melin (ed). Helsinki: Kikimora Publications, 77-98.

Thurlow, Crispin (2009), Speaking of Difference: Language, Inequality and Interculturality. *Handbook of Critical Intercultural Communication.* R. Hallawi & T. Namyama (eds). Oxford: Blackwell.

Thurlow, Crispin & Jaworski, Adam (2009), Silence is Golden: Elitism, Linguascaping and "anti-communication" in luxury tourism. *Semiotic Landscapes: Language, Image, Space.* A. Jaworski & C. Thurlow (eds). London: Continuum.

Top Sites Blog (2014), top 20 most popular websites in Russia, available at http://topsitesblog.com/russian-websites/ (accessed 20 January 2014).

Tumarkin, Nina (1994), *The Living and the Dead: The Rise and Fall of the Cult of World War II in Russia.* BasicBooks.

Turner, Victor (1974), *Dramas, Fields, and Metaphors: Symbolic Action in Human Society.* Cornell University Press.

Umland, Andreas (2009), Ponimanie Oranzhevoy revoliutsii: demokratizatsiia Ukrainy v zerkale Rossii, *Polit.ru*, 30 December 30 2009, available at http://www.polit.ru/institutes/2009/12/30/orange.html (accessed 20 January 2014).

Umland, Andreas (2010), "Oranzhevaia revoliutsiia", russkoe antizapadnichestvo i evolyutsiia rossiiskogo politicheskogo rezhima poslednykh let. *Polit.ru*, 14 January 2010, available at http://www.polit.ru/ institutes/2010/01/14/umland.html (accessed 20 January 2014).

Valtioneuvoston innovaatiopoliittinen selonteko eduskunnalle (2008) (Report of Innovation Policy by the Council of State of Finland for the Finnish Parliament), available at https://www.tem.fi/files/20298/INNOPOL_ SELONTEKO.pdf (accessed 20 January 2014).

Vanderford, Marsa L. (1989), Vilification and Social Movements: A Case Study of Pro-Life and Pro-Life Rhetoric. *Quarterly Journal of Speech* (75), 166-182.

Vanhala-Aniszewski, Marjatta (2005), Tendetsii razvitiia postsovetskogo me-dia-teksta. *Re-reading Soviet and Post-Soviet Texts.* Learning by Doing 4. Natalia Baschmakoff & Marjatta Vanhala-Aniszewski (eds). Joensuu: University of Joensuu, Russian Department, 140-155.

Vanhala-Aniszewski, Marjatta (2007), Eurokaput. Venäläisen media-tekstin keskustelunomaistuminen. *Puhe ja kieli* 1/2007: 9-24

VTSIOM (2005), "NASHI" v gorode: *Rossiiane o molodëzhnykh organizatsiiakh* (30 March 2005), available at http://wciom.ru/index.php?id=4 59&uid=1156 (accessed 20 January 2014).

Vul'fov, Boris & Ivanov, Valery (1989), *Komsomol. Uchitel. Uchenik.* Moskva: Pedagogika.

Wodak, Ruth (Rudolf de Cillia, Martin Reisigl & Karin Liebhart) (1999), *The Discursive Construction of National Identity.* Edinburgh: Edinburgh University Press.

Wilson, Andrew (2005), *Virtual Politics. Faking Democracy in the Post-Soviet World.* New Haven and London: Yale University Press.

Yurchak, Alexei (2000), Privatize your name: Symbolic work in a post-Soviet linguistic market. *Journal of Sociolinguistics* 4/3, 2000, 406-434.

Yurchak, Alexei (2003), Russian Neoliberal: The Entrepreneurial Ethic and the Spirit of "True Careerism." *Russian Review.* Vol. 62, No. 1, 72-90.

Yurchak, Alexei (2006), *Everything Was Forever, Until It Was No More. The Last Soviet Generation.* Princeton & Oxford: Princeton University Press.

Yurchak, Alexei (2008), Necro-Utopia. The Politics of Indistinction and the Aesthetics of the Non-Soviet. *Current Anthropology.* Volume 49, Number 2, April 2008.

Zima, ukhodi! (2012), Documentary film on protests in Russia in 2011-12. Produced by Marina Razbezhkina. Available at http://www.hdkinoteatr.c om/documetary/9016-zima-uhodi.html (accessed 22 January 2014).

Zherebkin Maksym (2009), In search of a theoretical approach to the analysis of the"Colour revolutions":Transition studies and discourse theory. *Communist and Post-Communist Studies* 42 (2009): 199-216.

# Appendices

Appendix 1: T-shirt "Ministry of Health recommends: Reproduction is nice and useful."
Shapovalova fashion collection catalogue (not available anymore on the web)

Appendix 1: T-shirt "I want three." From Shapovalova fashion collection catalogue (not available anymore on the web)

Appendix 3: Shapovalova T-shirt "Love Russian" and bikini "Vova, I'm with you!" Available at http://www.liveinternet.ru/users/time-traveler/post86636688/ (accessed 20 January 2014)

Appendix 4: Shapovalova t-shirt "Thanks Iura! The space is OURS!", originally available at http://nashi.su/shop/card/435 (accessed 24 February 2010, not available anymore).

# SOVIET AND POST-SOVIET POLITICS AND SOCIETY

Edited by Dr. Andreas Umland

ISSN 1614-3515

*ibidem*-Verlag / *ibidem* Press
Melchiorstr. 15
70439 Stuttgart
Germany

ibidem@ibidem.eu
www.ibidem-verlag.com
www.ibidem.eu